THE GODFATHER OF
TABLOID

THE GODFATHER OF
TABLOID

GENEROSO POPE JR. AND
THE *NATIONAL ENQUIRER*

JACK VITEK

THE UNIVERSITY PRESS OF KENTUCKY

Scholarly publisher for the Commonwealth,
serving Bellarmine University, Berea College, Centre College of Kentucky,
Eastern Kentucky University, The Filson Historical Society, Georgetown College,
Kentucky Historical Society, Kentucky State University, Morehead State University, Murray
State University, Northern Kentucky University, Transylvania University,
University of Kentucky, University of Louisville, and Western Kentucky University.
All rights reserved.

Editorial and Sales Offices: The University Press of Kentucky
663 South Limestone Street, Lexington, Kentucky 40508-4008
www.kentuckypress.com

   12 11 10 09 08   5 4 3 2 1

Library of Congress Cataloging-in-Publication Data
Vitek, Jack.
  The godfather of tabloid : Generoso Pope Jr. and the National enquirer
/ Jack Vitek.
     p. cm.
  Includes bibliographical references and index.
  ISBN 978-0-8131-2503-9 (acid-free paper)
  1. Pope, Generoso, 1927–1988. 2. Publishers and publishing—United States— Biography.
3. National enquirer (New York, N.Y. : 1957)—History. 4. Newspaper publishing—United
States—History—20th century. 5. Tabloid newspapers—United States—History. I. Title.
  Z473.P57V58 2008
  070.5092—dc22
  [B]   2008016855

This book is printed on acid-free recycled paper meeting
the requirements of the American National Standard
for Permanence in Paper for Printed Library Materials.

Manufactured in the United States of America.

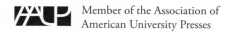

Member of the Association of
American University Presses

We shoulda filmed the deal.
—*Old Hollywood saying*

CONTENTS

CONTENTS

INTRODUCTION

Generoso Pope Jr. denied all his life that he had any connections with the Mafia, most publicly when he was questioned about such links by Mike Wallace on *60 Minutes* in 1976. Wallace noted that Pope had known Frank Costello, Joseph Pravachi, and Albert Anastasia, which Pope readily admitted, and commented that Pope owned 100 percent of the *National Enquirer*'s stock and ran the paper like a "godfather."

Wallace went on: "And you know as well as I do that there are allegations that Mafia money had been behind the *Enquirer* since the beginning?"

Pope: "Right, I've heard—I've read that, heard it."

Wallace: "Answer?"

Pope: "Well, I think it's pretty obvious to anyone who understands or reads or knows anything about this organization, whatever it is, that if there were, there still would be."

Wallace: "Because?"

Pope: "Because they never let go once they get their hooks into you. And that obviously has not happened."[1]

Significantly, Pope managed to stumble through his denial without actually using the word *Mafia*. And Wallace, one of journalism's most aggressive reporters, let Pope off, saying to the program's wide audience, "The plain fact is no one has ever been able to prove a Mafia-*Enquirer* connection." And no one ever did.

Nearly all mafiosi denied that they were associated with the Mafia: Joseph Bonanno said he stayed away from the word because it caused too much "confusion." Costello's lawyer, George Wolf, who represented many famous mobsters in criminal court, noted that he never heard any of his clients use the word. Famously, the word Mafia was banned from the pages of the *Enquirer* (as were stories about the dangers of smoking), and the chain-smoking Pope once stopped a press run to replate a page to eliminate the offending word. There was, he insisted, no such thing as the Mafia. But Pope knew better than to get into that with Wallace.

There's no doubt that Frank Costello was a close associate of Pope's father and was widely reputed to be young Gene's godfather. Pope Jr. made the front page of the *New York Times* twice before he was thirty, both times in connection with Costello, the so-called prime minister of the underworld. The first was in his wheeler-dealer political era and concerned the election of a New York City mayor, and the second was when he was having dinner with "Uncle" Frank in a Manhattan restaurant on the 1957 May evening that Costello was shot and wounded in the head by an unsuccessful assassin. Costello, by many accounts, loaned Pope money to buy the *Enquirer* in 1952 and, according to one of Pope's earliest associates, loaned him more money to keep going during several early years of red ink. In return, according to the source, the *Enquirer* published the week's numbers for the mob game. Pope's grown-up son Paul came to believe that his father moved the paper to small-town Florida to shake his mob connections.

Pope's father, Generoso Sr., published *Il Progresso*, New York's Italian-language newspaper, and became a kingmaker in association with Carmine DeSapio, the first Italian American boss of Tammany Hall, and Costello. The night Pope Jr. died of a heart attack in 1988 he might have read a review published that Sunday in the *New York Times* of a book raking up long-forgotten secrets, fingering his father as the murderer by contract of his left-wing publishing rival, Carlo Tresca, who was fatally shot on a dark, lonely Manhattan street in 1943.

Young Pope seemed preternaturally patriarchal. In his front-page photo in the *New York Times* in 1950, just before his twenty-fourth birthday, he looks like a man twice his age. His manner later as publisher and hands-on editor of the *Enquirer* was aloof, distant, tyrannical, at once whimsically generous and whimsically ruthless. He made decisions (and reversed them) imperiously and never bothered to explain his logic to anyone, if there was any logic at all.

Pope kept a low profile outside his small circle, so successfully that he was hardly known outside the circle of tabloid writers and editors. He moved in the shadows and even served a few months as a CIA officer—in psychological warfare—probably exploiting a little-understood connection between the Mafia and American intelligence operations. New hires at the *Enquirer* were warned that they could mistake him—at their peril!—for the janitor. People said he bought his undistinguished polyester clothes out of a Sears catalog, or his wife Lois bought them at Kmart. He could behave like the Queen of Hearts from *Alice in Wonderland* and fire a dozen reporters on a Friday afternoon. He hid the *Enquirer* in a small working-class town near Palm Beach, Florida, and hid the sprawling, one-story, utilitarian building in a seven-acre bower of tropical plants, a sort of Emerald City, which was ironic because Pope could be described as a real-life Wizard of Oz .

Like the ventriloquist Wizard of Oz, Pope affected a sort of projected voice, a deep, flat tough-guy voice, sort of a cross between Jack Webb and Humphrey Bogart, so distinctive that whenever people quoted GP stories, they imitated his strange intonations, talking out of the side of their mouth, as he did. That was the workplace voice; others often found him shy and soft-spoken, especially in his younger days. In an era of drastic downsizing in the journalistic mainstream (a sort of professional tornado), lost souls flocked to him by the dozens, including many of the profession's rusting tin men and cowardly lions, all the way from Britain and her far-flung colonies.

In the end Pope was riddled with weakness; this sedentary, workaholic chain-smoker who feared and avoided doctors died suddenly at sixty-one of a massive heart attack. The ironies reverberated. His two tabloids had gone a long way toward creating junk medical science and never dealt at all with the consequences of smoking. Pope died in a special ambulance he had donated, on his way from his home to nearby JFK Medical Center's state-of-the-art DeBakey Cardiac Care Unit, to which he had donated millions, suggesting he had some foreboding of his manner of death.

Our present public notion of the Mafia is mostly a cultural construction created by our entertainment media. But if one were to read all the books—fiction and nonfiction—and see all the gangster and Godfather movies and *Sopranos* programs about the mob and then imagine how a newspaper run by a godfather would look, the result could very well be something like the *National Enquirer*.

ONE

THE MAN IN PERSPECTIVE

Generoso Pope Jr. is virtually unknown to the American public as well as to academic circles, including even the discipline of American culture studies, yet ultimately he has had an immense and continuing effect on our everyday lives and our culture. Pope, who founded the *National Enquirer* and edited it for thirty-six years until his sudden death in 1988, will be seen, when the full story is known, as the man who invented and fostered the ever-widening brand of tabloid culture that surrounds us now. A critical biography of Pope is in order for several reasons, and the first and simplest is to bring that story to light for the first time. It is also a raucous and entertaining narrative in itself, and the backstage story of tabloid journalism is more tabloid than tabloid itself.

One scholarly rationale for this project is to explore why Pope's influence on American journalism is so underestimated and undervalued. The circulation of Pope's publication in its best days—more than five million a week, occasionally spiking into the six millions, more if we include the one million of the *Enquirer*'s weird sister publication, the *Weekly World News*—was comparable to that of Joseph Pulitzer's and William Randolph Hearst's papers. Pope followed Pulitzer's and Hearst's lead in sensationalism and in reaching down and extending his readership to the commonest man and woman. Pope self-consciously modeled himself on the two newspaper greats and read and recommended their biographies. Yet Pope did not cut the public figure in his time that they did in theirs. Now and then the press, enamored of its clichés, tried to stick the label *flamboyant* on him, but Pope refused to wear it. He was as low profile as a true Mafia godfather, as a man living on the wrong side of the law. What was flamboyant was what he published, not his dull lifestyle as a small-town, blue-collar millionaire. His dour personality was a nucleus, and the entities that revolved around him provided a virtual circus. He was probably as rich as Hearst and Pulitzer, and Pope's considerable wealth was vastly underestimated even by *Fortune* magazine, until he died and the *Enquirer* was sold for far more than anyone had thought it was worth. Although Hearst's magazine and newspaper empire loomed larger, it was stretched thin and debt-ridden. In the end there is an excellent case for elevating Pope to the pantheon alongside those two moguls, who were also undervalued in their own lifetimes and looked down on, too, as mere popularizers.

Pope ruled his paper with such obsessiveness and dominated his talented and often widely experienced reporters and editors with such passion that his figurative DNA was stamped on every *Enquirer* story. So intrusive was Pope's personality that, after the Jonestown mass Kool-Aid suicides in Guyana in 1978, one of his editors took to calling the *Enquirer* Popestown, mocking Pope's tyrannical rule—out of his hearing. One of the ironies of the situation is that Pope rarely if ever wrote for his own paper (except for a high-minded manifesto or two in the very early days) though he habitually read, reread, and editorially reshaped many times over every word he published. The *Enquirer* was widely imitated, and of the six major American supermarket tabloids that survived the turn of the new century as a communications monopoly, two of the originals were Pope's: the *Enquirer* and the black-and-white *Weekly World*

Pope's preference for working with paper is reflected by his cluttered desk in his walnut-paneled inner sanctum. (Photo by Ken Steinhoff / *Palm Beach Post*)

News, which he founded in 1979 to make use of his idled monochrome presses when he took the *Enquirer* to color.

The U.S. tabloid monopoly that survived the first years of the twenty-first century was a consolidation around Pope's old empire, which had included the flagship original, the *Enquirer,* the *Weekly World News,* and—often overlooked—the actual racks Pope owned in tens of thousands of the nation's supermarkets and convenience stores. His private GP Group has been sold and resold, renamed, taken public, bought back, and its managements changed twice. For an initial one-time profit the first of the new owners sold off racks and delivery operations, key ingredients in Pope's original, stunning business success, and then watched their papers' circulations dwindle. Few consumers realized that Pope made money off the competing tabloids that so slavishly imitated his formula by renting them space on his racks, where the prime top spots were reserved for his own products.

The *Globe,* the *Examiner,* and the *Sun* were virtual clones, operated under Canadian Mike Rosenbloom's ownership, first in Montreal, then in South Florida, where Rosenbloom moved his tabloids to escape a union drive and to employ mostly recycled *Enquirer* staffers from a rich tabloid labor pool Pope had inadvertently created by capriciously hiring and firing so many reporters and editors. Rupert Murdoch founded his *Star* in 1973 in the *Enquirer's* wake and image, then bought the *New York Post* a few years later, going on to become a second force in tabloid culture, although he was relegated to a distant second place in the United States during Pope's lifetime. In 1986, two years before Pope's death, Murdoch founded the tabloid TV news show *Current Affair* and launched *The Late Show* with Joan Rivers. Murdoch continued to carry the tabloid genre into television, a medium at which Pope had so stubbornly balked, eventually turning Fox into our fourth national network, America's first new one since ABC began in 1951. To head up Fox News, Murdoch picked one of Pope's most interesting alumni, former *Enquirer* reporter Steve Chao, a Harvard classics major and one of the whiz kids Pope recruited from the Ivy League in the early eighties. Chao has been credited with inventing Fox's reality programs *Cops* and *America's Most Wanted*.

Murdoch's News Corporation, which is already capable of beaming Chinese-language news and entertainment via satellite to most of Asia from its studios in Hong Kong, appears to be on the verge of extending the empire of tabloid beyond Britain, Australia, and the United States. So far tabloid culture has manifested itself mostly in English, very much including the Internet, whose colorful Web pages and punchy writing owe much to tabloid journalism and Pope's original formula. If Murdoch, or any media mogul, can overcome the obstacles of language and culture, which so far have prevented any truly global media empire, China, with its billion-plus population, looks promising for the site of the next explosion of tabloid culture.

But until his fatal heart attack, Pope was without a doubt the driving force behind our first and foremost supermarket tabloid and the inventor of a kind of culture (a British-American hybrid, as we shall see) that has spread far beyond the grocery checkout counter into nearly all other forms of our popular media. That the original supermarket tabloids survive as an increasingly antiquated subgenre with dwindling circulations does not mean that tabloid culture is in decline, merely that it has spread so widely into other media that the supermarket checkout no longer holds the monopoly.

The story of the *Enquirer* would be far simpler, but much less interesting and eventful, if Pope were a man of vision who brainstormed or theorized the *Enquirer* into existence. Far from that, the *Enquirer* evolved through a series of dialogues—between Pope and his readers, between Pope and his editors and reporters, between the paper and the supermarket, between the paper and the subjects of its reportage, especially the celebrities it preyed upon, and between the paper and the major legal apparatus that regulates publishing in this democratic republic, libel law and the courts.

The story of the *Enquirer* and the biography of Pope are virtually the same thing, so little life did Pope have outside the paper and so tyrannically did he rule over his publication. Attempts have been made to write Pope's biography and the colorful tale of the *National Enquirer,* but until now they have failed to achieve publication and all have foundered in one way or another.*

Pope's son Paul commissioned a biography in the nineties, when he was in his thirties, intended to prove that his father was murdered, his will destroyed, and that Paul was the true heir to his father's publishing empire. The project sparked interest in publishing circles and was written and researched by former *Enquirer* staffers, who certainly knew how to write to order and hype material. But even they failed to find proof of this quintessentially tabloid tale.

---

* There was even a TV movie made about Pope, though he was fictionalized and played by the seventy-two-year-old Burt Lancaster. The 1985 film, *Scandal Sheet,* a flop, had started out as a witty memoir of a former *Enquirer* reporter, published in *Rolling Stone* and optioned for a movie. By the time the scriptwriters had their way, it was a soppy romance between the tabloid editor and his new star reporter. The premise was that the hot-writing and -looking female lead was going to show the boss how to improve his paper. It was totally improbable because everyone who knew Pope knew he was likely to fire any employee who suggested too strenuously that his paper needed improving. The only bright spot was a minor role played by Frances McDormand.

Having failed to publish, Paul Pope offered a million-dollar prize to anyone who could come forth with conclusive evidence of his father's murder.

Tom Kuncl was once given a six-figure advance to write a tell-all book after he resigned as executive editor of the *Enquirer* in the early 1980s. But his insider role proved to be a handicap:

> So I wrote a couple of pages, and it came flying back to me; these guys [the book executives and editors] sound too nice and too smart. And they are nice and they are smart, but the only thing they wanted was what scumbags we were. So I'm saying, well, look, if everybody there is a scumbag, I just left there, and I'm the chief scumbag. So what do they want from me, a confession? I couldn't do it. The place was good, we did good work. If you like the paper, fine, and if you don't, don't read it. I stood by every story that ever went through there on my watch.[1]

Other formidable obstacles to a biography of Gene Pope lie in his social isolation; his incapacity for intimacy, which apparently extended even to his own close family; and the ironic fact, considering he was a publisher, that he seemed seriously inarticulate.

A discussion of whether, for instance, the *Enquirer* should cover British or European royals—which the paper didn't at first—would be settled with an epigrammatic comment from Pope: "Americans don't care about royalty." Later the paper would publish many stories about Prince Charles and Princess Di and their privileged circle in great detail, many of them cover stories, but it was coverage that likely evolved through the interests and enthusiasms of its

British reporters rather than any editorial strategy discussions involving Pope. Recounted conversations with Pope, whether firsthand, thirdhand, or overheard, consisted almost entirely of short sardonic sentences, phrases, observations, and judgments, generally quoted in an imitation of his voice and manner, so distinctive was his mode of expression. This behavior suggests that to some extent everyone who worked close to Pope in some sense internalized him, since their workday life consisted of second-guessing his wishes.

Pope's tough-guy stance against the world precluded his sharing his thoughts or elaborating on his feelings. As for feelings, he seemed by the period of his greatest success even to be anhedonic—unable to experience pleasure at all except in the most remote and vicarious ways. He was, most people thought, humorless.

After he was so successful as a tabloid publisher, in the late seventies and eighties, Pope granted interviews fairly generously, though he tended to give the same interview, more or less, over and over. In such situations reporters tend to cannibalize earlier published interviews, so eventually a sort of short standard history of Pope and the *Enquirer* emerged, with quotations that seemed to have become standardized. There was also a standard mainstream attitude toward the paper—it was tongue-in-cheek fun—and the interviews were always puffs. Pope's accessible biography, including these limited interview performances, remains almost totally intertwined with the *Enquirer,* and even after that backstage drama is revealed, he will likely remain personally an enigma.

Pope shows many symptoms of Asperger's syndrome, first recognized by the American Psychiatric Association in 1994, or of high-functioning autism. The indications include Pope's lack of social skills, his capacity for obsession, his inability to articulate his inner states (he once told an interviewer that he didn't try to figure himself out), his sensitivity to eye contact, and his childhood precocity, including his memory of his father *allowing* him to verify and write payout checks for *Il Progresso* when he was fifteen. Pope's obsession with the length of the grass on the *Enquirer* grounds and his home, with the absolute correctness of the temperature on the *Enquirer* billboard, and the minute timing of the automatic sprinklers could be interpreted as parts of a pathological cluster. We know from the recovered microrecorder he used as a personal notebook that he was inordinately concerned that his sprinklers came on five minutes early as he returned home from work his last Friday on Earth.

Pope also kept something like a daybook or objective log, not a diary in the sense that it would make notes of his moods or thoughts, but something that would be useful for a biographer. "It was a dated listing of contacts, phone calls, people he had lunch with," said Val Virga, former chief of photo. "I know exactly where it is, but it's in the Boca building"—the building in Boca Raton that is still infected with anthrax from the famous 2001 incident; no one has been inside for years.

We sometimes read scientific insights from such behavioral clusters and pathologies back into the biographies of outstanding and productive figures, and Pope is an excellent candidate for such a study. Screenwriter, director, and playwright David Mamet, in his book *Bambi vs. Godzilla,* allows: "It is not impossible that Asperger's syndrome helped make the movies. The symptoms of this developmental disorder include early precocity, a great ability to maintain masses of information, a lack of ability to mix with groups in age-appropriate ways, ignorance of or indifference to social norms, high intelligence, and difficulty with transitions, married to a preternatural ability to concentrate on the minutia of the task at hand."[2]

If Pope were to be posthumously diagnosed with Asperger's, what difference would that make? It would probably help us understand Asperger's more than it would help us understand Pope. But it would also help support the view that Pope was not a visionary who theorized the *Enquirer* into existence, but that he acted as the central catalyst in the long and varied cultural dialogue that produced it. He was the only central character in the drama of the *Enquirer:* everyone else came and went, almost always as victims of his imperious will. The only important editorial employee who stuck with him was Iain Calder, who started with Pope in 1964 and remained after Pope's death to preside over the first years of a cataclysmic decline. The most obvious conclusion is that it was Pope's figurative DNA, or his Asperger's traits, or simply his obsessive, eccentric personality, that kept the paper moving, changing, and prospering.

Inevitably the biography of Pope is the consummate tabloid story, and the recounting of it invites a style that is itself tabloidish. The tabloidization of our culture in all media has gone far enough to influence the idiom of our era and has infused an Elizabethan exuberance and energy into English.

TWO

FAMILY CONNECTIONS

Generoso Pope Jr. was the namesake, third, youngest, and favorite son of Generoso Pope Sr., who came to New York City in his early teens in 1906 on the S.S. *Madonna* from a farming village near Naples, with only a few words of English in his vocabulary and, as he later told a reporter, only a few dollars in his pocket. Bearing the family name Papa, which he later changed, he made his way with meager jobs, variously described as water boy in a piano factory and water boy for the men constructing the East River Tunnel. He worked his way up to shoveler then to foreman of a sand and gravel company and, when the company was threatened with bankruptcy in 1916, convinced creditors to give him a chance to pull the company out of the red. The stocky, energetic immigrant emerged as president, half owner, and eventually sole owner of the country's largest sand and gravel company, renamed Colonial Sand and Stone, which provided the raw material for much of Manhattan's avenues and skyline.

The elder Pope married Catherine Richichi in 1916 and started a family. Four years later his name appeared in a *New York Times* report of a lawsuit for $50,000 damages brought by Frieda Weber, a Florida woman who alleged that Pope had proposed marriage, promised an engagement ring, and agreed to buy her a country home. Weber's mother investigated Pope, according to the *Times*, and found that he was already married; she said that Pope contended he was

This 1937 photo of Generoso Pope Sr. (center) giving the fascist salute after decorating Rome's Tomb of the Unknown Soldier caused political trouble. (Bettmann/Corbis)

waiting for a divorce, which was false. Weber said Pope had been trying to induce her to settle her claim against him for a small sum.[1] Pope remained married to Richichi until his death in 1950. If he was a womanizer, as this vignette suggests, he did not pass the trait on to his son, who appeared unburdened with the complications of philandering, at least during the long stretch when he was running the *Enquirer* and was married to his third wife, Lois.

The younger Pope often told a bare-bones version of the story of his immigrant father, so that it sounded like a Horatio Alger story. Like many Americans, Pope liked these rags-to-riches stories, and they became a favorite *Enquirer* genre by the seventies. They became part of the paper's winning formula, as were the closely related success-without-college stories, which also applied to the senior Pope, who had little formal education. But when Gene Pope retold the story of his father, the middle part, which told how exactly Pope Sr. became a millionaire by the age of thirty-seven, was always missing. The story Americans like to hear is one of hard work, determination, frugality, and self-sacrifice: Generoso Pope Sr.'s story contained all that and much more.

In 1928 the elder Pope bought *Il Progresso Italo-Americano*, America's largest Italian-language daily, for over $2 million. Newspapers were rarely really lucrative, but they conferred something more precious than money on those who knew how to wield it: influence and its corollary, power. New York supported several Italian-language newspapers, both left- and right-wing, in those times, and they had close political links to the old country as well. The elder Pope visited Italy in 1931 to counter reports that he was an unreliable opportunist with connections to Tammany Hall and the Mafia. He was ultimately successful in proving his loyalty to the Italian government.[2]

Dorothy Gallagher's *All the Right Enemies: The Life and Murder of Carlo Tresca* fingers Pope Sr. as the prime suspect in the murder by contract of Carlo Tresca, a once well-known anarchist and the editor of a rival Italian-language newspaper. Tresca was all the more attractive to many because he was left-wing without being communist. Gallagher portrays Pope Sr. as a godfather type who made offers that "couldn't be refused." She quotes Tresca's description of the elder Pope in the October 28, 1934, issue of his own paper, *Il Martello*, under the headline "We Accuse Generoso Pope . . . of Being a Gangster and a Racketeer":

There's the man for you: abusive, presumptuous and violent. But that is not enough. Up until now, given his quality as director of

Fascist papers . . . his relations with the more presentable parts of Tammany, his intimate friendship with New York mayor Jimmy Walker . . . nobody has ever dreamed of lifting his mask: of presenting him to the public as a gangster and a racketeer. We are forced to do it because . . . he is using against us and all anti-Fascists the same methods of gangster and racketeer that he has been using up to now to impose his monopolistic will on all possible rivals. . . . If one of our own is struck, the author of the blow is known: it is Generoso Pope. . . . We have denounced him before public opinion. There isn't a city editor of the New York dailies who does not know today who Generoso Pope is and what gangster methods he employs.[3]

After the article was published, Tresca told friends about the visit of one of Pope's henchmen, Frank Garofalo, who told him that Pope had been too patient with him and that if the attacks on Pope's character continued, Tresca would pay with his life. Meanwhile, Pope raised $800,000 for Mussolini's invasion of Ethiopia and, as one of the handful who controlled the Italian vote in New York City, wielded influence in Albany, the state capital, and Washington.

As a consummate mover and shaker, the elder Pope was famous for his lavish entertaining; he took judges to steak dinners in upscale hotels and treated politicians to the big boxing matches in Madison Square Garden. In 1936 Pope met in Washington with Senator Robert Wagner, Secretary of State Harold Ickes, and President Franklin Roosevelt himself, according to Gallagher. (Pope's long obituary in the *New York Times* noted that he had been received by Roosevelt several times.) Afterward Pope Sr. told Roosevelt, facing reelection: "My newspapers will spare no effort to give their readers all information in news and editorial . . . on your behalf. . . . They are at your disposal."[4] But Pope's politics contained a contradiction he would eventually have to resolve. In 1936 he participated in a Madison Square Garden tribute to Mussolini. The following year he visited Rome, where he was received by Mussolini, awarded the title Grand Officer of the Crown of Italy, and photographed with his arm raised in the Fascist salute. Pope Sr.'s continued support of Mussolini remained a problem to his Washington connections.

In 1941, Pope finally publicly repudiated Fascism and Mussolini, who had signed a treaty with Hitler. In an editorial in *Il Progresso* he wrote: "I am against any government that is against the government of the United States. I am unequivocally against any diffusion of all foreign and anti-Americanism in this country, whether it be communism, Nazism or fascism."[5] He turned *Il Progresso* over to one of his older sons—Fortune or Anthony, since Generoso Jr. was only fourteen. By the forties, the elder Pope was the third member of New York City's powerful ruling triumvirate, whose other two members were Carmine De Sapio, the old-style chieftain of Tammany Hall, and Frank Costello, who became known as the prime minister of the underworld.[6]

The enmity between Pope and the unforgiving Tresca flared one last time, according to Gallagher's account, at a dinner under the auspices of the War Bond Savings Committee of Americans of Italian Origin, on September 10, 1942. Tresca had gone under the impression that Pope would not be attending. But Pope arrived with Frank Garofalo, the henchman who had threatened Tresca's life, and Garofalo's girlfriend, Dolores Facconte, an assistant U.S. attorney—a relationship that openly advertised the intertwining of crime and law enforcement in New York City. "Tresca rose from his seat," according to Gallagher: "In a voice loud enough to be heard by dozens of people, he called out: 'Not only a Fascist is here, but also his gangster! This is too much! I'm leaving!' He continued to speak loudly as he left the room, calling Garofalo a notorious killer."[7]

Four months later, on the night of January 11, 1943, Tresca was shot twice and killed as he walked in lower Manhattan. Police soon discovered evidence that the shooter was Carmine Galante, a thug who had served eight years in Sing Sing. Galante was arrested and held on parole violations, but after a year he was released. Roger Baldwin, one of Tresca's friends and a founder of the American Civil Liberties Union, wrote John Dos Passos about the case in 1945: "I share the conclusion . . . that the investigation is being blocked by powerful forces or political connections. I think they got the right man in Galante. . . . But Galante, a hired gunman, could not be made to talk even with the third degree! The trail through him would lead directly to Pope and he is, as you know, a powerful Tammany figure."[8] Alfred Kazin's review of Gallagher's book in the Sunday *New York Times* revealed that Dos Passos had lunched with Tresca the day he was murdered.[9] The case remains officially unsolved to this day.

Galante continued an eventful career in organized crime that included a stint in Lewisburg Penitentiary's privileged cell block G, known as Mafia Row, on narcotics convictions. In 1977 he was charged with parole violations and was defended by Roy Cohn, who seemed always to be on the dark side of every case and was closely associated with both the junior and senior Popes.

Two years later Galante, aged sixty-seven, was shot to death as he ate lunch on the patio of a Brooklyn restaurant.

Young Gene would have been sixteen when Tresca was shot. It might not seem likely that Generoso would have discussed strong-arm tactics, threats, and assassination plots with his teenage son, but considering the premature responsibilities his favored son was given by the time he was nineteen, it is not entirely unlikely. Many subtle attitudes would have been telegraphed, character traits perceived and shaped in the smithy of the family. This is not difficult to imagine for anyone who has watched Anthony Jr. and Meadow grow up in our latest and most thoroughly constructed fictional Mafia family, the Sopranos. All his life Gene Pope talked like a tough guy, and while some saw that as a bluff, considering how relatively tame his life as a publisher was, he was formed in the shadow of a real tough guy.

His father wore the mantle of power and earned it in a tough arena. The elder Pope wasn't talented in the usual sense; certainly he wasn't wise in the educated or philosophical sense. Though he could influence elections and manipulate high appointments, he never ran for election or held a high office himself. He wasn't the likely subject of a biography, and his considerable power in the shadows seems to have melted away with hardly a trace. Yet the Pope patriarch passed something to his youngest son, something that is a consideration in the formation of the character of a publishing mogul whose editorial outlook—it was never really a vision—narrowed to something we have come to call tabloid. The editorial product wasn't high-minded, nor was it ideological. It definitely had a satirical edge, and it looked at its subjects from a low—rather than high—angle. It didn't mince words, and it satisfied basic appetites. It gave people what they wanted, even when they didn't want to admit it.

Generoso Pope Jr. was born on January 13, 1927, in the Bronx, but by the time he went to the city's prestigious Horace Mann School in Manhattan, the family had moved to 1040 Fifth Avenue, at the corner of Eighty-fifth Street. In 1930 his father had purchased the ninth and tenth floors of the newly built cooperative, with a total of twenty-two rooms, including six baths. Gene rode to school in a chauffeured limousine, often accompanied by his schoolmate Roy Cohn, whose father was a liberal Democratic judge sitting on the New York State Supreme Court.* The two boys lived a few blocks apart—Cohn lived on Park Avenue at Ninety-second Street—and, according to Nicholas Von Hoffman, Gene Pope was one of two boys Roy always invited to his parties.[10] "Roy's father was a judge and every Friday night I would go over to his house for dinner," Pope told reporter Sid Kirchheimer. "I met all the judges, the DA that way." A cluster of alumni from Pope and Cohn's class at Horace Mann showed particular distinction in journalism. Si Newhouse, who was also a classmate in the boys' circle, came to head the Condé Nast publishing empire, which eventually included the *New Yorker* and *Vanity Fair*. Another Horace Mann classmate was Anthony Lewis, son of Kassel Lewis, formerly

---

* Roy Cohn later became notorious for serving as Senator Joseph McCarthy's chief counsel during his 1950s witch hunt for Communists in government and the army. Cohn was pitted against another young attorney, Robert Kennedy, with whom he had a lifelong feud that was still fiercely alive when Kennedy was assassinated in 1968. In later life Cohn became a legal dealer and fixer of the sort that led biographer Nicholas Von Hoffman to tag him as "high society's junkyard watchdog."

Oshinsky, owner of a leading garment district firm. "At Horace Mann I had no closer buddy than Tony Lewis," Cohn told reporter Sidney Zion, dictating his "autobiography" as he lay dying of AIDS. "Yes, the very Anthony Lewis who won two Pulitzers, and ran the London bureau and then wrote a column for the *New York Times*."[11]

Both Cohn biographers, Von Hoffman and Zion (whose books were reviewed together on the front page of the *New York Times Books Review* by Tom Wolfe), tell the story of how a precocious teenage Roy Cohn fronted Pope Sr.'s purchase of the New York City radio station WHOM. They also recount his strange intimate friendship with the elder Pope. Von Hoffman says Cohn believed Pope Sr. was "with the Mafia,"[12] though saying it that way overlooks the subtle circumlocutions in how the mob defined itself. George Wolf, Frank Costello's lawyer for most of the mobster kingpin's life, described in his book about Costello how the terminology worked: "I never heard Frank—or any of my other high underworld clients—mention the word Mafia, or Cosa Nostra. The key word that always denoted the Mafia was not a noun but a verb: 'connected.' In describing a stranger to me Frank might say, briefly, 'He's connected.' And then I knew. The Mafia is not organized like a business corporation."[13]

Joe Bonanno, another mobster described as a mafioso, a rare one who died of natural causes at ninety-seven, also eschewed the use of the word Mafia (although his son and successor, Bill, the subject of Gay Talese's bestselling work of New Journalism, *Honor Thy Father,* seemed to accept it). The term *connected,* said the elder Bonanno, who godfathered one of the so-called Five Families in New York during Costello's era, "refers to a process, a special set of relationships among men." His Associated Press obituary quoted him as saying in his ghosted memoir, *A Man of Honor,* "I stay away from the term [Mafia] because it creates more confusion than it's worth."[14]

Pope Sr. was undoubtedly "connected," and the avoidance of the word Mafia possibly even left room for Pope Jr. to plausibly deny, at least in his own mind, that he had Mafia associations. Whatever the word games, by 1943, according to Wolf, Costello "literally owned New York, appointing judges and district attorneys and even mayors."[15] But, as Cohn pointed out in his memoir, Costello remained in the shadows and operated through De Sapio, who functioned as his "stooge."[16]

"I had a very special relationship with Generoso Pope [Sr.]," the bedridden Cohn told Zion in the last weeks of his life. "He was really a second father to me and had been almost since the day I met him in 1941 when I was 14 and he was 45." Cohn described Pope as the man "who practically ran Tammany, was tight with President Roosevelt, and was one of the most powerful Italian-Americans in the country."[17] Cohn told Zion, "A night didn't go by when I wasn't on the phone with Mr. Pope before bedtime and that was after a good half-dozen calls during the day. We didn't talk about the weather—these conversations roamed from politics to business to intimate personal things. In that way, at least—on the personal stuff—he was closer to me than my father, who was not one to share his innermost thoughts"[18]

This December-May friendship with Pope's favored son's equally precocious schoolmate was described as part of a "pattern" by Cohn: "All my life I've been able to work well and closely with older powerful men—Joe McCarthy, Cardinal Spellman, J. Edgar Hoover, Lewis Rosensteil, to name a significant few."[19] Cohn described for Zion how one night when he was fifteen he proposed that he front Pope's purchase of WHOM, because Pope was afraid the price would go up when it was known he was bidding.

> At dinner at his house one night, it must have been 1942, he mentioned that he wanted to buy a New York radio station, WHOM. He said it was worth $400,000, big money in those days. I said, "What's the highest price you'll pay?" He smiled. He asked why I wanted to know. I said, "I'd like to take a crack at getting it for you." He said, "If you can buy it for $350,000 you've got ten grand."[20]

Cohn said he accomplished the deal with the help of his uncle, Bernie Marcus, who had done time in Sing Sing over the failure of the family bank. Uncle Bernie introduced young Cohn to the general counsel for WHOM, "and in record time we had it and I made $10,000."[21] Although his generous parents could well afford to put him through college, Cohn said he used Pope's money to finance his undergraduate and legal education at Columbia University because "I wanted independence . . . I didn't want to think I owed them anything"[22]

One of the most illustrative stories Cohn told Zion on his deathbed about Generoso Pope Sr. was how Pope engineered the appointment of Irving Saypol, Cohn's close personal friend, as U.S. attorney for the Southern District of New York. Cohn, then twenty-one, went to see Pope to propose Saypol's name.

"Do you vouch for him?" Pope asked in a dialogue that reads like Marlon Brando's in Francis Ford Coppola's *Godfather.*

"I said, 'Sure. He's a good guy.' What did I know about the word 'vouch'?

I was 21 years old. It really meant I was putting my name on the line for Saypol. If it went wrong it could have been my head.

"'We hear bad things about him. We hear his word is no good, that we can't trust him, that if he gets in there he's liable to knock our brains out. But you say he's OK, you vouch for him, yes?'

"'Absolutely.'

"'Then it's done.'"[23]

Later Cohn learned much more about what went on in the shadows of power—it became his métier. As the wiser, older Cohn told Zion: "What I didn't know was that Frank Costello was running Tammany for the mob, that Carmine DeSapio was his stooge, that the mob had for years before (and years afterwards) decided the appointment of the U.S. Attorney and that Costello—at Pope's behest—had chosen Irving Saypol."[24] A few years later Cohn became a U.S. attorney under Saypol and was one of his chief assistants during the prosecution of Julius and Ethel Rosenberg on charges of spying for the Soviet Union.

Roy Cohn grew up to become one of the strangest men of the twentieth century, the gay-hating homosexual who lived, according to his biographer Zion, in a "closet with neon lights"[25] the friend of the powerful FBI director who nevertheless specialized in defending wealthy crooks, the social outcast with high-class connections. As an assistant U.S. attorney under Saypol, Cohn even played a small part in the prosecution of Alger Hiss. Then he rose to become Saypol's first lieutenant in the prosecution of the Rosenbergs, showing an early knack for picking the sinister side of sensational political cases.

Since it's commonly believed that our sexual proclivities are formed during puberty, if not before, Cohn's homosexuality needs to be dealt with (though inevitably inconclusively) in the context of his early close friendship with Gene Pope, which lasted on into young adulthood. No one has ever proposed that Pope was a homosexual—it's almost unimaginable to anyone who knew him at all—yet he was best friends with one of our culture's most famous gays. Cohn was by anyone's account a twisted man of self-contradictions, an anti-Semitic Jew as well as an antigay gay who partook boisterously of the gay bacchanal that flourished in the seventies and eighties, until the AIDS crisis changed gay culture—and eventually claimed his life in 1986.

In his daily life, Pope was hypermacho. And so was Cohn. Most of us know, in this era when gay marriage is discussed nationwide, that in gay circles the male butch persona can be just as viable a role choice as that of the femme, a continuum that now stretches all the way to the transsexual who can pass as a woman. But the perception was different in the fifties, and Von Hoffman speculates that in his youth Cohn felt he could plausibly deny he was gay because he wasn't feminine, or swish. In the fifties a homosexual was defined as a limp-wristed sissy, and Cohn wasn't that: "It appears that for Roy [in his youth] the definition of a homosexual was a man with womanish mannerisms,"[26] writes Von Hoffman, who elsewhere cites a distinction between being homosexual and gay, defining the first as a gender preference and the second as the folkways and byways of a particular time and culture. Von Hoffman even allows for the possibility that Cohn did not practice, or only rarely practiced, his homosexuality in his early career, when many of his acquaintances and friends remembered him as asexual.

But even after that conception of homosexuality was well past, Cohn continued to deny that he was gay. Mike Wallace interviewed both Pope and Cohn, and neither parted with their secrets. Cohn was interviewed twice, the second time a year before he died. In that final interview he refused, in the face of Wallace's signature badgering, to admit that he was homosexual or that he had AIDS. Cohn continued to deny that he was gay or had AIDS even to some of his closest friends, who were deeply hurt when they found out he had lied to them to the very end.

Both young Roy and Gene affected toughness, or really were tough; Cohn was or became homosexual and Pope wasn't homosexual, so it's unlikely that Cohn—in light of what we know of him—ever confided his homosexuality to his early best friend or that Pope had any inkling of Cohn's homosexuality in his youth. Later it's more than likely that Pope knew, as knowing people's secrets was what he treasured and traded in as the world's foremost tabloid publisher.

THREE

KID WHEELER-DEALER

After Horace Mann, Pope breezed through MIT in two and a half years, by way of an accelerated wartime program, and earned, at age nineteen, a degree in mechanical engineering that he never used. Though he described himself as a "science nut," Pope also said he never wanted to be an engineer but went to MIT because engineering fascinated him, that studying engineering taught him to think logically.[1] Cohn outpaced Pope, graduating from Columbia through a similar accelerated program with both his bachelor's and law degrees by the time he was twenty.[2] After young Gene graduated from MIT in 1946, his father made him editor and publisher of *Il Progresso,* probably displacing one of his favored son's older brothers. He also made his teenage son vice president of Colonial Sand and Stone, as well as general manager of WHOM.[3] Pope always told interviewers that printer's ink got in his blood at *Il Progresso,* but the sand-and-gravel business, he said, "didn't intrigue me."[4] This is also the period when, Pope acknowledged, he fell deeply under the influence of Cohn. "I did nothing but wheel and deal," he recalled in an interview with the *New York Daily News.*[5] And what better teacher than Cohn, who Nicholas Von Hoffman said was already fixing traffic tickets for his teachers in high school. This is probably the period when Pope attended the New York School of Law, as noted in the *New York Times* announcement of his first marriage to Patricia McManus in 1951, but he did not get a degree. In those wheeler-dealer years Pope was invited to lunch at the White House with Harry Truman, a reminder that the Pope family continued to be a power in the Democratic Party by virtue of their influence over New York's Italian vote, through *Il Progresso* and the important connections it fostered.

Pope's early close association with Roy Cohn helps us understand where Pope went after the pair parted ways. Had Pope finished his law degree, he would have been even better outfitted than Cohn to be a fixer, dealmaker, and powerbroker on the dark side of politics—one with a mob godfather no less. But Pope's motivation at this point appears to be more about getting away from things than going toward anything. There's little evidence that Pope had a master plan (he's educated as an engineer but never practices) and that helps explain why the development of his life's major project, the *National Enquirer,* seems so serendipitous. But his parting with Cohn was clearly a fork in his life's road.

Cohn stuck much closer to the example of Generoso Sr., the older, powerful male he so admired in his youth. He was ruthless and unprincipled by almost everyone's account, a man who dodged taxes, stole from his clients, failed to repay loans, and came within a hair of being disbarred.

Cohn was even reputed to have connections with the underworld good enough to have people whacked, and he was dogged all his life by rumors that he had murdered a gay lover in scuttling a yacht for insurance money. Von Hoffman, his biographer, found nothing to substantiate such gossip; it seemed merely part of Cohn's wicked image. In the early days of the *Enquirer* Pope also had the reputation of being capable of having people rubbed out, according to his longtime associate Iain Calder, but that part of his godfather image faded after he moved the paper to Florida. Reporters who crossed him would be summarily fired, but at least they didn't feel they would be whacked as well.

The Pope family's power was centered in politics and publishing. Like Hearst and Pulitzer, Pope Sr. thought of his readers as voters, a quantity he could broker and deal in. He made his money in construction, but he gained his power when he bought *Il Progresso,* and later the radio station. Sometimes it is easiest to see how a political machine works when it breaks down and the inner wheels and pulleys are exposed. Such an opportunity came on October 26, 1950, when young Pope's face appeared on the front page of the *New York Times.*[6] He was attempting to fill the shoes of his father, who had died five months earlier, and the *Times* story indicates that those wingtips were too big. The story concerned a scandal that erupted when acting mayor Vincent Impellitteri accused Gene Pope of acting as an emissary for Frank Costello, "a gambler and racketeer," following two conversations they had in the corridors of city hall concerning *Il Progresso*'s endorsement of New York Supreme Court justice Ferdinand Pecora for mayor. The preponderance of Italian names makes it obvious how much power the Italian-language papers wielded in New York City politics.

Impellitteri had been seeking *Il Progresso*'s endorsement for the job, and when Pope declined to back him, he took revenge in withdrawing privileges within his power, privileges that had been bestowed by the former mayor, Bill O'Dwyer, who had been forced to resign after a police corruption scandal. Pope disputed the version of the conversations given to the *Times* by the acting mayor, who quoted him as saying, "Costello told me he's going along with Pecora, so I'm going along with Pecora, too." The paper also noted that Pope had attended a dinner given by the Mafia kingpin at the Copacabana to raise money for the Salvation Army.

As a result of his association with Costello, Pope was required to turn in his shield as a deputy police commissioner, which entitled him to salutes from police patrolmen and, maybe even more important in teeming Manhattan, allowed him to park anywhere in the city. The article also notes that Pope was in danger of losing his position on the board of higher education.* The princely parking privileges and salutes were largely symbolic; the damage was the publicity, the exposure of what ordinarily went on in the shadows.

Impellitteri went on to win the election, and it appears that the Pope family's power was disintegrating following the death of the elder Pope. Despite the patriarch's attempt to groom his namesake for the succession, it appears the heir was too young, and the older brothers were not capable or interested. The family continued to own the newspaper, but there was evidence that their fortunes were declining. There was evidence that Costello's power was waning as well.

In 1950 the elder Pope, who had been in poor health since a severe case of pneu-

---

* Young Gene's appointment to a nine-year term on the board, the policymaking body for the city's four municipal colleges, was decried by the Teachers Union of the United Public Workers, which asserted that O'Dwyer used the board "as an agency for the crude award of political favors," according to a June 10, 1950, *New York Times* article ("Pope and Ohrbach in School Posts"). The union protested that the appointments revealed a "contempt for the city's municipal colleges that can only end in their complete degradation," adding, "It is singularly unfitting that the youthful Mr. Generoso Pope Jr. should now sit to evaluate recommendations for promotions of scientists and creative scholars of experience and maturity."

monia four years before, died of a heart attack at age fifty-nine. With his two-column, twenty-two-paragraph obituary, the *New York Times* ran a 1946 photo of a rotund, energetic-looking Pope Sr. wearing a pinstripe suit, slicked-back hair, and a garish tie, seemingly about to break into laughter. (His namesake, by contrast, always photographed gloomily; the lower halves of their faces are remarkably similar, however, and both had dark hair and eyes.)

The Pope patriarch tied up $4 million of his $5 million fortune in a foundation to be administered by his widow, Gene, and his two older brothers, Anthony and Fortune. The Generoso Pope Foundation was to help the "aged, sick, and infirm, to assist in the study and promotion of the arts and sciences, to establish scholarships and research awards to induce intellectual attainments, and to study and promote religion and morality."[7] The widow was to receive one-third of the remaining estate, and the rest was to be held in trust for the three sons. The inheritances were probably structured in such a way as to minimize taxes.

The foundation, which took up the bulk of the patriarch's fortune, appeared to be a serious charity, however, not just a front. Later, the *Enquirer,* in its supermarket stage, also had a charitable function, funneling thousands of dollars in small amounts to the sick and suffering in the form of stories that encouraged write-in donations. Those sympathetic tearjerkers about hard luck and tragedy were almost entirely lost under subsequent owners and largely forgotten. Now the *Enquirer* is noted for its celebrity gossip, but under Pope the paper offered a much wider menu.

Pope Sr. was an honorary deputy police commissioner, too, and that entitled him to be buried with the full honors of that rank. He was interred in Woodlawn Cemetery after a requiem mass at St. Patrick's Cathedral attended by former mayor Bill O'Dwyer, the police commissioner, and three thousand others. Ten blocks of Fifth Avenue were closed to traffic as the cortège arrived with the police band playing Beethoven's *Funeral March.* As police and firemen stood at attention, the mayor, the commissioner, and staff doffed their hats to the tune of "Lead, Kindly Light."[8] It was an incredible showing for a man whose name is largely remembered now only through his namesake son, whose own memorial service by comparison was mostly a quiet affair for tabloid insiders.

Gene Pope soon fell out with his brothers and mother and severed relations with his family. His name was taken off the masthead of *Il Progresso.*[9] Without the patriarch to impose order, family war broke out, much of it possibly fueled by pent-up resentments over the father's favoritism. Pope eventually stopped speaking to his mother, who outlived him. Neither she nor his two brothers came to his funeral. The family breakup after the death of the patriarch lasted a lifetime. "They decided I was going to work for them," Pope told *Forbes,* "and I told them to take a walk." In recounting the story to the *Washington Post,* Pope said: "I'm not going to get anywhere in this deal. It's two to one."[10] The quote suggests that his brothers ganged up on him, and his mother, to his disgust, sided with them.

But really it was Pope who walked, and when he did, he started over from pretty close to zero. By the time he died, he possessed a fortune that had been estimated three years earlier by *Fortune* magazine at $130 million.[11] Even that estimate was more than three times too low, as the terms of the sale of the *Enquirer* in 1989—for $412.5 million—made clear. Because the family fortune was tied up in charity and young Gene walked away from his family, he is a cultural anomaly. Since he started over again with close to nothing at the age of twenty-three, he qualifies as a second-generation self-made millionaire, a man who went from riches to rags (sort of) and back to riches. But young Gene started over with some privileges, including his elite education and experience—and his connections for securing loans from underworld sources.

The similarities between father and namesake went deep. Gene Pope orphaned himself in turning away from his mother and brothers, just as his father was orphaned when he sailed alone to the United States and suffered the immigrant's alienation from his home culture. It's tantalizing to speculate just how much Pope Jr. was a chip off the old block, how much genes, family nurturing, and his sense of entitlement had produced a similar character. Were his strange mannerisms and eccentric personality modeled after his father?

Gene Pope seems never to have been young. In his photo on the front page of the *New York Times,* the young man filling his father's shoes at *Il Progresso* and walking the corridors of city hall seems already to have assumed the dignity and poise of an older, successful male. At the *Enquirer* Pope never invited familiarity; there was always an enormous gulf between Pope and his employees. To his face, his reporters and editors called him "Mr. Pope," and out of his hearing he was referred to as "the boss" or "GP," never by his first name. Only family and close friends were privileged to call him by his nickname, Gene.

Pope had a direct inside phone line to every editor's desk—a sort of presidential hotline—and when he summoned anyone, the employee dropped whatever he was doing and ran, even if he was in the middle of an important deadline. *Enquirer* reporter Frank Zahour, formerly of the *Chicago Tribune,* had never seen anything like it: "They treated it like a fire bell. Whatever you were doing, Pope was the priority. If he wanted you for something, others were given your tasks, even if it meant going over your notes for a story, whatever."[12]

Pope was also singularly lacking in humor or playfulness—a youthful trait—and hardly ever seemed to unbend, except perhaps a tiny bit with his editorial cadre on Saturday mornings. Then he came to the office wearing slippers and attire variously described as shorts, a bathing suit (he had a pool and lived on the beach), or pajamas,[13] which seemed to offer an uncharacteristic intimacy. But wasn't that more like treating employees like the privileged courtiers invited into Louis XIV's bedroom? Saturdays he would play the kind of music he liked—old warhorses like "Victory at Sea"—loud enough to be heard by his nearby colleagues.[14] Certainly no one was going to suggest a change in the musical fare or play any other music.

FOUR

FRIENDS IN LOW PLACES

In 1951, Pope went to Washington and landed a job as a CIA officer in psych ops, or psychological warfare, in those days when the cold war was at arctic temperatures and a shooting war was going on in Korea. The Pope family's Mafia connections likely had quite a lot to do with young Gene's job with the CIA. The connection between the Mafia and Washington went beyond elective politics and the Italian American vote. During World War II the Office of Naval Intelligence had strong connections with the Mafia that did not surface until after the war. Before the Allied invasion of Italy, Naval Intelligence collaborated with the Mafia to gather information about Sicily from recent immigrants and to maintain peace on the strategically important New York waterfront, where in 1942 a strike was averted with the Mafia's help.[1] Gay Talese notes in *Honor Thy Father* that Naval Intelligence cooperated with the Mafia after the *Normandy* burned and sank in her berth where she was awaiting conversion into a troopship, an incident of suspected sabotage.[2] Then after Churchill and Roosevelt agreed in 1943 at Casablanca to invade Sicily, the Office of Naval Intelligence–Mafia project became even more important. Gallagher quotes Michele Pantaleone, a Sicilian who served as a Socialist deputy in Palermo:

Even while the war was still being fought, the reconstitution of old [Mafia] groups was inaugurated by American gangster leaders . . . who got in touch with their old friends on the island before the Allied landings in order to induce them to help the Allies. . . . It is a historical fact that the Mafia, in agreement with American gangsterism, did its best to clear the way right across the island and so enable the invading troops to advance into central Italy with remarkable safety. . . . Clandestine landings of Sicilo-Americans also took place in the small Mafia-controlled fishing ports between Balestrate and Castellammare. . . . These are ports which years later would play an important part in the drug traffic between American gangsters and the Sicilian Mafia.[3]

At the center of the U.S. Navy's dealings with the Mafia, according to both Gallagher and Talese, was Lucky Luciano, who had been convicted and imprisoned on pandering charges by special prosecutor Thomas E. Dewey. While there is no written proof that Luciano bargained the Mafia's cooperation for personal favors, as files of the operation were destroyed, if they ever existed, Luciano was moved to a better location in prison, allowed special visitors, and eventually paroled. Then in 1946 Dewey commuted Luciano's sentence. He was deported to Italy, where he remained the rest of his life. Dewey, dogged by rumors that he had been paid off by the Mafia, convened the Herlands Commission ten years later to clear himself, then kept the 2,600-page report secret for another twenty years. However, in spite of denials by the navy, Judge William B. Herlands concluded, "The evidence demonstrates that Luciano's assistance and cooperation were secured by Naval Intelligence."[4]

The Italian connection with military intelligence, which at that time was only a few years back, may have been part of the deal. Although it was not widely known, Pope spoke fluent Italian, and both his parents were native speakers born in southern Italy, which he visited several times in his youth. But Pope didn't like working for the CIA at all. The bureaucracy chilled him more than any cold war. He left before the year was out. "I really got fed up with government bureaucracy," he said. "You'd spend weeks trying to get things done and then you couldn't do it."[5] So, he said, "I'd sit there and read the newspapers."[6] It's doubtful from what Pope said about his tenure there that the agency had much influence on his personality or methods, and his testimony is one small indication of why the CIA might have been inefficient enough to fail to predict the end of the cold war in the collapse of the Soviet Union. The public's image of the CIA is, like its perception of the Mafia, a fiction of the media. At any rate, the CIA seems a much less fruitful place to look for influences on Pope than the Mafia, the Cohn connection, and his early exposure to high-level political wheeling and dealing.

Washington was by then also the arena of Pope's fellow wheeler-dealer Roy Cohn, who was making a reputation hunting down Communists. Cohn had secured an appointment as special counsel in the Justice Department, where his portfolio was to get Owen Lattimore, a left-wing Johns Hopkins University professor whom Joseph McCarthy called "the top Russian" spy.[7] That trail soon grew cold, but Cohn quickly became the Red-baiting Wisconsin senator's chief counsel; in contrast to Pope's bureaucratic fate, this must have seemed like riding with Genghis Khan. It would be easy to believe that Cohn, with his Red-baiting credentials, had a hand in Gene Pope's landing a job with the CIA, whose task during the fifties was to fight and thwart Communism at every opportunity. At any rate, it's unlikely that Gene Pope could have been happy in any of Washington's bureaucracies. He left the employ of the CIA before a full year was out.

The CIA stint is a puzzling interlude in Pope's life, but it is a digression that fits in with a number of points in understanding his biography. It is yet more evidence for his lack of a master plan, evidence that he was confused and struggling. It fits in with the collapse of the Pope family's underground political network following the death of Pope Sr. and the election of Vincent Impellitteri as mayor, in that it is likely that there wasn't any more wheeling and dealing for young Pope. And there is the possibility of another angle: the twenty-four-year-old Pope may have been enlisted in the reserves or the National Guard following ROTC at MIT, and he may have chosen the CIA to avoid serving in the army during the Korean War. Eventually he heeded the summons of the printer's ink in his blood, though he no longer wanted to work in any capacity with his brothers at *Il Progresso,* which remained in the family's hands.

When he returned to New York from Washington, Pope evidently had time for romance. He married Patty McManus, an aspiring actress, who soon gave birth to a son, Generoso Pope III. The young father was pretty near broke, and there's little evidence he knew where he was headed. Again, he seemed to be more motivated by what he was trying to escape—Washington's intelligence bureaucracy, where he had clearly decided he didn't fit in.

In New York Pope soon heard, perhaps from Uncle Frank, that the widow of the owner of the *New York Enquirer* was putting the paper up for sale. The deceased owner, William Griffin, a former advertising man, hadn't approved of the U.S. entering World War II and was notable for once having been threatened with sedition charges in connection with expressing those sentiments.[8] The *Enquirer* had been founded, with some financial backing from Hearst, in 1926 as a weekly and as a venue for experimentation. Part of the experiment had to do with filling the gap in the news cycle between Saturday afternoon, when most dailies closed their Sunday editions, and Monday morning, when they came alive again. The paper's greatest scoop had been when the bombing of Pearl Harbor occurred on its brief news cycle, within this gap. A weekly also had the luxury of watching a hot story in the dailies unravel itself for a few days and could write more reflectively—or jazzily—on the news of the week. In this it would perform what the Week in Review section of the Sunday edition of the *New York Times* does these days.

The paper also had a reputation for faking stories, which was ironic considering where Pope was to take it. Part of the impulse toward faking and hyping was related to the position of a weekly against the dailies. A weekly wasn't able to compete with the dailies on breaking news, so the pressure was to put a "perspective," or new angle, or mere spin on the stories to make up for the absence of new information. Most of America's newsweeklies have gone out of business, except in small towns and rural areas. The last really interesting one, Dow Jones's *National Observer,* went down in 1977. Pope's *Enquirer,* first as a gore paper, then as a supermarket tabloid, became one robust branch in the family tree of weekly journalism, which has many enfeebled and dead branches, including the strangely short-lived free-press movement of the sixties and Al Goldstein's sex tabloid, *Screw,* which for a few years brought cheap newsprint porn to the people.

To make the purchase, Pope put down whatever cash he had left from his millionaire father's sole slim cash legacy—possibly as little as $5,000—

and borrowed another $20,000 toward the down payment on the $75,000 total.[9] Pope never publicly revealed where he got the money. But he told how he spent his "last buck" on the deal: "I took a cab to the lawyer's office on Wall Street, and I didn't have the money to pay the cab. I had a lucky silver dollar, so I paid the cab with it and went up to close the deal, more on nerve than anything else."[10] The spell of the lucky dollar wouldn't appear for a long time, but eventually Pope would run into a streak of prosperity that could be characterized as spectacular good luck.

Many sources have indicated that Pope had turned to the mob and Costello for the loan.[11] Roy Cohn also claimed he loaned Pope money toward the paper's purchase, but his recollection of the numbers doesn't square with Pope's account. Cohn was dying of AIDS when he related the story to his biographer Sid Zion, who said Cohn's mind occasionally wandered into hallucination. Zion said he assumed the virus had affected Cohn's brain,[12] a well-noted phenomenon in death from AIDS. Cohn said Pope bought the *Enquirer* for $40,000 and that he loaned Pope $10,000. "If I'd taken a piece, which he offered, I certainly wouldn't have had 20 years of trouble with the Internal Revenue Service," he told Zion. "No regrets. I wasn't brought up to take pieces of favors, and I've been more than recompensed by Gene's unswerving loyalty to me."[13] Aside from the problem with the amounts, there seems little reason to doubt that Cohn loaned Pope money on the *Enquirer,* though his help could have come later, because for the next few years Pope continued to borrow money, almost certainly from Costello, to keep the paper afloat.

Pope had grand ambitions for his paper. He told the *New York Times* he wanted to take the paper national, with bureaus in Chicago and San Francisco.[14]

It would be a news-feature weekly and would drop the paper's formula of sports, politics, theatrical news, and personality stories. The mission statement of his first issue indicated the magnitude of his ambitions (and perhaps contained an echo from his recent employment as a CIA propagandist): "In an age darkened by the menace of totalitarian tyranny and war, the *New York Enquirer* will fight for the rights of man, the rights of the individual, and will champion human decency and dignity, freedom and peace."[15] This fulsome manifesto is a rare example of something that Pope probably wrote himself. By the time the paper had morphed into a supermarket tabloid, no one remembered him writing a single story, column, or photo cutline. During the short period when he practiced a more conventional journalism, Pope might have exercised his publisher's prerogative and written editorials, but if he did, they seem lost in the shifting sands of memory.

How little Pope wrote is illustrated by an observation made years later by executive editor Tom Kuncl when he was in the hospital and received a handwritten Christmas note from Pope. Pope had signed his full name, and Kuncl realized that over the years, as he rose in the paper's editorial ranks, he had never seen more than his boss's habitual initial signoff, GP. Pope even communicated in initials: for instance, N.G., for "no good" on a rejected story idea. His story approval was a crimson Zorro-like slash. (Pope forbade anyone else at the *Enquirer* to use red ink.)[16] Though he probably used computers as early as anyone in journalism, Pope always liked to handle stories on paper so he could hold them, initial them, and give his one and only mark of approval. Unlike many editors and publishers, Pope seemed to have no vanity about his writing talents, no wish to write himself.

The revitalized paper would also, Pope told the *Times,* have a worldwide intelligence column, an interesting idea coming from a recent employee of the CIA. He also said that the paper, which was eventually to be called the *Weekly Enquirer,* would *not* become a tabloid, although less than a year later he announced that the paper, still called the *New York Enquirer,* would after all go to a tabloid format to better display its "feature content." Pope was never afraid to change his mind or contradict himself, and as a result the wake of his progress often transcribed a zigzag.

Pope's first years of publishing the *Enquirer* were harrowing. "I couldn't pay the rent," he recalled. "I spent 90 percent of my first six years borrowing from one guy to pay off the other guy. I was thrown out of more banks, because all the checks used to bounce."[17] Eventually the debt reached a quarter of a million dollars, and no one would take his checks. "The printer wouldn't take checks. The employees wouldn't take checks. Everything had to be in cash. I'd be carrying around $10,000 in my pocket to pay the printer, but I couldn't pay my rent. I was getting eviction notices from my apartment every month. When my first son was born," Pope recalled, "I had to go out that night and borrow money to get him out of the hospital."[18] As Dino Gallo, Pope's oldest publishing cohort (all the way back to *Il Progresso*) remembered it, those $10,000 pocketfuls came from Frank Costello. Costello would advance Pope the cash, and the next week Gallo would meet Costello's right-hand man, Big Jim, at the Waldorf's barbershop or grill with an envelope of cash from newsstand sales.

"Gene always needed more money," said Gallo, "so even though we were paying Costello back, Frank was always helping him pay the bills."[19] Pope was performing a tightrope act that was made possible by the fact that a newspaper with a decent circulation was a cash cow, and cash could be moved and manipulated to make it go further. He survived. But the paper did not honestly make its way into the black ink until 1958,[20] when its circulation reached 250,000.[21]

Pope and Costello traded favors, Mafia-style, according to Gallo. A weekly like the *Enquirer* depended in those days on the mom-and-pop newsstands that also dealt in candy and tobacco. Some of them refused to carry the *Enquirer* as it moved deeper into its gore stage, so Gene called upon his mob connections to persuade the proprietors otherwise, according to Gallo. In return for help from the mob musclemen, the *Enquirer* published the figures for their numbers racket. And when Judge Samuel Leibowitz ran for mayor on an anti-mob platform, Gene assigned a reporter to do a three-part exposé on him, Gallo recalled.[22] Also, Costello's constant infusions of cash could very well have been construed as a useful money-laundering operation.

A weekly paper can be put out on a shoestring, and in those years Pope no doubt found out most of what could be known about journalistic shortcuts. Understaffed underdog papers usually do a great deal of rewriting and cannibalizing of their competitors, a downward spiral usually, a tailspin that wasn't new with the declining *New York Enquirer*. Since sinking papers have a hard time getting an exclusive, they tend to hype stories, and the *Enquirer* had a reputation for that before Pope bought it. Pope said that, at the times he was down to one reporter, he put that reporter on police stories. "I discovered a huge amount of crime news in New York was never being reported," Pope told a reporter a little more than a year before he died. "So, while I had only one full-time employee, I used to have the police reporters for other papers to file stories for us. I latched onto a guy called Johnny Miller. He was hotter than Winchell, I'll tell you. He was 17 at the time."[23]

Police stories are easy to get. In a city like New York the police blotters are always full of names, and the stories of their tragedies and ironies are contained in the preliminary police paperwork, a public document. A reporter need only canvass the blotters, read the reports, and contact witnesses and perhaps the arresting officers, if they are willing to talk. A quick police reporter could go a long way toward filling up a thin weekly like the *Enquirer*. Feasting on Rotten Gotham's police stories was a necessary first step in Pope's evolution into the gore stage.

Pope was also learning how interested city reporters for other publications were in freelancing, or double-dipping. Chronically underpaid reporters were always close to the action, and if they were careful, they could file the same story to two or more papers. Pope continued to encourage and employ double-dippers the rest of his career. Later it amused him that while *Enquirer* reporters were being treated like pariahs, he had a list of reporters working at the *New York Times,* the *Wall Street Journal,* and other prestigious papers, the best in the business, who were secretly filing stories to his *Enquirer.*

On May 3, 1957, Pope was again prominently mentioned in a *New York Times* front-page story, and again the link was Frank Costello, who had survived an underworld hit in the lobby of his apartment building the night before. Pope and his wife had been having dinner with Costello and his wife at the Monsignore Restaurant on Fifty-fifth Street near Madison Avenue. Costello said he had to return to his apartment on Central Park West to make some phone calls about the marker he had in his pocket for $434,695, which police later discovered precisely matched the take from the gambling tables of the Tropicana Hotel in Las Vegas. Phil Kennedy, described by the *Times* as the operator of a model agency, had been at the restaurant as well. Kennedy described dropping Costello off in a taxi, then rushing back when he heard the shot ring out. According to witnesses, a big man in a dark suit had arrived in a Cadillac and slipped into the building's lobby, where he waited and then shot Costello at close range. The big man ran back to the Cadillac, which sped away. Kennedy found Costello collapsed on a couch, but quite alive. The bullet had entered behind his left ear and, failing to penetrate his skull, traveled under his scalp and exited near his right ear, a type of wound common enough not to surprise those familiar with head shots from small caliber pistols. Police later found the .32 slug, probably from a Colt Pocket Auto, a small flat semiautomatic favored by gangsters (and noir films) of the period.

Costello was rushed to the emergency room. He emerged less than two hours later wearing a bandage and his bloodstained clothes, which police had rifled while he was being treated. When reporters asked him about his assailant, he said, famously, "I didn't see no one."[24] He continued to say this until he was held in contempt of court and sentenced to thirty days in jail. Costello served fifteen days before lawyer George Wolf got him out. Sixty-six detectives—a record of sorts—scoured the city looking for his alleged assailant, who eventually turned himself in.

But at the trial Costello refused to identify Vincent "the Chin" Gigante, a former prizefighter, as his assailant. As a result Gigante was acquitted, according to lawyer Wolf in his book. After the verdict Gigante walked over to Costello and said, "Thanks, Frank." Costello seems to have borne Gigante no personal grudge. He apparently saw Gigante as an obedient soldier just doing his job for his capo. Wolf remembered going to dinner later at Costello's and discovering Gigante seated at the dinner table as an honored guest.[25] In the way he handled the assassination attempt, Costello transcended the Mafia code of feud and vengeance, and the reward for his fifteen days in jail was a rare longevity for a man in his high-profile position. Eventually he became widely known as the prime minister of the underworld, as Wolf relates in his book, for wielding what power and influence he had left so judiciously and diplomatically.

However, both of the front-page *Times* stories mentioning Gene Pope—the first in 1950 and this one in 1957—were probably markers in the relentless decline of his fortunes. Soon after the 1950 story Vincent Impellitteri won the mayoral election, which probably marked the destruction of the Pope family's political base. Understanding Mafia politics is like reading tea leaves, but it's likely that the failed assassination of Costello marked a decline in his fortunes, and by extension Pope's. Failing to finger Gigante and holding off on getting even with whoever ordered the hit bought Costello his life, but it couldn't have gained him any better standing in the vicious Mafia underworld.

Costello, against the odds of the era, died peacefully in bed at home at the age of eighty-two. Phil Kennedy, present along with Pope at the intimate dinner at the Monsignore the night of the assassination attempt, had the honor of accompanying Mrs. Costello to Frank's funeral, according to Wolf. Given the close association of the Popes with Costello, it seems more than likely that Gene Pope, as godson, would have been invited, too. But did he go? Obviously, Pope would not advertise his attendance at a gangster godfather's funeral, but he could have discreetly flown to New York. The legend that Pope's fear of flying made him incapable of traveling by air was untrue, as we shall see. It's even possible that he cultivated that legend so he could fly. At any rate, only fifty of Costello's close friends and associates attended the private funeral on February 21, 1973, but Wolf discreetly named no one aside from himself, Mrs. Costello, and Kennedy in his account.[26]

Pope never denied he was with Costello the night he was shot, but somehow Pope managed to pass the fact off as an amazing coincidence. In fact, he contended this coincidence was the source of the "rumor," as he put it, that he had Mafia connections, a line of reasoning he used when Mike Wallace interviewed him for *60 Minutes*.[27] Yet connecting the intimate private dinner date with the front-page *Times* story seven years earlier, when the acting mayor denounced Pope for acting as Costello's emissary, it seems obvious that Pope was (in the language lawyer Wolf witnessed) *connected.*

The fifties were a turgid period of Pope's life, in stark contrast to his later life as tyrannical tycoon and staid married (to his third wife) blue-collar millionaire, a workaholic who thrived on routine. Those years very much included a stormy love life.

After the birth of their son, Patty McManus became depressed, and her postpartum depression deepened into a clinical variety of melancholia that required her institutionalization. Eventually she was diagnosed as schizophrenic. All of her teeth were pulled in the hope that her headaches were linked to the mercury in her fillings or other dental maladies. This had to be a terrible blow to a beautiful, still-young woman, and it's possible that this radical cure was administered without her consent, since she had been legally committed. Finally she committed suicide by overdosing after Gene divorced her in Mexico and married Edith, or Sandy, Moore, a beautiful model. In 1961 a daughter, Gina, was born to Sandy and Gene. His troubled marriage to Moore did not last long. Pope was divorced from Moore by 1965, when he married his third wife, Lois, and adopted her two small girls by George Wood, Michelle and Maria. It's possible he courted Lois after he was separated from Moore but before he was divorced. Eventually, Pope had two children by Lois, Paul David, born in 1967, and Lorraine, who had Down syndrome and was eventually institutionalized, born in 1972.

FIVE

FROM GORE TO GROCERIES

After several years as a hand-to-mouth newspaper publisher, Pope experienced an epiphany that was to guide him into lucrative new territory. Certainly he was ready for something else. When the Soviet Union crushed the Hungarian revolution of 1956 he printed ten thousand extra copies. They didn't sell.[1] This was one of the key moments that convinced him, as he was to say more firmly later, that politics and religion were "dead." Such pronouncements go a long way toward explaining why Pope's later tabloid journalism was so politically bland. Trying to exploit the Sunday news gap wasn't working out; that was an obsolete strategy that reached back to the paper's founding in 1926, when the medium of print dominated and the city had many newspapers that people read on the street, before radio news was much more than a novelty and before TV even existed.

The inspiration for the next step came when Pope passed a particularly gory traffic accident, a story Pope often recounted: he was watching not the accident—he always said accidents made him sick—but the rubberneckers so eagerly watching, and he came to understand the nearly universal appeal that sort of situation has for most of us. "I noticed hundreds of people looking at the horrifying scene—it was too awful for me to look at—and it suddenly hit me," he said. "That's what people want to see, that's what I'll give them, blood and gore."[2]

It was, of course, the troubling appeal of the abject, the horror we cannot face in our lives. As Pope noticed, few can turn away from the scene of a bloody accident. Newspapers have always covered accidents, but few have ever taken the genre as far as Pope did in those years. When he started to do gore, "that's when the circulation began to climb," Pope said.[3] "We decided to go ahead and see where we'd level off. With that formula, we got up to a million copies." This was also the point where Pope decided to take his weekly national, cutting his ties with the city. Gore was for everyone; it transcended geography. The deeper the gore, the more the circulation went up, at least to that point of six zeroes, where the paper stubbornly plateaued, even with its national circulation.

Pope ran a story about a madman who cut up his date and put her body in the freezer, and the one that every historian of tabloid journalism remembers, the mother who used her son's face as an ashtray. One headline read, "Passion Pills Fan Rape Wave," and was accompanied by a photo of Indian fanatics scouring their chests with barbed wire.[4] Stories were often made up around a photo from an entirely different context: photos in this predigital age didn't lie, but stories could transgress from truth to fiction. The mismatch of stories and photos was often implausible: who could believe that these skinny, ascetic Indian fakirs had sex on their minds? But readers didn't seem to care. This broached one of tabloid journalism's enduring mysteries: Did people really believe these stories or care whether they were true or not? Did this new tabloid territory exist in the same realm as the kind of spectator wrestling where audiences knew the punches and falls were choreographed but enjoyed the spectacle just the same? Winning or losing wasn't the point there, and true or false didn't seem the point of Pope's hyped stories. You could enjoy an Elvis impersonator without believing he was Elvis.

Some of the paper's stories would seem to be a variety of Ripley's Believe It or Not. (Did Ripley ever document his material?) The *National Enquirer* offered a story headlined "I Put My Baby in a Waste Basket and Poured Concrete Over Her."[5] Most of the stories were hyped, though many started out with more than a few grains of truth. It was part of tabloid's art to blur the line between truth and fiction, and some of the stories were even, believe it or not, *true.* The subject of a story, with year-to-year photos, about an eleven-year-old who died of old age, was probably a victim of progeria, a well-documented disease that causes premature death and "aging." The paper dealt in certified freaks of nature, such as conjoined twins and two-headed calves, snakes, and other animals. (The two-headed animals stuck in people's minds, and the memory of those stories haunted the *Enquirer* long after it had changed its formula.) Copies flew off the stands when Pope published the gory photos of Lee Harvey Oswald's autopsy. Pope went far beyond the borders of good taste, where others feared to go: he published a photo of a cop wearing a rubber glove and carrying by the hair a head severed in a subway accident.

No magazine or daily published the last picture of Princess Diana after her fatal crash, although at least one of the paparazzi shot her horribly disfigured face when their pursuing pack arrived on the scene. However, the photograph did appear on the Internet, which has a lunatic fringe with no rules at all. Would the old *Enquirer* have published Diana's last photo in the days of high gore? It's an open question, because Pope continued to flout the rules of good taste, decorum, and privacy, most notably in his greatest triumph and record-selling issue with the cover head shot of Elvis in his bier.

It's difficult to recover the editorial practices of that era, but much can be inferred from the way Pope ran the *Weekly World News,* the *Enquirer's* sister paper he founded in 1979 to make use of his idled black-and-white presses when he took the *Enquirer* to color. The *News* worked a way-out territory written from clips culled from mainstream papers and hyped to the maximum. When there weren't enough clips, the Wacky World News, as insiders called it, also hyped or totally made up its own UFO, Loch Ness monster, Bigfoot, Atlantis, Bermuda Triangle, multiple births, world's fattest cat, fattest boy, and psychic prediction stories, as well as such "way-outs" as "B-29 Bomber Found on Moon," the marshmallow diet, and, so famously, "Elvis Is Alive."

However, at that point the *Weekly World News* was highly profitable, with its editorial staff not much more than a baker's dozen, and Pope could easily afford to give its writers and editors salary parity with the *Enquirer.* He could also just as easily have not raised *News* salaries by more than $10,000 or, in some cases, $20,000 a year, but he was truly generous in such ways, living up to his name. (Though overpaying his journalists apparently left him feeling free to fire them at will.) Perhaps the million mark in circulation was a natural saturation point for way-out journalism, since both the gore *Enquirer* and the *News* stuck at that point.

Then in 1982 Canadian Mike Rosenbloom, owner of Globe Communications, founded a clone paper, the *Sun,* to chase the *News* and split its market. The *Weekly World News* always remained substantially in the lead, though from that point its circulation slowly declined. The conventional wisdom in split markets is that one publication alone in its field creates an appetite that is not completely satisfied, so the familiar doubling of publications—the *Time* and *Newsweek* phenomenon—exploits a larger market. The sum of the split market is greater than the original market.

Pope used to tell *News* staffers that they were having all the fun and that he missed the old days when the *Enquirer* worked a similar formula. There was some nostalgia-tinted ambivalence there, though, because elsewhere Pope said of the old *Enquirer*, "It bothered the hell out of me running that kind of paper, but it was paying the bills and after all those lean years it was a good feeling to have some money in the bank."[6]*

The offices Pope inherited in 1952 were rundown and rat infested, with odors and accumulations of years of cigarette smoke, with wobbly chairs and broken typewriters. "It was a dump, literally a dump," recalled Dino Gallo. "I mean the chairs were on three legs."[7] Pope couldn't pay the rent anyway, so the only rolling stock he was interested in was the half of the ten or twelve typewriters that worked. Gallo remembers that the red ink was so deep that when the debt collectors came, he climbed on Pope's shoulders and hid the typewriters in a loft.

Manhattan department stores had not rushed to buy ads in Pope's failing *New York Enquirer,* so Pope accepted a panoply of oddball product ads, in-

---

* Perhaps the sleaziness of the early *Enquirer* bothered some of its writers, too. On a gray day, April 15, 1968, Damon Runyon Jr., who had been writing for the paper, threw himself to his death from a precipice in Washington, D.C.'s Rock Creek Park. There were other problems in the life of this experienced reporter, who wrote a biography of his father called *In the Steps of His Father,* but it couldn't have helped his depression to compare his own writings for the *Enquirer* with his reporter father's masterful stories of Broadway in the twenties.

cluding tackily sketched rupture trusses, as well as geeky lonely-hearts classifieds from men and women seeking companions. The ad situation never really improved much, and Pope formed the uncommon habit early on of attempting to sustain the paper on its cover price. A typical magazine, in contrast, gets 60 percent of its revenue from advertisements.[8] The *Enquirer's* relationship with the ad industry is one of the interactions that shaped it. When he was independent of the pressures of advertisers, Pope could be as down and dirty as he wanted. He cleaned up the paper when he went into the supermarkets, but never spick-and-span enough for the classiest ads. He never, for instance, got high-end cosmetic ads, even though it was well known that most of his readers were women.

All his professional life Pope hired and fired reporters and most of his staffers too quickly and impulsively to inspire loyalty. Dino Gallo was the rare exception who remained with Pope, on the business side, until Pope's death. He was the only employee known to have lasted with Pope until retirement age, though after Pope died, the new ownership took his pension away, reaffirming journalism as the most unstable of professions.[9] Dino, who had reportedly worked with Pope on *Il Progresso,* was from another world, one—judging from his early role as the *Enquirer's* bagman—more connected to Frank Costello and the tribal loyalties of the Mafia than the slippery and competitive brotherhood of reporting.

One night in the mid-sixties Pope went to hear the widow of a friend sing at a midtown Manhattan club. Lois, who had been married to the late George Woods of the William Morris talent agency, had cool Grace Kelly looks that knocked the separated or divorced Pope off his feet. She had appeared onstage and in TV and film under her professional name of Lois O'Brien. When Pope left the club that night, he told his pals how much Lois had impressed him: "I walked outside and the two guys I was with almost fainted when I said, 'I'm going to marry that girl.'" It was yet another of the sudden, life-altering decisions that came like thunderbolts, and further evidence of the single-mindedness of which he was capable. "Two weeks later I asked her to marry me, and she thought I was a nut."[10] They were married two years later, in May 1965.

With his new hype-and-horror formula in hand, Pope concentrated on making it work on a national basis. At first this was a matter of distributing the paper on big-city newsstands. The paper went truly national when it entered the supermarkets. Stories of the sort he then dealt in were easier to put over in a national paper. Such exaggerated wonders and horrors as the *Enquirer* announced required a wider venue: it was easier to believe a way-out story if it happened somewhere else. A national weekly could also better exploit city drugstore and tobacco shop newsstands, where the tabloid freak-and-horror paper came to be sold. No one had as yet succeeded in the timely printing and delivery of a national daily. The *Wall Street Journal,* which eventually was the first American daily to surmount the problem, was then relying on the U.S. Postal Service, and copies typically arrived a day or two late.

Pope began paying better and better salaries; unlike most publishers of schlock and pulp, he understood the value of talent and the need to pay for it (as William Randolph Hearst had in his days of yellow journalism). "I feel very strongly that if we're making money, [the employees] deserve a part of it."[11] This is an important point, since understanding how the *Enquirer* came into such cultural prominence involves tracking certain discourses, one of the strongest being the complicated dialectic between Pope and his reporters and editors. Pope attracted talent and soon acquired a taste, also like Hearst, for raiding other publications, offering much higher salaries, often an eye-popping "double what you're making now," to people already at the top of their profession. But his habit of hiring and firing very quickly (like Joseph Pulitzer) heated up the whole process.

Chris Currie, Pope's accountant, who had to cut the checks, remembers a telling incident from the 1970s: "Pope brought a photo editor from some European magazine and signed a three-year contract for an astronomical amount of money, and paid to relocate his family here. And then he promptly fired him—five or six weeks later. I think he was paying him a quarter of a million dollars a year. I think Pope enjoyed the power of doing that sort of thing."[12]

Pope might have remained comfortably in his pulp niche for years, stabilized in the evolutionary process like the detective and romance magazines, which remained the same for decades after their formula was worked out. Pope could have made a handsome living, if not a fortune, at the million mark; only a handful of national publications could top that. But it was in Pope's nature to remain always on the march, at least in that time of his life. (As an older man he would balk at the clear opportunity to move into tabloid TV.) In the late sixties and early seventies the paper's editorial direction took many sharp turns, but even later, when the course was more or less set, Pope was always tweaking his formula.

It has been commonly assumed even in the tabloid community that the step into the supermarket was a stroke of genius on Pope's part, one that changed our culture drastically by submitting every American grocery shopper to a barrage of lurid headlines at the checkout. Even the thoroughly skeptical and determined found it hard to avert their eyes from the *Enquirer*'s covers, and once their curiosity was piqued, it was tempting to dig for a few extra coins. Digging for a few coins for a short stint of entertainment was what popular culture was about—the circus, vaudeville, most Hollywood film, especially in the early days when admissions were cheap. Another way of looking at Pope's gore epiphany and the subsequent freak formula was that it was a move from being a newspaper—an increasingly factually challenged one—to a vehicle for entertainment. Pope was pioneering a movement in a direction that disturbs so many about our engulfment by tabloid culture and manifests itself, for instance, in the vast reduction of hard news in network TV programming. But the move to the supermarkets was not exactly brainstormed, at least not by Pope. That was not the way Pope worked, despite the fact that he was capable of bold action once he made up his mind.

Tom Kuncl, who joined the paper in the early seventies, when Pope was still tuning his editorial content for the new readership that flowed across the nation's checkout counters, recalled:

The idea of putting the paper in supermarkets was not Pope's own. It came from a guy named Bill Hall. Bill Hall was a guy who'd been with a food chain somewhere [Kroger] and knew supermarkets. Bill Hall went out on a hustle and told supermarkets we'll cut out the stories about how I used my baby's head for an ashtray, and if we do will you put it in here? And one by one he got the chains to take it in. Bill Hall put that whole thing together. His name vanished from the pantheon later on. Pope would never say, I came up with that idea, but it was so far back in history everybody assumed he had.[13]

The story of Bill Hall, who left in 1974, was an example of how Pope interacted with the rich and varied pool of talent that passed through the revolving door of his employ. "If a person was good, his salary was ten times what it would be anywhere else," said Kuncl (with a dash of tabloid hyperbole). But if that person displeased Pope, he was gone in a flash. However, that person's ideas remained behind with Pope.

SIX

A SECOND START

When Pope made the move from the New York area—his editorial offices were in Englewood Cliffs, New Jersey, from 1962 to 1971, aside from a brief time on Madison Avenue—to Florida, he dumped practically his whole editorial staff and started over.[1] As noted, Pope never had trouble firing people. Iain Calder recalls Pope firing his whole editorial staff, except for his two top executives, after he heard reports that his employees were interested in unionizing. Pope was so trigger-happy, so much of a godfather, it was considered unlucky to even look him in the eye when passing him. According to legend he once fired a man for stepping into an elevator ahead of him, only to be told, "I don't work for you—I was just delivering lunch."[2] In his tabloid memoir Calder describes the atmosphere in the Madison Avenue offices as "Stalinesque."

In Florida Pope began a new cycle of hiring and firing. Calder, who followed Pope to Florida, said that by the late seventies and early eighties the *Enquirer*'s pool of fired employees "could have filled Carnegie Hall, maybe Yankee Stadium."[3] Pope even helped establish a small British colony in South Florida—his own little Fleet Street—because he soon began hiring and firing reporters from London who liked Florida so much they stayed on. He inadvertently created a pool of tabloid talent that his competitor Mike Rosenbloom decided to exploit by moving his *Enquirer* clones from Montreal to the

The chain-smoking publisher and editor strides through the *Enquirer* newsroom, cigarette in hand. (Photo by Ken Steinhoff / *Palm Beach Post*)

West Palm Beach area. It was also Rosenbloom's way of escaping a union drive in Montreal, and he, too, left nearly all his editorial employees behind. Those who followed him into the Sunbelt got no moving expenses, aside from a few key people, like John Vader, a former Montreal taxi driver who founded the *Examiner* and, eventually, the *Sun* for Rosenbloom.* There was certainly something fly-by-night about tabloids, and tabloid journalists seemed to be regarded as a renewable resource that could be "churned and burned," as the lively inside *Enquirer* slang described Pope's process of strip mining their of-

---

* When the transvestite Devine in John Waters's underground classic *Pink Flamingoes* summons America's tabloid editors for a press conference, Vader is one of the editors depicted and mentioned by name. Waters was one of the few people to have a mail subscription to the *Enquirer;* in his memoir, *Crackpot,* he said it made him feel closer to the mainstream.

ten considerable talents. For several months his *Globe* and *Examiner* paid his new staff on a daily freelance rate—until the Internal Revenue Service stepped in and required management to start withholding taxes. Thus was created Florida's "Tabloid Triangle," where all six supermarket tabloids came to roost, eventually even including the *Star,* whose editorial offices had been in Tarrytown, New York.

If the transfer to a small town in Florida wasn't a stroke of genius, it was certainly a typical Gene Pope masterstroke, right down to the eccentricity of it. There were solid reasons for the move as well. He was having trouble with his unionized Teamster truckers, and his son Paul is probably right that he wanted to sever all connections with the mob, possibly including pressures to launder money through the paper. The powers of his Mafia protector, Frank Costello, had been on the decline for years.

The bonus was that living was cheap and sweet in Lantana, basically a working-class town of about seven thousand. Across the drawbridge over the Intracoastal Waterway was South Palm Beach, where a three-mile stretch of beachfront was being developed for condos for retirees from the North. South Palm and Manalapan formed the southern tip of the barrier island that farther north was the real Palm Beach, the wealthy enclave developed by Henry Flagler, who built his railroad resort there in the twenties. Also across the narrow waterway from Lantana was the favorite bar of *Enquirer* employees, at an old beach motel that had been grandfathered in amidst the condo zoning. The Hawaiian was always crowded with *Enquirer* reporters at happy hour, and on weekends it served them as a country club, with its restaurant overlooking the ocean, its gorgeous stretch of wide white beach where the sea turtles still lumbered up on summer nights to lay their eggs. It had a terrace with tables and a pool, into which many a drunken *Enquirer* reporter had fallen or been pushed. It also served as temporary housing for reporters and editors on their six-week tryouts. Pope's lively crew made the motel's terrace, pool, and beach a local hot spot, where the Florida beauties flocked in their bikinis and thongs to display themselves and tan.

Manalapan, where Pope lived, was a few miles south, an enclave of low-profile wealth, as distinguished from flashier Palm Beach to the north, with its Raiders' Row of grand ocean-front imitation European villas. Pope chose his house before the site for the paper; he wanted to make sure he had a short commute. Pope drove through only two traffic lights to get to work, not counting the drawbridge where he sometimes waited for a passing yacht. He could get to work within five to seven minutes. Pope was low profile all the way. The low, sprawling house Pope built overlooked a shallow bluff on the oceanfront and had a virtually private beach, though Pope evidently didn't use the beach or his pool much—he was as pale as a prison inmate 365 days a year. There Pope lived a strangely circumscribed and modest life. He dressed down, drove a series of white Chevrolets, and came home from work six days a week and watched TV, especially prime-time soaps and comedy series. He was a creature of routine who liked to eat dinner early and then read story leads until prime time. He seemed to have more money than he needed. He wasn't greedy, and when an interviewer asked him why he wasn't eager to exploit the possibilities of tabloid TV, meaning in the context why he didn't want to make more money, he answered, "Well, how many cheeseburgers can I eat?"[4] It was a line he repeated many times. He told the *Bergen County Record* in 1964, "Fame and money are means, not ends."[5]

Palm Beach itself—three miles north—was created as high society's

American Riviera and made accessible by Henry Flagler, a genius of another sort. In Flagler's era at the turn of the twentieth century millionaires traveled down in private railway cars and parked them along Worth Avenue. Now only Flagler's railroad car remains, parked near his old mansion, currently a museum that houses his art collection. Worth Avenue, with its own Tiffany's, Louis Vuitton, Hermès, and other expensive boutiques, is the Southeast's equivalent of Rodeo Drive. Palm Beach was a moated enclave of American wealth, with only two bridges to it over the Intracoastal, and scored socially on a par with Newport Beach. It had a season from Thanksgiving to Washington's Birthday in February, when its wealthy revelers moved on to Newport for the next step in the U.S. social season. It was conservative, anti-Semitic, and the kind of place where Donald Trump, when he bought his prime piece of real estate, Mar-a-Lago, was regarded as an upstart. People like Pope were hardly even on the scale, though Trump brought his own scale: his yacht was so big it couldn't get through the Intracoastal's inlet to anchor outside his home. No problem: he had a helicopter on board.

There was plenty of prime Florida real estate to go around, and even working-class Lantana owned a recreational stretch of municipal beach across the Intracoastal bridge on the Atlantic. In the early nineties Ritz-Carlton built a world-class hotel next to the town's simple public beachfront, confirming that it was indeed a charmed patch of white Florida sand. The first wave, and even the second, of new *Enquirer* staffers enjoyed a golden age of Florida real estate and bought houses with Pope's generous salaries that would have been far, far above the means of reporters in cities where national journalism was ordinarily practiced.

Pope immediately became a benefactor of the *Enquirer*'s blue-collar neighborhood. In his way a genuine man of the people, he erected a series of World's Tallest Christmas Trees on the *Enquirer* grounds and financed a world-class fireworks display each Fourth of July. He donated millions of dollars for nursing scholarships and threw a lavish party every Christmas for staff and patients at John F. Kennedy Medical Center, the main object of his philanthropy, where he also served on the board of trustees. The year before he died, Pope donated part of the new DeBakey Cardiac Care Unit, to which he so ironically didn't make it on the morning he died of his heart attack.

Before he moved to Florida, Pope had serendipitously discovered Fleet Street, and Fleet Street discovered Pope. The Fleet Streeters who flocked to Florida were experienced tabloid reporters, and they brought new energy and strategies to Pope's enterprise. The mix also included Australians, largely by way of Fleet Street, who emerged as the most buccaneering of journalists, and now and then a white South African. The Brits, as they were all called, found Pope's pay scale lavish beyond their wildest dreams. One of the originals, Liverpudlian Vince Eckersley, said, "I think somebody worked it out that we were like $5,000 ahead of the Prime Minister of England."[6] Another of the originals, Harold Lewis, carried the stub from one of his paychecks around in his wallet, which he would pull out in bars at the slightest provocation. Lewis, himself an anomalous tabloid dandy in elegant suits, also liked to talk about how he'd been running around England with a check for a million pounds in his pocket made out to Anthony Armstrong-Jones. That was the price Pope was willing to pay for Armstrong-Jones's memoirs of his love affair with Princess Margaret, though the check never sufficiently tempted the royal swain.[7]

The Brits' influence in this rapid evolutionary period of the supermarket tabloid was deep and wide, enough that it is no exaggeration to say that the American supermarket tabloid is a British-American hybrid. Aside from Pope's money, the Brits loved the sun of South Florida as passionately as Englishmen have always loved the sun of Spain and Italy. When Sir Freddie Laker began offering really cheap flights between Britain and the United States in the early eighties—under $250 for a round-trip—thousands of British tourists flowed into Florida—so many that when Pope ended John Bell's reign as executive editor, Bell started up his own tabloid just for his fellow countrymen visiting as tourists. Bell started the enterprise, which he sold in South Florida hotels, after he got an overwhelming response posting British soccer scores in the Breakers and other Palm Beach hotels. Bell's short-lived but lively tabloid, which he put out with his wife and delivered from the trunk of his car, even featured a bare-breasted Page 3 girl, just like home, and was no doubt read with curiosity by non-Brits as well. It's unlikely that Pope would have attracted so many British reporters if he hadn't moved his paper to Florida's subtropical climate. Like Bell, the Brits who stayed on in Florida were resourceful, and they continued to exert their cultural influence as well in Rosenbloom's tabloids, the *Globe, Examiner,* and *Sun,* where they quickly found work (sometimes as soon as the next day) after Pope fired them. Several of the Brits eventually went all the way in their recolonization of America by becoming citizens.

Pope was still a bit of a wheeler-dealer, and he worked out a way to bend the immigration laws to permit the rapid influx of British journalists he needed. In 1981 he briefly faced criminal charges from the U.S. attorney's office "for fraudulently obtaining United States residency status for more than 50 foreign reporters and other employees."[8] The complaint charged that the tabloid set up a dummy London company, News Enquirer Ltd., that ostensibly supplied stories to the paper but in actuality "was used to obtain residency status for foreign journalists entering the United States," according to the *New York Times;* "On admission they went to work for the tabloid." In all, the practice amounted, it was alleged, to fraudulently "aiding and abetting the commission of a violation" of the laws pertaining to visas, permits, or entry documents. But the fine, on conviction, would be only $2,000, far less than the cost of renting the Learjets that transported Pope's reporters to and from the big stories. At any rate Pope had formed the habit of hiring the finest legal talent, and the matter was smoothed over without another ripple in the press or among his Fleet Streeters. In fact, by the eighties Pope's restless romance with the Brits was somewhat in decline.

Fleet Street reporters were generally working class and streetwise, not university graduates. They were amused at how seriously many better-educated American journalists took themselves, amazed at the Americans' high-minded ideals regarding truth and objectivity. The British tabloid reporters came from a brand of journalism that understood itself as a form of entertainment. They also allowed for many gray areas in their practices in regard to the border between truth and fiction. They were aggressive, cunning, and resourceful, and they had a big bag of tricks, ranging from delivering flowers to get access to scenes of tragedy to dressing up as priests and waiters at celebrity funerals and weddings. Pope valued the British reporters for qualities of resourcefulness Americans considered their own and on which they did not like to concede ground (perhaps reflecting how much the American character must have been founded on such hardy British rootstock from colonial times).

"Mr. Pope liked the Brits more because they were chillingly relentless in the pursuit of a story," said Art Golden, an American who served the *Enquirer* as a writer at the peak of Pope's infatuation with Fleet Streeters. "He used to say that British reporters were more resourceful than their American colleagues, and that they would do just about anything to get an exclusive interview or dig up a fact that would make a story complete."[9] The Brits were also serious pub crawlers and soon had a major impact on the Lantana nightlife. "You could go into the New England Oyster House on a Friday night—they had a small bar—and all you could hear were British accents," said Phil Brennan, who began working at the *Enquirer* as a writer a few months after Pope's move to Lantana.[10]

Photographer Vince Eckersley arrived in Lantana around 1973. "Pope's feeling was the British were a dab hand at tabloid," he observed, "and it was what they were brought up to do." Although Eckersley went to university, he points out that most of his colleagues didn't: "Very few of them were college- or university-trained journalists. They learned on the job, or with agencies. Papers like the *Daily Mirror* had training programs. They'd work on a regional paper, then move up to an agency. The holy prayer was to get on a newspaper on Fleet Street."[11] Eckersley points out that the British reporters knew Pitman shorthand: "They were impeccable shorthand-takers. If you were doing court reporting in Britain, you weren't allowed to use a tape recorder." Eckersley also commented on the level of Brit efficiency: "The thing was to get the story, get it done, and get in the pub. They performed with something of a lighter touch. They didn't take their job seriously to the point it affected their enjoyment of it. They'd also been brought up with much more sense of co-operation and camaraderie." According to Eckersley's portrait of the breed, a certain friction was almost inevitable between the British reporters, who regarded journalism as a trade, and the college-educated Americans, who thought of it as a lofty profession, even as they condescended to write tabloid.

Eckersley was among Pope's original photographers, and he remained closely associated with the paper through Pope's death and beyond. Eckersley was a staff photographer at first, then a freelancer, and then eventually a photo editor on his return. One of his earliest assignments as a staff photographer came in 1974 when Pope sent him to Cape Town, South Africa, to photograph the Rosenkowitz sextuplets, born after their mother, Susan, took fertility drugs, then the world's first full set to survive. Pope was probably more difficult to work with for photographers than for writers: words were easier to mold to Pope's will than were the subjects of pictures, especially babies. Pope often started with a concept, which he dictated to his photographers or writers, and their job was to make reality conform to Pope's vision. Eckersley discovered Pope's vision on this story was to have "the mother standing behind all six babies lined up, like the Virgin Mary with her arms down."

Eckersley knew there would be problems:

> We're talking about week-old babies. They don't have much spine to sit up with. Then the doctor said, "I'm only going to let them out of the incubators two at a time." We thought, oh God, it'll be six weeks before we get them all together. I called up and said, "We've got this problem; the doctor is only going to let two out every two weeks because he doesn't want any infection. If one gets a cold we don't want all six to get it." We said, "There's plenty of other stories we could be doing." But Pope said, "No, sit right

there." And we did. I didn't even get my cameras out. We sat right there in Cape Town. Eventually we got all the kids out and took the picture with six people hiding under a table, each one with his hand up a sweater like a sloth puppet in a Punch and Judy show to keep them from falling over. I finally got the picture.[12]

It wouldn't have done any good for Eckersley to explain to Pope that the picture he had in mind wasn't really feasible for babies that age. Eckersley's personal strategy, to which he attributes his longevity of employment under Pope, was never to switch signals on the boss but to do what Pope wanted in addition to shooting other angles, rather than trying to talk Pope out of his original vision: "He never restricted you. He wasn't worried about how much film you used. So, yes, you would do his picture and then do what you wanted to do." Eckersley and most other successful *Enquirer* journalists came to understand that Pope knew what kind of story or picture he wanted but had no idea of how to get it. He had always worked as an editor, from the tender age of nineteen, and almost surely had never worked a story in his whole life in journalism. Even when he was down to one reporter and neck deep in red ink, he was a publisher.

The Rosenkowitz sextuplets were a big story for the *Enquirer,* and Pope was eager for the pictures. Getting them to Lantana in those primitive times was slow. Eckersley was at the bottom of the world. Pan Am Airways had two around-the-world flights, one through Rio de Janeiro and another through London. Since he didn't know which was faster, Eckersley was planning to send two sets of pictures, one through Rio and the other through London, but that wasn't fast enough for the eager Pope.

Photo editor Bob Young was acting as the go-between, as Eckersley remembers it. Characteristically Pope did not speak directly to Eckersley. Young gave Eckersley this account of how it went with Pope, when he told him the timetable he and Eckersley had worked out:

"Well, the only other way we can do it, Mr. Pope, is if we charter a plane."

"Well, have you investigated that, Bob?"

"Well, coming from Cape Town we'll be needing a pretty big plane."

"Well, Boeing makes some very big planes."[13]

By the time Young had worked out a charter, the film was almost to Miami anyway. But Eckersley was amazed at the expenses Pope was willing to pay: "He was seriously thinking of chartering a plane from Cape Town, which was about as far as you can get from Lantana, short of the Antarctic and Australia. He had no hesitation in chartering a bloody plane from Cape Town for three rolls of film." Soon Pope did charter Learjets for important stories like Elvis's funeral and Princess Grace's death in a car accident. Both yielded record-setting covers, not only for the paper but also for all American tabloids and newspapers.

The photo of the sextuplets ran on the cover. "We had the rights for, I think, six years," Eckersley remembers. "I used to go back to do the birthday parties." Eckersley also observed that once he had bought or established rights to a picture, Pope rarely resold the photos, which was common practice for publications once they had had their exclusive, to recoup some of the expenses they had paid up front. Sometimes a publication could even make money on resales. That's definitely what happened with one of the rare exceptions to Pope's policies, when Gamma Liaison was retained to market the secondary rights to the photos of Gary Hart with Donna Rice on his knee—which ran on the cover and in the center spread on June 2, 1987—for which the *Enquirer* had paid Rice's friend with a camera $50,000. Politics may have had more to do with the decision to further publicize the humiliating exposure of Hart's behavior than financial gain, but with sales to *Paris Match* and magazines in Italy and Germany, secondary rights were expected to generate more than $100,000 in a month.[14] But generally, Pope's exclusives, as Eckersley observed, were exclusives forever. The first pictures of the Rosenkowitz sextuplets were not published elsewhere, nor was the Elvis funeral picture.

"Pope never sold anything," Eckersley said. "He didn't want anybody to have anything. He spent a ton of money getting the Elvis picture and he never sold it to anybody. It's still locked up in a safe. I understand he was offered a lot of money. Somebody offered a lot of money to reprint the *Enquirer* cover, and he wouldn't even do that."[15]

SEVEN

ROCKETING UP

Within a year of the move to Florida and the change in formula, the *Enquirer*'s circulation rose to two million, and it gained nearly a million a year for the next four years.[1] The nation's press pricked up its ears; *Time* and *Newsweek* started covering the paper's spectacular rise and the hairpin turns Pope was making with its editorial content. In 1975 *Newsweek* summarized the developments:

> [The *Enquirer*] used to be a weirdo's delight. Specializing in tales of mutilation, perversion, and gore, the *National Enquirer* mesmerized its one million readers a decade ago with such headlines as Mom Uses Son's Face for an Ashtray and personal ads for everyone from the sadomasochistic set to foot fetishists. But now, in the libertine seventies, the *Enquirer* is peddling a morally upright product, so blameless it could be handed out in Sunday schools. The current issue of the nation's top-selling newspaper, for example, features a helpful essay on household repairs, some nostrums on relieving backache, an analysis of pet names as clues to the owner's hidden feelings, . . . a reassuring survey indicating that most high-school students still support such "traditional values" as

virginity and regular churchgoing, a report on an "army of crazed monkeys" that attacked villagers in Somalia, and a warm, winsome profile of Ambassador Shirley Temple Black.[2]

The *Newsweek* article observed that the paper's editorial staff had zoomed from 35 to 150 and noted Pope's editorial profligacy: "Pope detailed 21 newsmen to cover the Onassis funeral via helicopter and limousine—and calmly footed the excursion's $50,000 tab." *Newsweek* quoted Pope as shooting for a circulation goal of twenty million internationally and noted that an edition with the Nixon-in-exile interview did not sell well. Yet again, Pope reflected that politics was dead. That couldn't really be true, but it was a reading of American culture that had to be taken seriously considering the enormous growth of the *Enquirer* from one million to five million in five years. The *Enquirer* had become, in terms of numbers alone, America's most influential national publication, aside from the *Wall Street Journal* (whose success showed that money and business were alive and well). Eventually Pope would advertise the *Enquirer,* on its cover, as having the "Biggest Circulation of Any Paper in America" (though some wouldn't consider it a newspaper at all).

As the early and mid-seventies witnessed the tabloid explosion that Pope had wrought, others were soon interested in getting in on this lucrative new market. As the Canadian publisher Rosenbloom tailored two of his shady Montreal tabloids into *Enquirer* clones and followed Pope into the American supermarkets, yet another, more ambitious publishing entrepreneur was becoming interested: Rupert Murdoch. It became known that he was looking to buy an American supermarket tabloid.

Roy Cohn would surface once again significantly in Pope's life when he emerged as a dealmaker who would try to broker the sale of the *Enquirer* to Murdoch, or so he claimed in the deathbed autobiography he dictated to Sid Zion. The negotiations were so discreetly managed that it was not widely known that Murdoch had attempted to buy the *Enquirer,* but Calder confirms Cohn's story in his own 2004 memoir.[3]

Murdoch started up his own paper, the *National Star,* in 1973 only after he had failed in his initial effort to buy an existing tabloid. Knowing the subsequent history of the *Enquirer,* it's hard to believe that Pope would have even considered selling it, since he was just starting a circulation boom that would blast him through the seventies and eighties. But at that time the memory of more than a decade of hard times and red ink might have left a deep imprint.

Cohn obviously believed the sale was possible, because he recalled being worried about not getting his commission: "These people are all my friends for years, and that's all well and good," he told Zion, "but I don't want to see this thing go through and I'm staring at a basket of fruit they send me." At a later meeting, Cohn said, Murdoch and Pope told him, just as he was about to broach the subject of a commission, "We know what you're going to say, we've already discussed it, and if the deal goes through, you get a million dollars."[4]

Politics could never really be dead, but the extent to which politics were irrelevant to Pope as a publisher is remarkable when he is compared to his mogul predecessors, Pulitzer and Hearst. They had both been deeply engaged with the politics of the vote—and even affairs of state in Hearst's crusading for war to "liberate" Cuba from Spain—and their yellow journalism often crusaded on issues of social change. Their mass circulations were slanted to the have-nots rather than the haves (like the members of St. Louis high society who hated Pulitzer's upstart *Post-Dispatch* from the beginning), but their sort of political formula no longer worked for Pope. The political demographics of America are continually shifting, and one of the remarkable changes is the extent to which have-nots have increasingly voted against their own class interests. This seems to have been sufficiently exploited by conservative strategists in this era by emphasizing conservative social and cultural issues—abortion or gay marriage recently—over economic matters.

So if the demographics of Pope's new and thus insufficiently understood circulation base was politically mixed, then an issue about Nixon, who narrowly won his first election, would appeal to only a portion of that base and, predictably, "not sell well." Pope appeared to be learning to stay away from politics. His Nietzschean pronouncements about the death of politics and religion made it clear why his paper didn't engage politics in the same way as those of his titanic predecessors, Hearst and Pulitzer, whose journalism otherwise had many uncanny similarities to Pope's. Pope was not an intellectual, he never elaborated quotably on his observations about politics and religion in journalism, but he was certainly capable of bold, direct action that capitalized on his astute insights.

When the *Enquirer*'s circulation hit five million, Pope was on a weekly basis neck and neck with the *Wall Street Journal,* which had in this period a daily circulation of one million, five days a week. The *Journal* wasn't a newspaper either, in the usual sense, because it specialized in financial news. So America's two most influential publications were heading in opposite directions, one totally topical and the other entirely serious business, and neither covered the news in the sense that the *New York Times* or the *Washington Post* did. The *Journal* and the *Enquirer* had both surmounted in their very different ways the problems of locality and found an editorial content that transcended geography to become truly national papers. This enabled them to command such enormous circulations.

Pope was suddenly casting a wide net for talent, and Phil Brennan, who had written the "Cato: From Washington Straight" column for the *National Review,* was one of the first to fall into it. Brennan, who was active in national and Republican politics, had just written a negative biography, *Claude Kirk: The Man and the Myth,* that he believed contributed to the defeat of the incumbent Florida governor:

"I was visiting a couple of friends [around 1970] at the *Enquirer* who had worked in the Washington intelligence community, when the chief writer grabbed me," he recalled. Brennan, who had moved from Washington to Florida with his wife and seven children, started working for Pope as a freelancer, "maybe two weeks out of a month." Then in 1974 Brennan went fulltime as an AE, or articles editor, the *Enquirer*'s title for a relatively independent editor who managed a circle of reporters and stringers. At that time most of the other articles editors and staff reporters were British. "I thought they were the best reporters in the U.S.," Brennan recalls. "While the American reporters were interviewing each other in bars, the Brits got the story. They got the story or they didn't come back. If you needed something, they got it for you."[5]

Brennan's link to the U.S. intelligence community is worth noting, considering his boss's year in the CIA. Another with spook connections was Bill Bates, a rangy, square-jawed fighter pilot who had flown Thunderbolts, Mitchell bombers, and bush planes as the youngest pilot in the Burma campaign's First Air Commando, the unit that had inspired Milton Caniff's *Terry and the Pirates* comic strip. Bates debunked the myth that Pope wouldn't fly, recalling that he used to ferry Pope and his inner circle in a small plane from Lantana to luncheon dates on Fridays. The *Enquirer* offices were only a few minutes from the municipal airport. In the early days in Florida, Pope and his crew soon exhausted the limited resources of the Lantana restaurants. "We used to fly to nearby towns," Bates remembered. "That was our thing in those days. All week long everyone was asking, 'Have you found a good new restaurant?'"6 It must have been a merry time, as the group drank a lot. Bates remembered that once when the group was coming back from a long beery afternoon, he had to go so badly that someone helped hold the controls while he urinated into a plastic bag. Perhaps after a few episodes with air commando Bates as pilot— half drunk, pissing into a bag, with his other hand on the joystick—Pope *was* afraid to fly.

The Fleet Streeters flowed in and out of Pope's employment with the ease and gaiety of men who appeared to look at life as basically a con. Few of them had trouble surviving on foreign soil. One Fleet Streeter worked for Pope, then did a stint in prison for bank robbery. When he got out he cofounded, with another marooned London journalist, a tabloid of his own that for a brief time achieved national circulation; it was called the *Get Rich Quick News.* They offered evidence that these Brits had come to understand why America would never have a true working class, in that many of us define ourselves more by our ambitions and fantasies than by the reality of our conditions.

Fleet Streeter Malcolm Balfour had a long run as an *Enquirer* reporter and editor. When he was inevitably fired, he too settled down in South Florida and began freelancing for British tabloids as their U.S. correspondent, as well as for Rupert Murdoch's *New York Post* and *Star.* Balfour was eventually piloting his own plane to chase down his stories on a beat that extended into the Caribbean islands.

As Brennan noted, most of the American reporters in Pope's employment at the time were from big-city papers, like the *New York Daily News.* Some American reporters had trouble adapting to Pope's exercise in popular culture, but the big-city tabloid reporters worked out better. Many American reporters had too lofty a conception of themselves to work for Pope, though they were attracted to the money he offered. By the late seventies Pope was paying among the highest salaries in American journalism, as Mike Wallace noted in his *60 Minutes* interview in 1976. The paper even attracted more than one Pulitzer Prize winner; Brennan even believed he remembered a reporter who had two Pulitzers.[7] The story of how one Pulitzer winner got fired was widely circulated as a cautionary tale about taking oneself too seriously.

This prizewinner, who labored under the impression that he was hired to improve the *Enquirer,* was put on the Lucky-the-dog beat, meaning he shadowed a mascot that had been rescued from the Animal Rescue League's death row. Lucky, who lived under cover under another name with an *Enquirer* editor (so even tabloid dogs had pseudonyms), often went to Hollywood to meet celebrity pets on what the *Enquirer* reporters called hydrant stops. He went to Washington to scratch and sniff with Nixon's King Timahoe and Amy Carter's spaniel, Gritz.[8] During Christmas season Lucky, a mixed-breed floor mop, posed with stars wearing Santa suits, Bob Hope being one of the most obliging. Johnny Carson was one of the least accommodating; his spokesperson once told a photo editor, "Johnny would rather have a picture of himself looking up Mother Teresa's skirt than to appear on the front page of the *Enquirer*."[9]

The prizewinner thought a jealous and resentful editor had put him on this humiliating beat in order to submerge his obvious talents, and, oblivious to warnings, he requested a personal interview with Pope to straighten the situation out. The prizewinner told Pope that he wanted to do better stories for the *Enquirer* and complained about being put on the lowly dog beat. Pope listened patiently then assured the prizewinner something would be done. When the prizewinner left, Pope went to the doorway of his paneled inner office and asked, "Who was that?" One of his close associates told him. "Well, get rid of him."[10] The Pope quotes in the story would always be rendered in his side-of-the-mouth, low tone.

"A Pulitzer Prize ain't going to win us two readers," Pope told *Newsweek*. "I don't care if other media respect us or not."[11] The Pulitzer Prize winner, or winners, cycled in and out of the paper so fast no one remembered their names. Tabloid journalism found prizewinners useless. Tabloid journalism, for that matter, had no prizewinners—there were no prizes at all.* Pope was renowned for turning down applicants and tryouts with distinguished backgrounds, and when one squeezed through, a distinguished investigative reporter and author, Pope asked, "If he's so good, what's he doing here?"[12] It seems Pope enjoyed his outlaw status with a dash of Groucho Marx.

---

* Frank Zahour, in an interview, said that he and another reporter, sent on a weekend think-tank-style retreat, returned and suggested the creation of a "Pope Prize" for tabloid reporting and writing.

The Pulitzer parable also illustrated another important rule of life at the *Enquirer:* stay out of Pope's sight. To request an interview was to court disaster. As George Hunter, a Scottish reporter and one of the Brits who survived after most of them were weeded out, explained, "You have to keep a low profile, mate. I keep my head down—I actually crouch down behind my keyboard so just the top of my head is showing."

The atmosphere of the *Enquirer's* newsroom in this era was like a pirate ship compared to the mainstream's regular navy. The Fleet Streeters, especially the Australians, were already the buccaneers of journalism, and the American reporters learned from them. The indigenous reporters had an additional kink: many of them had captured and lost good jobs in long careers that ended in the downsizing brought on by the era's media mergers. One veteran *Enquirer* reporter had been chief of the Associated Press's Rome bureau, another had covered Washington politics and had been to the White House. Newspaper mergers generally meant the weaker paper was scuttled, even as its name survived in a newly hyphenated masthead. So Pope's Americans were like sailors who no longer had to stand watches or formations: they were free of the rules of journalism. Pope's personal rules were absolute, but otherwise he flouted the mainstream's ethics and standards.

So, according to Pope's rules, if an *Enquirer* reporter asked a survivor of some ordeal whether he called out to God as he drowned, or looked into the face of death as the snapping jaws of the bear came closer, and the subject gave something that could be construed as an affirmation—a nod, a grunt, perhaps even the consent of silence—then those words the reporter had just uttered would be put in the subject's mouth and quoted. This was policy, a technique passed from editor to reporter and eventually written into the *Enquirer* handbook material. In this kind of journalism a reporter could do the talking and all the subject had to do was nod. Or remain silent. So you had to be careful not only what you said to an Enquirer reporter but also what an *Enquirer* reporter said to you. A reporter could go even further in manufacturing quotes for *Enquirer* stories once he learned the ropes and the even shadier unofficial practices.

The practical fact is there is no legal penalty for making up quotes, as long as the fiction does no harm. This is illustrated by a lawsuit discussed in detail by Elizabeth Bird in her study of tabloids.[13] A commuter airline pilot, Henry Dempsey, was sucked out of his plane when its door popped open. Dempsey managed to get back inside without serious injuries after clinging to the plane for a quarter hour. He refused interviews to the *Star* and the *Enquirer*, but both ran vivid stories anyway, filled with colorful direct quotes about how Dempsey prayed, how the wind tore at his face, how he called out to God, how he stared death in the face. Dempsey sued both papers for invasion of privacy.

The *Star* settled out of court for an undisclosed sum. This was a standard cost of doing business for tabloids, including Pope's two papers, as long as the settlement wasn't too high. It was known that many nuisance suits, as they were regarded, would be settled out of court for $10,000. But the *Enquirer* fought Dempsey's lawsuit to its conclusion, claiming to have pieced the story together by interviewing unnamed friends of the pilot. The judge dismissed the case on the ground that the account could not be considered "highly objectionable to a reasonable person,"[14] even if it were fictionalized. In other words, it did no demonstrable harm. Legal decisions like that enlarged the gray zone where tabloids could operate.

Eventually most of the *Enquirer*'s quotes about celebrities, who rarely spoke to Pope's reporters, were attributed to unnamed friends and associates. But sometimes those stories were backed up by aggressive reporting. The *Enquirer* loved to interview fired household employees (and paid them handsomely for their stories), such as Rock Hudson's former valet or butler who offered a poignant vision of the fading star sitting alone drunkenly in his private home theater running his old movies and muttering, "Garbage . . . garbage . . . garbage."

After Mike Wallace had grilled Pope in 1976 about his alleged Mafia connection on *60 Minutes,* he went on to attack some of the paper's dubious practices. He moved on to batter Pope, who had Iain Calder and other staffers with him, over hyping, cooking, and piping stories: for instance, attributing quotes to Raquel Welch that she personally denounced on the program as fabricated. It was the first major assault on the *Enquirer*'s credibility and more or less the last. Wallace accused Pope of doctoring a cover picture of Welch and Freddie Prinze together and publishing Walter Cronkite's purported salary ($750,000), which Cronkite, in a video or film clip, said was wrong: "Not half that do I earn," intoned America's most trusted journalist.[15]

Calder claimed that this was the first time the *Enquirer* had spliced separate celebrity pictures, and also learned how Wallace earned his reputation as broadcast journalism's attack dog. After Calder apologized for the spliced photos, in a fairly gentle exchange, Wallace turned the cameras on himself and rerecorded his initially milder-mannered questioning of Calder, this time in a "fierce and accusatory" tone: *Mr. Calder, what's your explanation for this phony picture?*[16]

Wallace's hatchet-job interview was about as close as the *Enquirer* came to sustained public humiliation, and as it turned out that wasn't so terribly close. As Wallace was discovering, the parodic elements of the *Enquirer* made it slippery prey. After all, the paper's slapdash practices were part of the fun, and Wallace, like many mainstream journalists, had some dubious practices of his own, as Calder had just witnessed. It was proving difficult for journalists to be too high-minded about tabloid journalism. In fact, overall Pope's *60 Minutes* appearance was good publicity, because one of the era's new tabloid truths was playing out: *any* publicity was good publicity in postmodern America.

If Wallace had sought to do harm, the effort had backfired. It was one of the earliest examples of the charmed life the *Enquirer* lived in regard to the mainstream press, whose exposés and articles routinely turned into light-hearted puffs. There was enough bogus in the serious press—Wallace's little trick is now banned at CBS—that its reporters could hardly bring themselves to humiliate a publication that was so earnestly over the top. To journalists less high-minded (or hypocritical) than Wallace, the *Enquirer* must have seemed at least a distant relative, a crazy cousin.

Wallace could have driven much harder at Pope's mob connections, but there was a certain justice in the way the story turned out. It's very likely Pope did drop his gangster friends when he went to Florida; he probably worked quite hard to clear up whatever debts he owed them and to disengage from any money-laundering favors, so he wouldn't be lying about the mob not having its "hooks" into the *Enquirer.*

In constructing his brief argument for Wallace and the public as to why the Mafia couldn't have its hooks into him, and the *Enquirer,* Pope came close to conceding that the Mafia did exist, even though he did not use the word *Mafia.* The *60 Minutes* interview was contained in Pope's CIA file, which former *Enquirer* reporter Frank Zahour obtained many years after filing a request under the Freedom of Information Act.

Visitors to the newsroom were struck by the energy and buzz. Pope at times acted like a pirate captain, offering cash bonuses for things he really wanted —for instance, $5,000 for a teenage photo of Steve McQueen for the leading man's obituary. It was as if he had nailed a gold doubloon to the mast for the first sailor who spotted the next victim on the horizon. Reporters scrambled into the figurative rigging, and before long one had located a high school yearbook with McQueen's senior picture, and collected his gold.

The *Enquirer*'s newsroom reflected, in a paradoxical way, Pope's personality. In mien he was a dour, gray man, yet he attracted a colorful circus of activity around him. But there was no denying his physical presence could cast a pall. Once Pope walked by when reporter Steve Chao was bent over with his pants around his ankles mooning another reporter. The immediate feeling was that Chao was in trouble. But Pope swept on without a blink. No indication that he had even noticed Chao's bare bum ever reached the newsroom floor. But incidents like that could go the other way. Pope once fired a reporter for spilling coffee on the carpet, according to a legend about which no one could quite remember the particulars. Ever afterward, *Enquirer* reporters and writers clamped a plastic lid on their coffee cups on the way back to their desks, even if the desk was only a few feet from the coffee setup. New hires were carefully instructed of this custom, which remained as a palpable trace of Pope's temper. Even the idle gaze of the boss might be scorching, apparently. Outside Pope's office window was a patch of grass the gardeners had to replace every few months. Some said it was a problem with the drainage or sprinklers, but the gardeners thought the problem was the boss's withering gaze.[17]

New hires were also cautioned that they could mistake Pope, with his Ollie North haircut and sloppy clothes, for the janitor. Pope was six-foot-two, a sallow, sedentary man who smoked three packs of Kents a day and was twenty pounds or so overweight. He worked six days a week and never took sick days and never, so the legend went, traveled more than thirty miles from home once he moved to Florida. He drove modest cars, which he sometimes kept for five or six years, and seemed to lack most of the usual vanities and vices of the rich and powerful. Pope wasn't tempted by hot cars, hot women, yachts, high society, clothes, art, shopping, fame, or travel. He wasn't greedy or miserly; he was a philanthropist and plowed much of his profits back into his cash-cow paper, which had the effect of making it ever more profitable.

Eventually there was a correction to the fast growth *Newsweek* had reported in the *Enquirer*'s staff. The later years of the seventies witnessed Pope's infamous mass firings of reporters and editors, the bloodbaths. They marked a particularly creative period in tabloid history, even if it was nerve-racking for the reporters who were axed, as well as for those who survived. In the beginning the firings happened on Fridays, in the last hour of the afternoon, which became known as the Hour of the Jackals. "You didn't want to answer your intercom on Friday afternoon after 3:00 p.m.," said Phil Brennan. "The editor next to me did and I never saw him again. You know, they sort of whisked you out of there."[18] Indeed, the drill was, then and forever after, that a fired employee was never out of sight of security once the ax came down, and was quickly bum-rushed out with nothing but purely personal possessions, certainly no files, lists, tapes, or documents. When Pope fired people, they virtually disappeared from the building (though they would soon surface in the Lantana bars to tell the tale). Brennan's turn was especially poignant. He was fired on his birthday. The cake was on the desk and the candles lit when he was summoned. The candles burned down, and Brennan never reappeared. "And the bastards ate my cake," he recalled.

Of course Brennan's cohorts ate his cake: there was an eat-drink-and-be-merry attitude in those buccaneering days. Besides, being fired could be a fortunate twist in the eventful lives of the tabloid breed. In those early days a tabloid reporter's life was so cheap Pope offered no life insurance in his benefits package. "One articles editor was fired and went to work for Jerry Ford," Brennan remembered, "and a few weeks later he dropped dead. It turns out they had a $1 million life insurance policy on him. If he hadn't been fired, his family would have been penniless." As to the reason for his own firing, Brennan says, "I never found out why. Pope never told you the reasons he did things. Sometimes you could figure it out." Talking back was a fairly certain way for a reporter or editor to get fired, according to Brennan: "Pope didn't like it." It's probable that Pope regarded talking back as a symptom of disloyalty or insubordination as well as an insult to his intellect. No doubt he was touchy. Iain Calder, who had been observing Pope since the gore days, remembered, "Telling Gene he was wrong was like handling weeping gelignite."[19]

Editors and reporters are expected to be the first line of defense against libel, but Pope's staffers were especially cagey about libel issues. No *Enquirer* reporter was told outright to hype a quote, though quotes were hyped by the dozens every day. Instead an editor might tell a reporter, "We need better quotes." Those who couldn't figure out things for themselves were soon left behind. Much of the *Enquirer*'s celebrity coverage occupied a legal gray area of romantic peccadilloes, changing boyfriends, or casual infidelities where it would be nearly impossible to show damages, even over made-up stories. It was harmless gossip, as we say, unless someone like Carol Burnett decided to make an issue of it, as she so famously did.

Paradoxically a reporter's best employment insurance under Pope could be having a libel suit filed against him, or better, more than one. The lawsuits usually took years to come to trial, especially with the delaying tactics of Pope's lawyers, and Pope wanted to make sure his reporter was still on the paper's side when it came time to testify. This was quite the reverse of mainstream journalism, where a libel suit was a personal disgrace and could render a reporter unemployable. But Pope needed to take risks to deliver the racy stories his readers craved, so he regarded libel suits as a cost of doing business.

Each week, Pope had an editorial meeting with his articles editors, and the question he always asked was, "What are Americans thinking about out there today?" according to Brennan. "I always wanted to answer, 'They're thinking about you, Mr. Pope,' but I didn't dare. I wanted to live."[20] Even a misdirected wisecrack at an editorial meeting might get an editor fired. Once when the notoriously humorless Pope asked what kind of shape the files were in, an editor, who had so far been one of Pope's favorites, made a shape like a box with his hands, meaning they were square. People chuckled. A few weeks later the editor was fired, and some thought his joke at Pope's expense was the reason. Australian Mike Hoy, serving what turned out to be a brief stint as executive editor, said he always kept a suitcase packed in his closet to remind him of the unsteady terms of his employment. When his head rolled, Hoy picked it up, set it back on his shoulders with aplomb, and within hours stepped on the plane back to London. The Aussies were proving the most adaptable of journalists, and the well-prepared Hoy landed on his feet. He soon became managing editor of Murdoch's London tabloid, the *Sun*.

Former Burma air commando Bill Bates, one of Pope's earliest photo editors, worked for Pope in New Jersey before the paper moved to Florida, one point about Bates being that *Enquirer* photo editors need not know anything much about photography. They were instead can-do people, masters of tracking down photos, finding photographers all over the world for assignments, and negotiating prices and fees with the paparazzi. Paparazzi existed long before the *Enquirer* called upon them, especially in Italy, as Federico Fellini's film *La Dolce Vita* (1960) shows, but the *Enquirer* certainly improved their living standard. Calder, in his memoir, says he regretted "creating a monster, who, more than any other journalist, made Jackie Onassis' life miserable."[21] He meant Ron Galella, who was eventually legally enjoined from coming too near Jackie O, so fiercely did he stalk her, often in the name of the *Enquirer*.

Eventually Pope decided it was not worthwhile having his own photographers; he would rely largely on freelancers. Vince Eckersley, who had worked for Fleet Street magazines and became one of Pope's original lensmen, explained the situation: "At one point we maxed out at eight or nine photographers, but then costs started getting prohibitive. To take a picture in the Midwest you're a day going there, and one job would take two or three days, and Pope would be paying hotel bills. People faded away."[22]

It was in his informal aviator role that photo editor Bates got on the wrong side of Pope. Someone had put Pope up to using a photographer in a helicopter, and Bates immediately told Pope the helicopter's prop wash, or slipstream, would spoil the shoot. Pope went ahead and, just as Bates predicted, the chopper's heavy downdraft created such chaos on the ground that the shoot was spoiled. Immediately Pope stopped speaking to Bates. A few weeks later, Pope fired him, and Bates assumed that the reason went back to their disagreement about prop wash. It was another cautionary tale against disagreeing with Pope, even if you meant well, and especially if you were right.*

Brennan theorized there often really was no reason, in the usual sense, for Pope's firings: "It was done to make an example, to frighten people." The sheer numbers were certainly frightening. Brennan remembers one Friday afternoon when thirteen reporters and editors disappeared at once. Calder recalls that whenever employees made plans for more than a week ahead in that era, they tagged on the phrase, "if we're still here."[23] Yet Pope seemed to feel nothing particularly personal was involved. He often took people back after a decent interval, and Brennan noted that he was fired from the *Enquirer* three times. It became common for reporters to get fired from the *Enquirer,* go work on one of Rosenbloom's tabloids or the *Star,* then return to the *Enquirer*—then maybe get fired again and start around the revolving

---

* Despite the prop wash problem, a new, virulent category of tabloid paparazzi eventually evolved, the chopperazzi. Hope of stealth was abandoned for the most aggressively intrusive means of all, a hovering helicopter. By that time the *Enquirer* was buying its pictures freelance. In 1985 it ran pictures of a chopperazzi invasion of Madonna's secret wedding to Sean Penn, which was almost spoiled by the invasion. The photos of these incursions featured tables swept clean of food and dishes by the prop wash, with guests cowering in nooks and corners and the women trying to hold their dresses down. In "Sex, Trash & Videotapes" (*Talk,* October 2001) *Enquirer* reporter Jay Cheshes says he was shot at by a security guard when he invaded Melanie Griffith's second wedding to Don Johnson in 1989 outside of Aspen, Colorado, in a chartered chopper, though at that time he was working for the *Star,* which was purchased by the *Enquirer* a year later.

door again. The employment merry-go-round of Florida's Tabloid Triangle certainly spread Pope's influence throughout the tabloids, as *Enquirer* experience was regarded as the gold standard of American tabloid journalism. The so-called Tabloid Triangle was the territory between Lantana and Boca Raton, where the *Globe, National Examiner,* and *Sun* were published; all the supermarket tabloids except the *Star,* in Tarrytown, New York, were within thirty miles of one another, not really in a triangle but in a straight line down Florida's Treasure coast. More to the point, the territory was like the Bermuda Triangle of legend, a place where people—tabloid journalists—disappeared and reappeared with regularity.

Not only did Pope fire often, he also fired at particularly inconvenient times, including birthdays and the Christmas season. It was also said to be very bad luck to buy a house while in Pope's employ. Phil Bunton's story was a classic illustration of why. Bunton was very much in Pope's favor as the founding editor of Pope's second tabloid in 1979, the *Weekly World News,* and then as managing editor of the *Enquirer.* Pope had bettered Bunton's salary at the *New York Post,* then owned by Murdoch, and after the successful startup of the *News* gave him a hefty raise—$20,000. "But people told me, whatever you do, don't buy a house," Bunton recalled. "In another three months I got another gigantic raise, another $20,000. I was making something like $120,000. I felt safe, and Pope seemed to like me. So we bought a house. But I didn't tell Pope."[24]

Nevertheless, just when Bunton was about to close on his new house, Pope called him in and said, "This just isn't working out." He offered to send Bunton back to the *Weekly World News* with a $40,000 salary cut. "I was shocked," said Bunton, "not so much because I had been demoted, but because I was about to buy this house I could no longer afford. But I went through with the closing. The real estate agent said, 'I've never seen such an unhappy person going through a closing—what's wrong?'" Bunton told him: "He later said, 'If I had known I maybe could have got you out of the deal.'"

Bunton got a call from Murdoch right away, and a week later was working on the *Star.* He never lived in the house. He rented it for more than a year then sold it at a small loss. The next editor of the *Weekly World News,* Lou Golden, did not buy a house, observed Bunton. "He lived in an apartment and socked away the money," said Bunton. "When he left, he took all that money and went and got married."

Pope built up an immense network of freelancers, or stringers—so called because their pay was long ago calculated by stringing together their copy and paying by the column inch. In theory this reportorial network was to be truly national, with a national network of sources as well. Pope paid handsomely for story ideas, submitted as punchy leads of three to five lines, and again for the stories themselves when they were researched, written, and published. Pope skimmed through hundreds of leads a week, after his editors had weeded them down, though Pope was the only one who had the authority to approve a lead. "I OK about 125," Pope told *Business Week,* "and maybe 40 make it in."[25] Often Pope's winnowing process for ideas and stories seemed nothing less than arbitrary. On a lead describing a South American tribe that once a year threw a virgin into a fiery volcano, Pope scrawled in red, "Happens every day."[26] Pope's personality, preferences, and obsessions were reflected in the leads he chose to develop. Just as stories about the dangers of smoking were tossed, as were downers in general, he ran many stories about avoiding constipation and remedies for it. Constipation stories were difficult to get through the system, as the boss usually had a lot of questions. It was a pretty good bet that Pope suffered from constipation.

The pay scale varied for top-of-the page leads and stories, and lesser ones played at the bottom, but the freelance rates were the best in the nation. A clever reporter for a mainstream newspaper could make an extra $500 with a few hours' work. Many of Pope's double-dippers did not want their bylines in the *Enquirer* because they worked for prestigious papers like the *New York Times,* the *Washington Post,* or the *Wall Street Journal.* No doubt it amused Pope to boast from time to time that he had some of the most distinguished journalists in the nation working for him, though he was not at liberty to reveal their names.

"I used to freelance stories to Pope during my lunch hour when I was a reporter for the *Miami Herald,*" said Colin Dangaard. "For what took me 30 minutes of work on the telephone for the *Enquirer* once a week, I was paid almost as much as I made for the entire week from the *Herald.*"[27] One of the ironies of the split between tabloid and mainstream journalism was these reporters working both sides of the street. Tabloid journalism and mainstream or "quality" journalism, as the Brits called it, might not be as far apart as they seemed in the popular perception. This is something to ponder in the context of the ongoing tabloidization of mainstream journalism.

A dedicated stringer, especially one with tabloid experience, could make a good living freelancing for the *Enquirer* alone, and many did—at one point too many, in Pope's perception, at least too many living in South Florida. After many Friday afternoon massacres Pope had created a pool of unemployed reporters in South Florida, many of them Brits who preferred to remain in Florida's sunny climate. Since they knew the ropes and had chums in the newsroom, the former staffers were especially efficient freelancers. Some of them claimed to have topped their already generous former salaries in freelance income, while living a much sweeter life. Aussie Brian Hogan said he spent so much time at the beach while making a living as an *Enquirer* freelancer that he had acquired a deep tan—too deep: "This created a certain resentment whenever I went to the office to visit a friend or drop off a story."[28] So, Hogan said, he started wearing a bit of his girlfriend's face powder to tone down the tan and dampen the resentment.

But the South Florida freelance pool lacked a benefits package, so the group formed a cooperative and bought its own medical plan. This, according to Brennan, annoyed Pope, who was proud of the generous benefits package he offered by that time. So Pope banned all South Florida freelancers in yet another of his "papal" decrees, as they were dubbed. To Brennan, there was a certain logic to this, as the national network of freelancers offered the paper significant diversity, while the heavily British local pool was becoming inbred.

Later Pope impulsively rehired the enterprising former staffer who had formed the benefits cooperative. And when Hogan was hospitalized after a serious auto accident, Pope paid his hospital bills, although he was under no legal obligation to do so. In another situation, when an editor was forced to leave the paper for medical reasons, Pope kept him at full pay for years. But when two highly regarded editors left Pope's employ to found their own venture, which quickly failed, Pope hired one back but not the other—and who knew his reasoning?

EIGHT

PERFECTING THE FORMULA

By the time Tom Kuncl rose to executive editor in the late seventies, there were more British than American reporters, and overall the editorial ranks appeared to have swollen beyond their most efficient capacity. Pope had even hired a journalist to publish a lively, gossipy house newspaper to keep track of what was going on in Popestown. Then he decided a few years later *not* to have a house organ. It appeared to be just another example of Pope changing his mind. Perhaps not coincidentally, the newsletter writer had recently bought a lovely house with a greenhouse bathroom and a sunken tub fit for an emperor, which the young couple had so enthusiastically showed off at their recent housewarming.

"One of my briefs when I took over was that Pope had become kind of disaffected with the lot of the Brits—not all of them, but with quite a few of them," Kuncl recalled. It was another reversal on Pope's part, but typically his zigzagging dialectics never got quite back to where he had been. This was part of the complexity of Pope's eccentric editorial course, which defied pat explanations. The British influence was already indelibly stamped on the paper. The *Enquirer,* and the supermarket clones that imitated it, was no doubt a British-American hybrid. Some British reporters were to become permanent members of Pope's staff, including Iain Calder, the Scot who served as Pope's

No. 2 man for years and took the helm after Pope's death. There was no denying that some British reporters were better, some worse, but in general Kuncl
disagreed with Phil Brennan's glowing assessment of the Brits as a whole.
Kuncl said that

> Pope was very impressed by the British reporters. They could talk
> you out of your underwear. Some of them were genuinely good
> people. But a lot of buddies came in the door, a lot of protégés,
> and a lot of hail-fellows-well-met, Guinness-stout drinkers. I can't
> bitch about that because I was capable myself. But some of these
> guys, that was their best skill. Their contribution? A hell of a lot
> of it was mythos. I was not all that impressed by the British—
> "Vicar Caught in Love Nest" and all that sort of thing. I thought
> we should be doing things with a harder edge. They were cheeki-
> er. I didn't find them more resourceful. And my view is you tell
> someone I'll give you 10,000 bucks for this, you don't have to be
> a crack journalist. I thought a lot of the Americans I put on-
> stream were better journalists. They would walk through walls.[1]

Kuncl was also in a position to explain a paradox in Pope's management
style. He was simultaneously hands-on and hands-off. His presence was felt
in every aspect of the editorial machinery. He read every story at every stage
of production and made all the editorial decisions, from picking the leads to
deciding the play of stories. It was well known that no one but Pope made
important editorial decisions, and under Pope all editorial decisions were important. So editors like Kuncl were reduced to second-guessing him. His

perceived presence was so intrusive that some employees were convinced that their phones were tapped, that they were under surveillance. It may have been a phantom feeling; the only evidence was circumstantial: how much Pope knew about his staff. He had a serious security department, though, and people weren't allowed to wander into security's offices.

As the weekly deadline loomed, Pope worked from a glass-enclosed booth in the newsroom, from which he could see everything. The office was arguably a version of the Panopticon, Jeremy Bentham's theoretical prison where the inmates felt they were under surveillance even when they weren't. It was believed that Pope was not above hiring shady private detectives and hackers for certain stories, so why not to check up on his staff?

Frank Zahour said it was commonly believed that Pope got a local police report on Monday mornings listing any of his staff who had had run-ins with the law, and it was likely that his philanthropy had bought some of the local police. As a consequence Pope was not the sort of boss who was ridiculed behind his back. Nor did he suffer any disrespectful or diminutive nicknames, not even the kind common in the military, expressing a certain fondness. Fondness was not an emotion that Pope was likely to arouse.

Yet a reporter, writer, or editor could go for weeks without speaking to him or personally encountering him. This put a heavy burden on a close circle around Pope, especially the executive editor. The unwelcome weight of the firings fell on Kuncl, who wanted to serve Pope loyally and found himself in a dilemma:

> There were times I had to carry out things he wanted done that I
> had to implement in a different way than he might have. Because

some of his orders were sometimes severe and almost went against logic, when it came to personnel. There were times when he would say, "This person is not doing good work." Well, I would know that they were, and that they had somehow made a misstep somewhere. I could play into the way he was presenting it, that they had somehow lost their steam. Or I could say to them, "Look, your number's up, okay, and I'm not going to insult you by saying you don't know what you're doing or that you're screwing up on the job. The best I can tell you is that your number came up." I did that several times. I couldn't feel myself in agreement with him on why he wanted someone out of the place. It would be bleak stuff—this guy's a jackass all of a sudden. One time it was a very cute young gal that I think maybe Lois took umbrage about. There was nothing going on, but it was enough. I don't want to say it was a Soprano decision . . . [2]

Kuncl was happier about playing the hatchet man when he could sometimes see the logic, or when he found someone who really deserved to be fired:

One of the things that went into my portfolio was to clean house. I agreed that we had to do it. We were overstaffed and we really had a bunch of dockwallopers who were not producing. So for a period of years I started looking everybody over. There were a lot of scoundrels. There were a lot of guys who were fucking us to death on expenses and stuff. So I did clean house, and it didn't make me very popular. I forget what the body count was, but it was significant. I tried not to do it on Fridays because that had become a legend. You know, Fearful Friday. And I tried to get people everything I could get them on the way out the door.[3]

Even after Kuncl's winnowing process the British reporters continued to have a major role in the paper they had helped shape. Never again were they a majority, but they were always a force and an influence. When reporter Steve Coz came on board near the end of Kuncl's reign, he still held the British reporters in high regard: "When I was first in the building, I thought the Brits were the go-to guys." Coz also thought that over the course of the eighties the Americans absorbed much from the Brits. "I think the Americans probably wanted to be a little more brash, and they admired the Fleet Streeters for the way they did things, their writing and their style. They'd already been in the trenches and they didn't have this undying respect for journalism. I think that was a good learning curve for the Americans."[4]

Pope's executive editors were pushed into a henchman role, and they were disliked and feared. It was the result, of course, of having so much blood spattered on them, even though everyone knew the man behind the firings was Pope. Kuncl saw Pope fire someone personally only once: Pope lost his cool, and, significantly, the issue was loyalty. Pope's behavior did not inspire true loyalty in his staffers, but he wanted it and was infuriated when he didn't get it. If it was discovered that an *Enquirer* staffer was looking elsewhere for work, Pope would fire him before he could make his move. Stealing even a little money from him on expense accounts, which were lavish by journalistic standards, enraged him out of all proportion. Kuncl recalled: "Pope thought M. was making payments to a girlfriend. As it turned out, I don't think he was. Or if he did, it was legitimate. Pope came out of his office and told him to get the hell out. It was like he was stealing. I saw Pope chew a lot of people's asses, but I never saw him fire anyone else. That was either me or Calder, and in my era it was me."[5]

Pope was still actively tuning his formula throughout Kuncl's tenure as executive editor, which ended when Kuncl and Mike Walker, the *Enquirer*'s chief writer, left to found their own popular publishing venture, ill-fated, as it turned out. As Kuncl noted, "Pope was a great admirer of the *Reader's Digest*," and he set his staff leafing through back issues for inspiration and story ideas. Brennan specifically recalled hearing Pope refer to the *Enquirer* as the poor man's *Reader's Digest*. "At one time I bought bound volumes from the original issue to the most current," said Kuncl. "We looked through them for ideas. When I left there, I said, 'What do you want me to do with them?' He said, 'Well, you like them, so you take them.' There were probably four or five thousand dollars' worth, which I ended up giving to the library in Norwood, New Jersey."

In regard to the formula, Brennan said Pope felt that there should always be at least two stories in the paper that interested everyone. Around these were several other generic stories. Said Kuncl: "When I went into the scheduling room to put together the paper, I had to make sure there was a ghost story, a rags-to-riches story, a reader's-participation story. There was a chart for what the mix needed to look like. And if we deviated from that mix because we didn't have a good-enough ghost story, Pope was aware of it and he didn't like it. Frankly some parts of the formula he was wrong about. But other parts he was dead right about."[6]

During his tenure as an articles editor, Phil Brennan specialized in two other areas of the formula chart: government waste and medicine. It was taken for granted in the *Enquirer*'s pages that the government wasted money outrageously. Brennan, formerly so active in Republican politics, was just the man to manage those stories. Here was a place where politics or ideology might have played some part in the *Enquirer.* The Popes, father and son, had long connections with the Democratic Party, and Pope kept a photo of Harry Truman in his office. It suggested that Pope's personal politics, largely concealed, were roughly center, against big government.

Pope also had connections with the Nixon administration: Melvin Laird pulled strings for him and eulogized Pope at his funeral. In an earlier political landscape the senior Pope was tight with Tammany Hall; young Gene Pope served in the CIA in the early cold war under Truman. He was a second-generation millionaire; his father epitomized the American dream, rising from rags to riches and power. Pope paid his reporters generously, in his best days more than union top scale, compared with the big mainstream papers, and he maintained strict control over editorial content. So importing British neo-Marxist ideas of social subversiveness to the analysis of tabloids—as the influential culture critic John Fiske does in his numerous books on media—seems seriously misguided.

The *Enquirer* and the *Weekly World News* were socially subversive in various ways, in their aesthetic of the abject, in their periodic elements, and in the *Enquirer*'s undermining of mainstream celebrity culture, but that could be better explained by the political paradox of the Mafia, which Gay Talese delineates in *Honor Thy Father.* Talese notes how the Mafia was both for and against the government. Talese wrote that mobsters supported the Vietnam War politically, insofar as they disapproved of young Bonanno's long hair and antiwar aspect, though as lawbreakers they clearly subverted the government that waged the war. Yet they didn't want to seriously undermine the government, because it provided the backbone of the social carcass they fed on like parasites. Pope subverted celebrity culture, but he needed its carcass in the same way the Bonanno mob needed the social order. It was a symbiotic subversive relationship.[7]

One of the *Enquirer*'s story categories was the "Hey, Martha!" (or alternately, a "Gee Whiz!"). A "Hey, Martha!" was the kind of offbeat story that moved a husband to call out across the kitchen table to his wife about it. It was, of course, an unconsciously sexist scenario, with the husband reading the paper, when, with the *Enquirer*'s demographics, it would more likely have been the wife. That situation also had the husband taking on a patriarchal role, doing the telling and teaching, and it wasn't too much of a step in this antique *Father Knows Best* setup to imagine hubby, as the *Enquirer* often called the man of the house, having a leisurely cup of coffee while the wife bent over the dishes or housework.

Pope's behavior toward women fit a sort of pre–Betty Friedan sensibility, and his sensibility was always reflected in the paper. Pope hired many female reporters and editors and fired them hardly less capriciously than their male cohorts. Personally, at this stage of his life, he remained above suspicion, neither a flirt nor a philanderer. Yet Pope's upper management was virtually entirely male, and the atmosphere of the paper was perceived as openly sexist by women working there. Many female clerks and assistants seemed to have been hired for their looks. The Fleet Street males brought a London working-class sexism to the newsroom. During the Brit rule of the seventies the whole newsroom fell silent when one of these beautiful flunkies flounced across the floor, then, when she had passed, broke into a murmur of appreciative evaluative commentary. One of Pope's most productive articles editors—an American—was so sexually abusive to his female reporters (including having public intercourse with a submissive tryout under the patio stairs at the *Enquirer's* beach-bar hangout) that Pope finally ruled the editor could no longer supervise any women reporters at all, though he remained on staff for years. Incredibly, it was an era when no sex abuse or discrimination lawsuits were spawned.

"Women at the Top" was a story category in Pope's formula. He also ran stories about deadbeat dads who failed to support their children. Yet, in significant ways the *Enquirer's* journalism supported a patriarchal attitude on feminist issues. Research finally confirmed what everyone already knew: most of *Enquirer* readers (65 percent) were female. That percentage might have been even greater in the early days, but the *Enquirer,* like most mainstream papers, did little demographic research in those times. Instead editors tended to rely on gut instincts and trial and error, the most primitive discourse between the publication and its readership. But who could say for sure that official figures would have made any difference? Gut instincts and trial and error might have more reliably courted female readers in the heartland, since it was possible, even common, to be female and antifeminist. To describe Pope as an anti-intellectual would be an understatement: he had little place for theory in his operating manual. In the eighties he would commission readership studies, circulate them among his employees, and patently ignore what the think tanks and focus groups concluded. He still listened to his own gut, and he was building a monumental circulation on the rumblings he heard there.

Early on Pope discovered the delights of covering medicine tabloid style. It began after he sent a dozen reporters to a medical conference in Washington to troll for story ideas. They were not to come back empty-handed, so the stories they wrote were naturally hyped in the usual tabloid way. Eventually Pope had an enormous role in founding a variety of postmodern "knowledge," junk science. His contribution reached back to the American tradition of frontier medicine shows and snake oil with stories about miracles, cures, and breakthroughs. The third-best-selling *Enquirer* cover story, after the Elvis funeral and Princess Grace's death, was "Drinking Beer Prevents Heart Attacks," which did especially well prominently displayed on supermarket racks. You could throw another six-pack in the cart. The issue sold 6.3 million.[8]

The *Enquirer* ran numerous crackpot stories on curing cancer, relieving arthritis, and preventing heart attacks. It hardly mattered that most of them never came true or that they repeated or contradicted something that had been written the week before. The tabloid narrative was about *now*—period. In tabloid neither the reader nor the writer had to worry about things adding up. Tabloid made people feel good now, and freelancers soon learned not to submit ideas for downers, stories that were not uplifting. Celebrity scandal was the exception, which suggests that readers took delight in the troubles of the mighty and rich. The paper's formula category of "The Mighty Brought Low," was obviously reassuring.

The *Enquirer* also ran stories that were 100 percent true; the paper even had a cooperative relationship with the American Cancer Society. Running true stories was an important part of the business of stretching the truth. There had to be gradations to keep people guessing and to keep the line between fiction and reality blurred.

Left entirely to his own whims Pope probably would have continued to take the *Enquirer* in the direction of a tabloid *Reader's Digest,* a paper with a great variety of hyped and simplified stories. The first free association most people have now to the words *National Enquirer* is invariably to conjure up some form of celebrity scandal, but Phil Brennan saw evidence in the mid-seventies that Pope was trying to get away from celebrity stories. "He tried to downplay the celebrities, but every time he did, circulation dropped," Brennan observed. After 1973, the *Star* was covering celebrities even more passionately and breathing down Pope's neck in their circulation war.

The *Enquirer* had existed for many years without so many celebrities, so why should Pope become overly interested in them at this point? As always, circulation would be the deciding factor, and this was Pope's bottom-line discourse with his readers: they appeared to want celebrity stories more than Pope. It's an important consideration, because both academic and casual media analysts tend to look through the wrong end of the telescope, as if the tabloids were foisting celebrity journalism upon the American public. But it's likely that Pope was reluctantly feeding a voracious appetite he had tapped. Calder observed that stories about celebrities never made up more than half the *Enquirer*'s mix before Pope died.[9] Later owners responded to public appetites and took the paper further in that direction, but it was a mistake. The formula grew monotonous and stale, and circulation continued to drop.

Celebrity journalism already existed in the form of dozens of fan magazines, which published puff pieces from studio public relations operatives. Pope couldn't offer the public anything much better in that overworked field, though he did do occasional puffs (often on Bob Hope and Sophia Loren) as well as scandal. But scandal was where the circulation was, and scandal was

legally dangerous. The significant predecessor of the *Enquirer* in that arena
was *Confidential* magazine, which ended badly. The fan magazines supported
the lie, for instance, that Hollywood closet gay Rock Hudson was heterosex-
ual, publishing photos of dating setups that Rock's studio, Universal, arranged for the fan press to cover, notably with fellow contract player Mamie
Van Doren, who became Hollywood's third-ranking platinum blonde after
Marilyn Monroe and Jayne Mansfield. But when Rock's agent, Henry Willson, and the studio publicists got a whiff that *Confidential* was about to out
their hunk in the spring of 1955, just as Rock was poised on the brink of real
stardom, they hastily arranged for him to get married—to Phyllis Gates,
Willson's secretary.[10]

In its heyday *Confidential* had a circulation of three million,[11] but by
1958 it had been gutted by a series of celebrity libel suits with damages total-
ing $40 million that drove it out of the scandal business.[12] That a repeat of
this story was a real and reasonable fear was demonstrated years later when
Carol Burnett sued the *Enquirer* and won a $1.6 million settlement over a
three-line 1976 gossip item that was judged to be libelous, in a widely publi-
cized lawsuit.[13]

Pope had to be especially responsive to circulation figures because the
Enquirer survived and prospered on its cover price. Despite the fact that he'd
made it into the supermarkets, Pope could not get national advertising, even
for the household products, that should have been his by rights because of the
female readership he commanded. As much as he cleaned up the *Enquirer,* it
wasn't enough for advertisers like Procter and Gamble. The *Enquirer* was still
too racy and lowbrow.

In the late seventies and early eighties the *Enquirer* would attain its highest circulation, consistently above five million, making it the largest-selling national publication after *TV Guide*.[14] Yet people were still afraid to admit they read the paper. Shoppers, mostly women, snatched the *Enquirer* from the checkout racks, buried it in their grocery bags and took it home—it was known as the "red-faced syndrome." Even if these secret readers hid the paper from the high-minded, the *Enquirer* circulation department believed it had a significant pass-along rate, three readers for every single issue. This pass-along statistic was based on anecdotal information, but it was widely believed in the paper's editorial offices. It suggested that the *Enquirer* was viewed by many readers as literary contraband, to be secretly circulated among friends.

NINE

LANTANA 33464

Pope remained a fair enigma even to his reporters and editors, who were ordinarily experts at figuring people out. They studied him hard and knew many little things about him, some he probably didn't know about himself. This was very plausible, since he once told a reporter, "I don't spend much time trying to figure myself out."[1] Writers knew they had to be careful about his sign in astrology copy (Pope was born January 13). Reporter Frank Zahour remembers having an item kicked back to have the Capricorn description pumped up: "When a feature called for a description of a Capricorn, you had to describe that sign in glowing terms. If the sign was facing some problems that day, or whatever, you would not say, 'A Capricorn may see some setbacks this week.' It had to be something like, 'The leadership skills of Capricorn will be tested this week.'"

Zahour also remembers that it was well known that Pope did not like crosswords but loved mazes. This was thought to be significant, since employees could imagine the paper as more of a maze than a puzzle (a puzzle could be solved, but a maze was an ongoing, disorienting experience). Zahour said the paper never ran a crossword in his six years there.[2] Meanwhile, the photo editors had learned that Pope would pass almost any photo that showed a tongue, whether a pretty girl's or a dog's, and a perusal of the *En-*

quirer during his era bears this out. One of his photo editors believed that Pope could not tell an original slide from a duplicate copy: "He would have to peel up the cardboard so he could see the exposure's edge." A seasoned photo editor could quickly discern a copy because the color balance would slip deeper into the red spectrum. The issue might be moot as far as any quality differences that would show up in the half-tone printing process, where at any rate photos were usually retouched for printing. The issue for Pope was originality; he wanted all his material to be exclusive. If Pope was some kind of a genius, he was certainly not a genius at everything, and his learning curve often seemed seriously lengthened by the ironic fact that in many ways he did not appear to have an enquiring mind.

Yet his employees were often stumped because it seemed impossible to tell Pope anything he didn't already know. For reporter Art Golden, that even included his own name. Golden recalled that he returned from lunch one afternoon and found the boss himself, who liked to tinker with the office hardware, standing on Golden's tiny reporter's desk adjusting an air-conditioning vent. "Who are you?" Pope demanded, and Golden replied, "I'm the new writer, Art." "Welcome aboard, Al," Pope said, and from then on Art was Al. "The mistake went uncorrected," said Golden. "On the *National Enquirer* you contradicted Mr. Pope at your own risk." [3]

Golden attended Pope's editorial meetings and listened to his jokes: "If you knew what was good for you, you chuckled, laughed, slapped your knees at the publisher's wit and openly marveled at his wisdom." Golden, who was at the *Enquirer* from 1975 to 1978, found himself surrounded by reporters with Liverpudlian lilts and Glaswegan burrs and saw the paper as "a place of fear and tension, where staffers worried that the slightest transgression would cost them their handsomely paid jobs." He found Pope "a man who delighted in publishing cruel photographs of aging actresses, who strived to give false hope to people suffering from incurable diseases, who seemed to enjoy reporting painfully embarrassing episodes in the lives of screen stars." Nor did Golden particularly enjoy his job as writer, where "ambiguity was shunned like a horrible out-of-body experience." Indeed, Golden tired of the simple tabloid fare: "Finally I could take no more. After completing a first-person account under the byline of a man who had been attacked by a grizzly bear—'I could feel his sweet and sour breath enveloping me. Saliva drooled from his opened mouth. The creature's fangs were white as death itself'—I decided to rejoin the real world. I found a reporting job on a small daily newspaper."[4]

On his last day Art's friends brought him a farewell cake inscribed "So long, Al." A few weeks after Pope's death Golden wrote a brief memoir of his years at the *Enquirer,* which was published in the *San Diego Union-Tribune.* By 1988 his perspective had changed: "In retrospect it was also a howlingly funny place, like a Mel Brooks movie run at breakneck speed, although I never thought so when I was one of Mr. Pope's employees." Significantly Golden continued to think of Pope as "Mr. Pope."

In the late seventies Pope began putting on a luxurious catered banquet on Fridays to celebrate the successful production of another issue. Reporter Frank Zahour said the practice evolved: "Pope had put a desk out on the newsroom floor then, and one day someone opened a bottle late Friday afternoon, and it was repeated the next Friday. People ordered in snacks, all the editors started competing with each other." When the practice was institutionalized, the banquet started at 4:00 p.m. on the dot. The food was lavish, the bar was free, and employees could schmooze with their colleagues, but Pope's presence put a pall on the gathering. Zahour remembered one reporter commenting as they were shuffling through the buffet line, "It's like being bitten by the hand that feeds you." On Friday afternoons, as at the weekly staff meeting, Pope's crew listened to his jokes and laughed on cue. It was one of the paradoxes of his dour personality that he liked to see his employees having fun, even if it was mostly a command performance. Could a man as oblivious to the shades and tones of emotion as Pope tell the difference between real fun and a puppet show for him?

If Pope noticed a staffer's absence, it was taken for granted he would resent it. Everyone attended. Wives and husbands of staff were not invited. If a husband was picking up his wife after work, he waited outside in the parking lot. That was part of the bizarre mix of barbarity, civility, and generosity at Popestown. Afterward, for many, the action moved raucously on to the Lantana bars or the Hawaiian beach bar, where the mellow Florida sunsets, reflected on the eastern clouds, seemed to last forever. Other popular bars included the Toucan, formerly a retirees' bar named the Nostalgia, with real toucans in a big glass cage at the entrance; the New England Oyster House, a franchise restaurant with a pleasant bar overlooking the Intracoastal Waterway; and, next to a bowling alley, the Whistle Stop, where the Brits flocked to play darts. Tabloid journalists enriched the pub life of Lantana and nearby Lake Worth and seemed hardly attracted to the tonier watering holes of Palm Beach, like Aux Bar, less than a twenty-minute drive away, where Willie Kennedy Smith met the woman who accused him of date rape.

One of the Brits' legendary members was a very short Fleet Streeter nicknamed the Poison Penguin, a brawler who liked to begin his peremptory assaults with an outrage, by pissing in someone's pocket. He was also reputedly a winner, as his tactic was to reach up and strike suddenly while his victim was still sputtering with indignation and disbelief.

The Friday banquets went on for several years; then suddenly they, too, ended. Pope changed his mind again.

Pope gave a yearly Christmas party as well, at first at the *Enquirer* offices, then at other nearby venues, and rather pointedly not at his house after a new reporter passed out and urinated on himself in the kitchen, after someone tested the theory that if you put an unconscious drunk's hand in warm water, he will wet his pants. It worked. To everyone's surprise, the victim—a former Marine who might have been resented for his military swagger and bluster—was not summarily dismissed when he was discovered cold, soggy, stinky, and abandoned on the floor. He survived his tryout and remained in the *Enquirer*'s editorial ranks long after Pope's death.

During Art Golden's tenure the Christmas party was held in the *Enquirer* offices:

> It was always a lavish spread. A big table in a conference room seemed to groan under the weight of platters crammed with caviar, shrimp, and lobster tails. Before the arrival [of Pope] at my first *Enquirer* yuletide party, I snatched a cracker and was about to scoop up a load of caviar, when a huge hand reached out and grabbed my wrist. The hand belonged to one of Mr. Pope's faithful retainers, a gigantic cigar-chewing accountant who had been with him for years. "Nobody eats till the boss eats!" the retainer hissed into my ear, squeezing my wrist.[5]

Reporters and writers functioned at the *Enquirer* somewhat as they did in the earlier days of newspapering, in the era connoted by the poster of a raffish reporter, hat cocked back, cigarette dangling, on the phone to the city desk: "Hey, baby, get me rewrite." *Enquirer* reporters more likely wore garish Hawaiian shirts and baseball caps, or were even women, but they functioned as legmen; reporters turned in files, often long compendiums of raw material. Reporters did not write their final stories. That was handled by a bank of three or four specialists, like Golden, who chafed at his daily menu of "horoscopes, miracle diets, the childhood of Jack Klugman." Despite Golden's condescending attitude, within the Tabloid Triangle writing in the tabloid style was regarded as an honorable and difficult specialty. One day the chief writer gave Golden "an assignment so demanding that [his] entire career at the *Enquirer* could very well depend on it.

"I held my breath," Golden recalled.

"'Golden,' he intoned, 'we want you to write a birthday card for Bob Hope.'

"It was my big chance. For the next week I labored over a birthday poem [which *Enquirer* readers would clip out and mail to Hope's Hollywood agent].

"When I finished I brought the poem to the chief writer for his approval. He read it. Then he shook his head. I thought I could detect tears glistening in his eyes.

"'Golden,' he said, 'this proves that when I hired you I made the right choice.'

"'My talent, eh, Mike?'

"'No,' he said. 'The poem shows you have no shame.'"[6]

There were arguments over whether Pope was a genius or an idiot—and plausible evidence could be offered for both positions. Or was he something in between, a kind of John Q. Public whose personal tastes reflected the middlebrow tastes of the nation, so that everything he touched turned to tabloid gold? Informed opinions tended to drift in this direction: Zahour thought Pope had an incredible instinct for what the American people wanted: "He knew they wanted simple stories with a beginning, middle, and end, and he was a great showman. He was a sort of P. T. Barnum of print." Ironically, one position that was not seriously entertained was that Pope's publishing enterprise was succeeding beyond anyone's wildest expectations simply because he was obsessed. It was too obvious. The point was not so much that Pope was smart or stupid or right or wrong about this or that, but rather that he cared so very much. Inevitably, that care—however insulated Pope was from the usual pathways to learning and change by his ego, his social ineptness, and his willfulness—furthered the strangely fruitful exchange Pope had with his editorial employees and his readers.

The more one knows about Pope the likelier it seems that as he made his right-angle turns, S-turns, and U-turn reversals of his editorial policies and judgments, he was not particularly aware that he was changing his mind, especially since few dared tell him so, and he resented it if they did. His staff was long conditioned to greet whatever idea he had on a given day as the best idea the boss ever had so far, whether it conflicted with a previous one or not.

One sure measure of the *Enquirer*'s success was the increasing volume of its mail. As the seventies progressed, the paper was getting so much mail from readers that it was granted its own postal zip code, 33464.[7] With its weekly call for readers' photos and its opinion polls and the usual interactive reaction with readers, the paper was getting as much as ten times as much mail as the whole town of Lantana.[8]

Tom Kuncl was a good observer of his boss's behavior, and as executive editor and Pope's head henchman, he had privileged access: "It's so hard to put Pope in a nutshell. I always have mixed feelings about him. He had a logical mind and he was very good at detail. He was very hands-on. He was very much the autocrat. I think he liked an aura of mystery about him, and I think he liked some of the legends about him. He was not very good with people. There were some people he treated like kings—and I was one of them—and others that he treated very harshly. I think he had a good heart in a context."[9]

Many *Enquirer* employees simply regarded Pope as a monster—for the mass firings, his cold personality, his tyrannical ways, his personal lack of style, his physical and social awkwardness, his obvious misjudgments, and his failure to own up to them. But for the more serious students of his personality it wouldn't be that simple. A central part of the trouble, as Kuncl notes, was Pope's serious social ineptness, which made his bad traits seem worse:

He was not in touch with the real world as the rest of us were. He seemed naïve. I don't want to say he was some kind of idiot because he wasn't. He had a very good mind. It was just where it was. When it got down to relationships and people I think it was just another example of him not being totally in touch. He was a very insular man. He lived in that guarded enclave out there. He was very much a hermit in some ways. Here was a guy who bought his clothes from Sears out of the catalog. He loved *The Flintstones*. He had a huge collection of videos back when it was Beta: *The Dukes of Hazard, Hogan's Heroes*. You had to think of that one a little bit, considering our place was a stalag. In terms of hard issues I don't think he was . . . connected.[10]

Pope always came into the office on the sixth day, Saturday mornings, after the week's edition had been finalized and shipped on Friday. Publications maintain a close watch during this period in their cycle, waiting and dreading a situation so bad that it required and justified the great expense of stopping the run. But 99.99 percent of the time it meant a high-level editor needed to be on call for the little glitches that inevitably cropped up at the last minute. At the *Enquirer* Pope himself would show up, and his inner circle was required to show as well. And any editors who wanted to impress Pope with their dedication would do well to be seen sitting at their desks, too. Said Kuncl: "Saturday mornings we had to go in and show the flag because he was there. I never did a damn thing. Then your phone would ring and he would say, 'You got a minute, Tom?' And then you'd have to wander down to his office and then God knows what you'd have to talk about. It could be anything from gardening ripping us off on the price of geraniums to how do you feel about life after death. Whatever was on his mind, you'd go away shaking your head."[11] Seeing Pope at times like this, when he might have been doing any number of other things with his family or friends (of whom there was no visible evidence) made Kuncl wonder what Pope got out of life. Pope had a hobby or two, and they were the hobbies of an obsessive: he collected electric trains and cars—apparently just to have them, since he commonly drove white Chevys, which he kept for several years. His sole concession to vanity on the road was his license plate with a single P, and perhaps that was more for security, so the local police would recognize him. Here was an echo of privilege the young Pope had experienced in New York City as an honorary deputy police commissioner. Also, his father had displayed what we now call a vanity tag long before they were widely fashionable. In 1935, when having a personal tag was unusual enough to be reported in the *New York Times,* Pope Sr.'s car bore the tag GP1.[12]

Since a kidnapping threat against one of his children, Pope kept bodyguards with him twenty-four hours a day. Charles Manson once threatened the *Enquirer* from jail, and a former writer who shot himself was discovered in his suicide note to have planned a going-postal episode that would take a list of *Enquirer* employees with him. Calder (who was high on the list) confided in his memoir that after the writer's suicide he always kept a loaded .357 magnum in his desk. One editor, a Vietnam combat veteran, was known to own a very elegant, fully automatic Swedish 9mm submachine gun. One day Pope asked if he could see it and seemed relieved when the editor assured him that, of course, he didn't keep it in his desk. Some believed that the editor did, however, at least some of the time. It wouldn't be too much of a stretch to imagine a gunfight in the *Enquirer* newsroom.

An armed man, usually a moonlighting off-duty Lantana policeman, stayed through the nights at Pope's Manalapan house. Security walked Pope to his car after work, where he had a special parking place in the *Enquirer* lot. It wasn't marked, but if a new hire accidentally parked in it, security soon found and hustled the offender to another spot. Lois once gave Pope a restored model of the car he owned when he met her, but he seemed never to drive it, or any of the others he collected. But the white Caprice with the P plate was known to all local police, his employees, and many of the general public.

Sometimes Pope put his collection of electric trains on display on the *Enquirer* grounds as part of his Christmas tableaux. There were dozens of engines and locomotives, yards and yards of small-gauge track winding spaghetti-like on a large platform. Once the set was a replica of the whole United States, with major architectural landmarks—Washington's Capitol, the Empire State Building—representing various cities. Another time the trains were set up as an old Western town. Local train collectors, backed by Pope, built the platforms and manned the exhibits, wearing railroad engineer caps, and the exhibit was billed, without any particular official sanction, as the World's Largest Portable Train Set. It was microcosmically Flagleresque, a railroad magnate's empire on a tiny scale. The trains seemed another venue to act out issues of control and obsession.

As Kuncl meditated: "It was hard for me to calculate what joy Pope got out of life, for everything he had. There was nothing pathetic about him, but I felt sorry because he was the kind of guy who had everything and at the same time didn't have that much. He wouldn't travel. He wouldn't go shopping. Yet somewhere in his own mind he was a media baron."[13]

TEN

THE MILLION-DOLLAR TREE: HO! HO! HO!

Soon after moving to Florida, Pope decided to erect "the World's Tallest Christmas Tree" on the *Enquirer* grounds, and thus was born a tradition that continued until his death. The tree was found each year in the forests of Washington State, felled, transported by railroad car, and erected on the *Enquirer*'s grounds. When decorated and lit up, it could be seen for miles. The Douglas firs averaged between 110 and 125 feet and were billed as the "world's tallest," though Pope was unable, despite the fullest efforts by several editors, to get any of his trees listed in the *Guinness Book of World Records*. "World's tallest," "biggest," or "greatest" was used in P. T. Barnum's sense, as there were too many other contenders for *Guinness* to grant him an official record. The main obstacle was that at some point a 150-foot Christmas tree was erected in an Oregon shopping mall, and Pope could never top that one. The editors, working under Pope's demanding lash, tried to squeeze in through various subcategories, but *Guinness* remained implacable. There was to be no tabloid hype in the most trustworthy of record books.

The annual *Enquirer* Christmas tree was much more of a feat than it looked. Each season it cost Pope nearly a million dollars, along with the tableaux and other displays, like Snoopy whirling in a tight circle in a mechanized Sopwith Camel on the roof of the *Enquirer* building, troops of little

Pope could never get his yearly Christmas trees in the *Guinness Book of World Records* despite their amazing scale. (Photo by Thomas Graves / *Palm Beach Post*)

green elves wearing space helmets, or the mechanical Bigfoot popping out of the shrubs. The acquisition of the tree was managed by Pope's lieutenant of longest tenure, Dino Gallo, and required long planning and overcoming serious obstacles. Each season a rough-looking gang of bikers roared into Lantana on their Harley hogs to muscle up and decorate the tree, for a reported sum of $5,000 apiece. Several of them bore tattoos of the tree or of the star that appeared on its top. The initials of each burly biker were scratched on the six-foot star with which they crowned the tree.

One of the first problems was that a conifer of that height had no lower branches, since they would be shed as the giant fir grew to greater heights. So batches of branches from other trees were brought down from Washington State as well and fixed to the naked lower trunk to shape the tree like a traditional Christmas pine. More than a thousand ornaments were fixed to the tree, along with 15,000 lights, a mile of garland, and 250 giant bows. On the *Enquirer* grounds 350,000 more Christmas lights twinkled.[1]

The whole setup proved there was plenty of P. T. Barnum in Pope, but unlike the circus king, Pope didn't charge admission. The area became so overcrowded that staffers who didn't get out before nightfall were parked in what Kuncl called a chromium graveyard. Busloads of gawkers arrived from Miami, Jacksonville, Tampa, and Pahokee. Florida's tourists, retirees, and children flocked to the display. Pope's attitude to the whole project was distant and aloof, even as he micromanaged it. But sometimes he roamed the grounds like a dour shadow, a kindly voyeur, the tabloid king moving incognito among his infantilized subjects. There was no danger whatsoever that he would be recognized. Perhaps he smiled, or his eyes twinkled.

Kuncl remembers being with Pope on the grounds when they saw Lois

Pope and her mother bypassing the huge line to see the tree. "Where do you think you're going?" Pope asked, and sent wife and mother-in-law back to wait in line. "This place is a democracy," he added, turning to Kuncl, who said his momentary horror turned to amusement at the very concept. Louis XIV, he thought, could hardly have been more tyrannical amid the gardens of Versailles.

Here, too, Pope fussed with every detail and imposed his titanium will, in some cases against his wife. Another of his lieutenants from the old days, the big, cigar-smoking Guy Galiardo, would get caught in the crossfire. Lois, who served as the *Enquirer*'s official art director, took a decorator's interest in the displays and would instruct Galiardo to make changes. But when Pope noticed, he would summon Galiardo, according to Kuncl's account, and ask,

"Why did you move that?"

"Because Lois told me to."

"See if you can get her to sign your paycheck next week. Meanwhile, move it back."

One evening near Christmas Pope noticed a small, unhappy boy struggling to stay in a van while the other boys were leaving to tour the grounds. Pope coaxed the boy out, bought him a Coke, and calmed him down. The next day Pope summoned reporter Frank Zahour and told him he needed to find the kid again. Pope hadn't got his name—all he remembered was the color of the van: beige. It was a reminder that Pope did not have the observational powers of a reporter, having never worked as one. By this time of his life he behaved like a fairy princess who simply waved or pointed her wand at what she wanted. Zahour found that one of Pope's security men had noted the license number. Since Pope had the Lantana police in his pocket, they traced the number for Zahour. "I found this small home for boys," Zahour recalled. "It was in an old, small, crumbling motel. The pool was cracked—it never had water in it. This young idealist ran it."[2]

Zahour reported his find to Pope, who told him to go back and ask the young proprietor what he needed.

"The young man who ran the home was astounded," according to Zahour.

"What does he [Pope] mean?" the man asked.

"I don't know. Make some requests. It appears he wants to give you some money."

The young man mentioned sports equipment and some other needs. Zahour relayed the requests to Pope. "Pope cut a check for around $10,000 to this struggling little outpost," Zahour said. "It certainly wasn't a high-profile charity. It had more good intentions—all from this young man—than anything. Pope told me to tell the man to call me whenever he needed anything. Over the next few years, the guy would call, and I would help him get a list together. I often encouraged him to ask for more." Pope also asked Zahour to check up on the home a time or two over the years:

> Over a period of years I would say Pope donated at least $50,000 to this home, all because GP found this kid one Christmas night, screaming that he didn't want to leave the van and look at the decorations. Pope never publicized it, never even mentioned it in the house newspaper. He just gave them the money when they called. Pope never said much in these short sessions. He just gave

orders: Find the kid. How much do they need? That was it. He just sat behind his big desk, saying as little as possible, never really reacting, never showing any emotion. Just calm.[3]

The young manager of the home never got over his amazement. "He always seemed a bit wary—I think he was used to fighting for every dollar," Zahour said. One day he showed up at the *Enquirer* with an award, a plaque for Pope. "I don't know why I took it in—I think the man just felt out of place doing it himself. He said, 'Check the back side.' I flipped it over and the back was a target and a note that said, 'Mr. Pope, if you ever get tired of awards, use this as a dartboard.' "

This small boy, isolated, orphaned, and unable to feel the delights of the common herd, touched Pope deeply and brought out his fatherly side, which his employees rarely saw. The other boys who came in the van and romped and enjoyed his Christmas wonderland didn't interest Pope particularly. Why did he hide his generosity and concern behind his gruffness and remoteness? Was it because this story, which stuck so poignantly in Zahour's memory, would reveal to his perceptive journalists that he, too, this sedentary, chain-smoking workaholic, was also isolated, unhappy, and unable to enjoy common pleasures?

One year the *Enquirer* was forbidden to cut the Douglas fir it had months before tagged in the northwestern forest for the World's Tallest Christmas Tree. There was a drought, and the friction of dragging the felled tree to the waiting railroad cars was considered too dangerous because it might spark a forest fire. Pope's tree-acquisition team immediately began negotiations with Indians on a nearby reservation, figuring that if Native Americans could sell tax-free cigarettes, kill game out of season, and run gambling operations, they could sell a bootleg tree to Pope. Price was no object. That avenue failed, however, as it turned out that Native Americans were not exempt from fire laws.

So Pope worked out—through emissaries, as always—a deal with state fire authorities. It involved putting fifty firefighters on his payroll and renting a tanker plane to circle overhead, ready to dump thousands of gallons of water on any spark that the firefighters failed to extinguish. Just in case, on call a minute away was an army Chinook helicopter capable of lifting a truck, a tank, or a very big tree and placing it on the railroad car. This story was related by Kuncl to the *Miami Herald* in 1989, when for the first time in fifteen years there would be no World's Tallest Christmas Tree at the *Enquirer,* following the benefactor's death and the paper's sale. Kuncl's story would have made a good Christmas-season film comedy, with Walter Matthau as Pope and Jack Lemmon as Iain Calder. In the real world the situation gave some sense of the implacability of Pope's will and the demands he put on his minions. When at last the feat was accomplished, even Calder, veteran of countless ordeals with Pope, felt relieved. Yes, there would be Christmas at the *Enquirer* this year after all, and the little working-class town of Lantana would be put on the map, for a few weeks at least, with a 110-foot tower of sparkle and color, visible for miles on the flat drained marshland of Florida. No doubt with some sense of accomplishment and pride, Calder told Pope the good news. The boss barely looked up: "So you cut down a tree. What's the big deal? We always cut down a tree."[4]

The Christmas season could also be a reminder that Pope's generosity was spotty. Yes, he spent nearly a million dollars on his seasonal tree and display, but he did not offer Christmas bonuses to his employees. He did not share the surpluses of his cash-cow paper in the manner of a Philadelphia law firm or a Wall Street brokerage. That would be to relinquish a portion of the control and discretion he relished. Employees got a canned ham or a fresh turkey, a bottle of Chivas Regal, and a lavishly catered Christmas party. Yet, said Kuncl, he was not tempted to ask Pope, "What, no Christmas bonus again this year?" Kuncl said when left the paper in 1981 his salary was nearly $200,000 a year, a fine paycheck in those days, and even these, three decades later, for a tabloid journalist whom society would label a hack.

Pope did not receive gifts well either, according to Kuncl's account. When an editor gave him a truly fine bottle of single-malt Scotch at Christmas, Pope reacted cruelly: "I had a sip of that cheap booze you gave me," he said to the editor during a staff meeting, possibly as a warning to others to keep their distance: "I must not be paying you enough. It tasted like kerosene. I used it to clean out the carb on the Chevy."[5] Such was life with the blue-collar millionaire, the man of the people.

Another reporter remembered another typical example of Pope's social ineptness. The employee met Pope by chance one Friday night at a public bar, where Pope was having a drink with Lois before their weekly dinner at their favorite Italian restaurant. Pope bought him a drink, and after an exchange of pleasantries there was an awkward silence. Eventually Pope turned to Lois and said, loud enough to be overheard: "I don't know what's wrong with him. I bought him a drink and now he won't go away." Lois was hardly any better. When one of her assistants presented her with a birthday cake in the presence of a few other employees, she blew out the candles and put the untouched cake back in its box, to take home at the end of the day. Ordinary people could hardly imagine what a couple so isolated from the ordinary give-and-take of daily life did or talked about when they were home alone.

Yet Kuncl recalls that when his osteomyelitis, a chronic bone infection, flared up and threatened the loss of his leg, Pope turned loose his staff's top medical reporters to find the best place to send their top editor. Then he flew Kuncl to Johns Hopkins Hospital in Baltimore, where Dr. Neil Solomon, syndicated medical columnist and medical adviser to the *Enquirer,* came to Kuncl's bedside every day to explain what the doctors were up to. Pope called every day. Then on Christmas Eve, said Kuncl, "a man who looked like he had just snowshoed his way down from Minsk sighed his way into my hospital room. He staggered under a load that included a miniaturized version of the big tree in Lantana, a gigantic fruit basket, a silk stuffed Santa, and an envelope that contained a Christmas card [on which Pope had scribbled], 'It might not be a 110-foot tree, but it's just as full of cheer and good wishes. Merry Christmas, Gene Pope.'" [6]

The man from Minsk, actually from the *Enquirer's* circulation operation, produced a Polaroid camera and took a picture. "I have to get one of these back out to the airport and down to the boss. He wanted to be sure the tree looked OK." Then the phone rang and it was Pope. "I'm surprised those jerks could find the hospital," he growled. Then, over the phone Kuncl heard his newsroom colleagues ("who," Kuncl said, "on any other day of the year would have eaten my liver") sing "On the Sidewalks of New York" and "The Marine Corps Hymn."

Pope's over-the-top generosities would be counterbalanced with acts of sudden cruelty. One day he saw a blonde secretary wearing her hair in cornrows, which he'd never seen before. "What's that?" he asked, and someone told him about the new fashion entering the mainstream from black culture. "Well, get rid of her." That was the sad end of that story, as it was for many such legendary horror stories. One of his favorite female reporters got a nose job; by all accounts she was an attractive woman who looked even better after her cosmetic surgery. For some reason the cosmetic surgery annoyed Pope. Finally, he decided to fire her. "She just didn't perform as well as she had with the old nose," he reportedly said.

Those stories showed why you didn't want to call attention to yourself when the boss was around. Whether these legends were exaggerated or true wasn't important from the point of view of the climate of employment under Pope. Many, like Phil Brennan, believed Pope was consciously creating that climate of fear. Much of this happened before employees in general became more litigious regarding their rights, especially in regard to race and gender; Pope was never successfully sued for a wrongful firing. After he died, that climate changed somewhat, but it was still difficult to sue the *Enquirer,* with its top-drawer lawyers. You would probably die before the suit was concluded, if Carol Burnett's libel suit was any indication.

Of course, no one was officially fired for having cornrows, or for having cosmetic surgery, or for the widely quoted reasons Pope so freely made clear to his henchmen. Routinely reporters were fired for problems with their expense accounts. Pope had a legendarily picky white South African accountant, Chris Currie, who scrutinized expense accounts. Currie deflects any description of being a henchman, however, and claims no special closeness to Pope. Currie says the secret to his longevity in Pope's employment was that he kept a low profile and rarely dealt with the man personally. When he did deal with Pope, Currie had a habit of asking questions aimed at discerning what results Pope wished. Since Pope so rarely shared his reasoning with anyone, this was admittedly dangerous. "I knew I was dealing with an imperious personality," Currie said, "but I would ask questions about what he wanted and focus on the objective."[7] When he succeeded in finding it, Currie was often able to deliver the objective, rather than floundering about, as many less-focused employees did. Currie lasted at the *Enquirer* long after Pope's death, resigning under the third owner.

Currie, an enthusiastic Hobiecat sailor who bought an old beachfront motel and made it into an elegant home, came aboard in 1976, in the midst of the Brit explosion, through a Fleet Streeter who also kept a catamaran on the beach. As a colonial, Currie did not share or sympathize with the cultural background of the British working class. Currie saw the British invasion as a sociological phenomenon that, among other things, presented a problem for him in carrying out his responsibilities:

> They were coming from Britain and had vaguely socialist back-grounds. They were encouraged in Britain to supplement their income . . . by cheating on their expenses. It was quite a habit of supplementing their income through their expense accounts. It took a while for it to get through that we didn't like it. It was quite a weaning process. Once in a while I had to make an example and a head would roll and they would all scurry for cover and behave themselves for a year or 18 months. Then they'd start stretching the envelope again. It was quite a weaning process and fairly much concentrated among the Brits.[8]

Currie was a bit of a detective, and his interrogations regarding expenses were well remembered, and resented. In fact, the legend grew up that Currie had been trained in terrorist interrogation techniques in the South African army. Currie acknowledged that he had

> stepped on a few toes—I rubbed people the wrong way, some of them quite high in the editorial offices. But I was always looking after the company's interests and whatever Pope wanted. Every once in a while you'd find something that was provable—you already knew they were exaggerating meals and tips. The most common thing I would catch people on would be entertainment receipts. Before we started insisting on credit cards, which are much harder to jimmy, they'd get these little cutoff stubs from the bottom of restaurant receipts. The restaurants wouldn't even fill them in, so they'd write off a $150 dinner when it was actually $15. I was occasionally able to verify them with the restaurant, because many of them were serially numbered. I'd be able to establish that such a receipt was for $15, when in fact they had submitted it for ten times more.[9]

But in the end, Currie observed, the issue was really loyalty: "Of course, we weren't ever really interested whether someone was stealing $15 or $150 or $15,000. Even if the amount was insignificant, it would result in a head rolling. Pope wanted loyalty. He maintained he was paying these astronomical salaries and they didn't really need to supplement them." Currie acknowledges that sometimes a reporter would be chosen just to make an example, which squares with Brennan's assessment that the firings weren't always for cause.

Brennan's feeling was that Pope would pick someone well liked, just to increase the impact. Currie also confirmed that Pope and his management would deliberately offer extra latitude to reporters who were exceptionally productive: "There were people who, let's say, deserved to be more profligate because we were getting something in return." Massacres and bloodbaths seem the right words, then, to describe editorial firings made as an arbitrary exercise in power. Even a careful and honest reporter might have a hard time staying clear of Currie's expert scrutiny if nothing more than a few dollars discrepancy was needed for a beheading.

Through the seventies and eighties Pope spent lavishly, especially on travel. The *Enquirer* kept its own in-house travel agent busy. Expense accounts were big and complicated. Pope liked to send reporters out on the Concorde, though Currie, overseeing the purse strings, disapproved: "I thought it was quite unnecessary, because they would arrive an hour and a half earlier than they would on a regular flight. But Pope liked his reporters to travel in style. I think he liked to treat them. Often he would charter a Learjet. The cost was astronomical. They were never under seven or eight thousand dollars for a short flight, and sometimes they were several tens of thousands of dollars. Was it really necessary? Probably not, but he wanted to make sure he got his people there at the right time."[10]

Currie confirmed that every reporter who left Lantana carried at least $1,000 in cash—all of which would have to be accounted for in receipts. (The *Enquirer*'s gamblers liked to catch reporters on the eve of their departure, as easy marks, and tried to tempt them into betting games of cards or darts.) In the real extravaganzas, like the Elvis or Princess Grace stories, Currie said he was fielding cash travel advances of between $10,000 and $20,000.

Often a reporter who came to work on a balmy subtropical morning could end the day watching the sunset in another climate zone, as did George Hunter, who found himself hounding celebrities on the ski slopes of Aspen wearing a short-sleeve shirt he'd put on to go to work at the *Enquirer*: "As soon as I got back to Aspen I bought this beautiful expensive down jacket, which I wore for the rest of the assignment." Hunter knew Currie would give him a hard time about the jacket, which he wanted to keep and didn't want to pay for. "So I put a bottle of Scotch on my entertainment bill. Currie disputed it. I defended it vigorously. Finally I gave in." Distracted by the Scotch, Currie let the expensive jacket slide. Hunter considered it a trophy from a rare victory over the paper's exacting bean counter.

It's clear that Currie enjoyed a good game of cat and mouse. Currie seemed to especially relish the game against such worthy opponents as the working-class Brits, who loved a good fiddle. Consider Currie's story about the vagaries of air travel out of Lantana:

You could fly out for $380 or for $1,600. If you knew you were going out to the West Coast in two or three weeks there was nothing to stop you from buying a $380 ticket, and then if you wangled it so the company bought you a ticket at full coach price there was nothing to stop you from putting that ticket in your pocket and flying out on the $380 ticket. You were never going to get a refund on your ticket, but there was nothing to stop you from turning around the next week and applying the $1,600 toward an airfare for you and your wife on a European vacation. I caught people doing that.[11]

ELEVEN

WASHINGTON GARBAGE

Sometime after midnight on Tuesday, July 1, 1975, *National Enquirer* reporter Jay Gourley stopped his car in front of Henry Kissinger's house in the Georgetown neighborhood of Washington, D.C., and started loading in five green trash bags awaiting the morning's pickup. The Secret Service agent standing on the nearby porch was unsure how to react, but he pulled himself together and told Gourley to desist. Gourley stood his ground. Talking into a mike in his left sleeve, the agent summoned his supervisor, and the choice was soon given to Gourley: put the trash bags back or go to jail.

"All right then, jail it is," said Gourley. "But first you really ought to check with your superiors."[1]

It wouldn't be apparent to an uninformed onlooker, but Gourley had the upper hand in this little chess game being played out on the sidewalks of Washington's most elite neighborhood. From this point he couldn't go wrong. Going to jail for picking trash might even be a better story, since up to this point Gourley had no idea what treasures Kissinger's garbage contained. Getting interrogated by the Secret Service would be a double plus.

Incredibly, Gourley had White House press credentials, as the growing assembly of heat—more Secret Service agents, Washington metropolitan police, and a young intelligence officer—discovered. So it was decided Gourley could leave with the bags, though security, law enforcement, and intelligence weren't happy about the trump card Gourley had played. Nevertheless, they had made the right judgment. Gourley's press credentials functioned like a Monopoly get-out-of-jail-free card; without press credentials and a powerful publication behind him, Gourley would surely have gone home empty-handed, or to jail. Gourley took home the bags—which had been instantly transformed from refuse to hot-ly contested property—sifted through them, and wrote a story.

For a week after the *Enquirer* was published, Gourley's lively tabloid inventory of the secretary of state's garbage obsessed the nation's press, which took the paradoxical position that Kissinger's garbage was *not* interesting. In the process the nation's press almost deconstructed itself with the absurd self-contradictions the situation aroused, as Gourley would point out later in an article for *Washington Monthly*. Among other things the story was a perfect example of how Pope continued to traffic in the abject even after he cleaned up his paper for the supermarkets, for what could be more classically abject than garbage?

Among the objects Gourley discovered were Maalox, aspirin, and barbiturate packages—suggestive of serious stress in the Kissinger household—as well as a memo indicating that Kissinger's Secret Service detail had accidentally left a shotgun in the Virgin Islands. A shopping list included a case of Jack Daniel's and a case of Ezra Brooks, "the poor man's Jack Daniel's." Gourley speculated that either Kissinger had two standards of bourbon, for A- and B-list guests, or he was filling the Jack Daniels bottles with Ezra Brooks. Gourley also found unused and unopened food: sticks of margarine, English muffins, cans of soup, jars of applesauce—for which he never found a "vaguely plausible" explanation. He also found discarded copies of Kissinger's old itineraries and daily schedules, which Gourley found of twofold interest:

"First, along with the memo about the misplaced gun, they indicated that in the current long lull between assassinations the Secret Service is getting sloppy again. Anyone wanting information about the daily behavior patterns of any terrorist's most desirable potential victim [Kissinger was secretary of state from 1973 to 1977] merely had to pick it up on Dumbarton Street."[2]

The itineraries and schedules also yielded privileged information: "For example, that on one day this summer Kissinger met with David Rockefeller, chairman of the Chase Manhattan Bank, followed shortly by Arthur Burns, chairman of the Federal Reserve Board," Gourley wrote. "Those who read the schedule put up by the State Department, or the articles written by reporters who relied on that schedule, were not so well informed."[3]

Nearly every major newspaper in the country prominently listed the contents of Kissinger's totally uninteresting garbage, often on page 1. The story led the trendy Style section of the *Washington Post,* which also ran an editorial headlined "Trash," comparing Gourley's journalism to child molesting—surely a quantum leap in logic—and called it "indefensible both as journalistic practice and as civilized behavior." That last phrase about civilized behavior made it clear that Gourley was in the ambiguous realm of the culturally degraded, while the story and editorial emphatically demonstrated how this inventory of rejected objects was so irresistibly fascinating. The State Department issued a statement: "This has caused grave anguish to Mrs. Kissinger, and the Secretary of State is really revolted by what he considers a violation of the privacy of his house."[5] Gourley said that of the nine hundred clips collected by the *Enquirer* from the nation's newspapers about the incident, none expressed doubt that the Kissingers experienced those emotions, disgust and revulsion. Gourley's question was whether anyone truly feels those emotions these days about things like garbage: "Now what public relations expert at the State Department dreamed up this Victorian scenario of the sensitive Lady Kissinger taking to her bed in anguish at the thought of some ruffian rifling through her garbage? Reporters are a cynical lot. I'm sure none of those who obligingly inserted this statement into their stories really believed it."[6] The border between the social and the abject had also shifted, suggested Gourley: "Those genteel fictions of an earlier era are thoughtlessly perpetuated: she is 'anguished,' he is 'revolted.' So who's publishing garbage?"[7] The cause of Kissinger's alleged revulsion was Gourley's alleged invasion of privacy, which, observed Gourley, came from "the man who as National Security Advisor helped bug the home phones of his own staff members [and] is one of our nation's leading practitioners" of wiretapping.[8]

Gourley's defense of the *Enquirer* and his attack on the hypocrisy of the mainstream press, especially his hometown paper, the *Washington Post,* in a prestigious, widely read monthly on journalism struck precisely at the border between mainstream and tabloid journalism and found the nerve running there. The tabloids have done many stories in far more questionable taste, but they have largely been forgotten. However, the story of Kissinger's garbage has become a legend of journalism. And perhaps, suggests Gourley, this border between the abject and the mainstream is precisely where the news is. Gourley reviewed the questionable reporting tactics of the *Washington Post's* team of Carl Bernstein and Bob Woodward on the Watergate stories: "One reason the *Post* got the Watergate story in the first place may be that the report of the original burglary came in on a weekend, so it was assigned to low-status reporters who were not afraid to use these unstatesmanlike techniques. Possibly now that its reputation as a respectable muckraker assures it of a steady flow of the kind of leaks which make for easy scoops, the *Washington Post* would like to call a moratorium on journalistic dirty tricks, and raise the tone of the profession."[9] Gourley continued drilling on the nerve: "Politicians and others are not averse to giving the public glimpses of their private lives when it suits their purposes. Kissinger has been especially skillful at molding a useful public image of his private self. Is it really fair for him to scream 'foul' when a reporter uses one of the few means at his disposal to determine what Kissinger's private life is really like?"[10]

That line of thinking went double when applied to the nation's media celebrities upon whom the *Enquirer* preyed, and such reasoning became the very credo of an *Enquirer* reporter. Stars and celebrities exploited the press to boost their ratings and sell their films, songs, books, and other wares, then protested when the press, especially the tabloid press, dug into their dalliances and divorces. Gourley's was a rationale for tabloid reporters who were weary of being consigned to the gutter press (though, as Gourley demonstrated, the gutter could be pretty damn interesting). Gourley threw the mainstream's definition of trash journalism back in the mainstream's face: "Which is Kissinger's real trash, and who is publishing it? Is it the *National Enquirer,* which did some harmless rummaging in his refuse bags, or is it the other elements of the national press, which accept and publish unquestioningly the official statements issued by the State Department and go along with the absurd deception involved in the repeating of trial balloons floated by 'a high U.S. official aboard the Kissinger airplane?'"[11]

In all, Gourley's *Washington Monthly* article was probably the most spirited and closely reasoned defense of the *Enquirer*'s style of journalism, rooted in the concrete facts of a perfectly illustrative incident.

TWELVE

MANUFACTURING "TRUTH"

Probably Pope's most embarrassing journalistic gaffe was occasioned by Australian Robin Leach, then freelancing for the *Enquirer*. Leach, who went on to found his famous TV program, *Lifestyles of the Rich and Famous,* placed a cover story—for which Pope always paid lavishly—on how *CBS Evening News* anchor Walter Cronkite had seen a UFO. That story, which Cronkite immediately debunked, nevertheless became one of Cronkite's favorite private war stories, which he eventually retold in 1997 on PBS's *Crossing the Line.* Cronkite's reminiscence jogged the memory of Neal Travis, who had cycled out of the *Enquirer* and was then writing a column for the *New York Post.* Thus, an almost lost story was recovered and enriched:

> Cronkite recalls that several decades ago, the *Enquirer* ran a cover story claiming to have interviewed him about his sighting of a UFO. The reporter was Robin Leach, and Cronkite says he called Leach in high dudgeon. What was this "interview" nonsense? Cronkite demanded to know. Leach wasn't at all fussed. He reminded America's Most Trusted Man that he (Leach) had approached Cronkite when the CBS anchor was leaving a function with Henry Kissinger. Well, yes, Cronkite recalls saying, but the

interview consisted of just one word. It's a nice story, but other reporters who were there at the time suggest Walter's account is something of a champagne dream. They clearly recall that Cronkite spoke at least several sentences to Leach as the intrepid reporter trailed him down the hall. Whatever did occur, Cronkite must have called the *Enquirer*'s Pope, because Leach got canned as a correspondent without a chance to defend himself.[1]

Travis's account is a reminder that any verifiable contact with an *Enquirer* reporter could be dangerous, entailing the risk of a my-word-against-your-word stalemate in the event of a conflict. Were Cronkite to file a lawsuit claiming, for instance, that his trustworthiness had been seriously undermined by the false story, the fact that witnesses saw him talking to Leach could soon boil down to a matter of whose word a jury or a judge would take. Leach could say there had been an interview, and Cronkite could say it had been one word, presumably "No!" Leach's defense would suggest that Cronkite was correctly quoted but that he denied what he said after he saw how silly it looked in publication, which might be plausible, since this denial scenario is acted out routinely in mainstream and tabloid journalism alike. In this particular case, of course, America's Most Trusted would have a great advantage over a tabloid reporter.

Cronkite did call Pope, according to Kuncl, who vividly recalled the incident. Before the story was ready to run, Kuncl had checked with Leach again, probably because the story seemed improbable even to those whose stock in trade was improbabilities:

I read the copy for the last time to Robin Leach, that wacko Australian. I was given the task of reading him back that story before it went. And I'm saying to him, "Cronkite said this, and you got this on tape. Right?" "Right." "Let me ask that again." "You bet." Jesus Christ, Cronkite picked up the phone and called Pope. And Pope was so embarrassed. I mean he had us in there and our asses were like spanked. And he put in the research department right after that. Robin Leach was a two-for-a-nickel stringer and his tape failed to operate that day when push came to shove. And Walter Cronkite just humiliated Pope. And Pope did not like it, trust me. And we had a meeting and it was, "This is the last time you people will ever," blah, blah, blah. We were sitting there thinking, "Hey, come on, we're living on the edge of a cliff every day; this shit can happen."[2]

Pope did trust Cronkite over a two-for-a-nickel stringer; the reliability of his stringers had been a problem all along. Sometimes they were conning Pope along with the *Enquirer*'s readers. Sometimes Pope obviously didn't concern himself over this; he got a good story and his hands were clean. The Leach-Cronkite incident was once again a reminder that reporters, and especially freelance reporters, were not employees in the usual sense of the word. They were more like independent subcontractors and their motives could be adversarial—they might want to place, and get paid for, a story contrary to management's interests. Pope wasn't likely angry just because the story was a lie. He was angry because it appeared to be an *obvious* lie and because *he* had been lied to, if not about what Cronkite said, certainly about the tape. No one at the *Enquirer,* not its cynical journalists and least of all Pope, who was after all a graduate of MIT, had to really believe these improbable stories about junk science, UFOs, and Bigfoot; all they had to believe was that someone else did, or *said* they did.*

So this was the point where "research," as the *Enquirer*'s fact-checking operation came to be called, arrived. Many publications have fact-checkers—Pope hired one of the best from *Time* to head his new operation—but Pope's crew faced some special problems. Fact-checkers can't verify that UFOs exist, only that some people think so, have claimed to have seen them or to have been abducted by them, or, like Fox Mulder of *The X-Files,* have claimed that their sisters were abducted by them. The main burden of this newly hired staff was listening to the tapes for every story the *Enquirer* published, from free-lancers and staff alike, except for celebrity stories, which significantly operated by an entirely different set of rules and pointedly did *not* require tapes. But otherwise, after research was installed, someone had to say on tape that he had seen a UFO, or whatever else the story said, and the tape had to be in hand before the story ran. Someone in research actually listened to the tape and cleared it before a story could run. Research, then, was clearly an adversarial branch within the editorial structure whose task was keeping the paper's

---

* Whenever *Enquirer* or *Weekly World News* staffers went on talk TV or radio, which was fairly often, this was their explanation for why they published so many outlandish and improbable stories of alien abductions and Bigfoot sightings, ignoring the fact that, especially in the case of the Wacky World News, these stories were made up in the office, along with the sources. The gambit of the tabloid reporter or writer, speaking to the public, was to blur the line between tabloid and mainstream journalism.

reporters "honest"—or at least making their job harder. It was an internal discourse that strengthened the *Enquirer*'s version of events and provided documentation that made the paper's stories more difficult to attack, even in court. The story could be fabricated, everyone could know or suspect it was fabricated, but nevertheless a convincing apparatus existed to support the story. Pope had developed, through painful trial and error, a way to manufacture "truth," a curiously postmodern development.

As Kuncl said:

> Once that research department got in place, there was a hell of a lot less chance of something that bad [the Cronkite debacle] happening. Because they would have demanded the tape. They would have said, "We have to have the tape in here before that story goes." And it made a better paper. But there was not a lot of that going on. This was a guy [Leach] who just took a ridiculously foolish chance. That was one of the worst times I ever saw Pope out of control. He was just purple. It affected him so deeply—it was like he thought everybody knew that Cronkite had called him and made a fool out of him. I mean nobody knew. The public didn't know. Cronkite didn't tell anybody. But Pope just felt like the whole world knew and was a witness to his humiliation. That was the worst I ever saw him.[3]

Leach went on to become gossip columnist for the *Globe,* the third-ranked tabloid after the *Enquirer* and the *Star,* which put him in position to launch his famous TV program. Leach was one of the many graduates of the supermarket tabloids who took his knowledge and practices to a wider world and other media with outstanding success.

It was significant that celebrity stories were exempted from the tape rule, indicating that there was more room to fictionalize there. Pope eventually carved out a gray area in the realm of celebrity gossip by fighting Carol Burnett's famous libel suit through the appeals process to the point where her victory was entirely Pyrrhic. And libel law was already tilted in favor of journalism in regard to celebrities, as the law stated that those who courted the limelight—"public personalities"—would have to suffer the slings and arrows of the press to a greater extent than ordinary private people. Simply put, celebrities had less right to privacy.

That the *Enquirer's* standard for celebrity stories was more lax became obvious in reading several of them at once. Celebrity quotes became next to impossible for the *Enquirer* to get firsthand, as the paper increasingly burned any celebrity sources or access it might have had. "Pope was really into celebrity cheating," said Val Virga, who served as photo editor during the eighties, eventually becoming chief of the photo department after Pope's death. Pope also delighted in catching celebrities looking bad and was first to develop that territory into a well-worked tabloid genre. Said Virga:

> You have to put yourself back. That stuff doesn't sound that thrilling now, but at the time it was, like Katharine Hepburn coming out of her apartment after she had her face lifted. Now we're so immune to celebs pumping gas and in their bikinis. But Pope had the first pictures of Liz Taylor and Richard Burton on a

yacht. The pictures were shot from a high angle, and they're lying on the boat and she's in her bikini, and that was a big deal. Pope loved Jackie O pictures, and he bought a lot of Ron Gallela's stuff. Pope ran a picture of Frank Sinatra sitting on the beach in Cannes—that was where everybody got nailed—and he was fat. There was a time of his life when Sinatra was fat. The headline was "Old Big Belly" instead of "Old Blue Eyes."[4]*

Celebrities simply didn't ordinarily talk to or cooperate with the *Enquirer*. But then they hardly talked to any journalists except in carefully arranged pieces that did them some good, when they had just released a record, book, or film. Celebrity quotes in *Enquirer* stories were mostly "as told to a friend," a hearsay standard of truth too sloppy for the mainstream press. Anyone who reads ten or twenty *Enquirer* celebrity stories of the era would see that the wording of these quotes is remarkably the same. As Jay Gourley wrote in his account of how he was thrown out of a Madison Avenue bar for photographing Harry Reasoner next to a beautiful bosomy blonde, "with the

---

* Pope loved to publish paparazzi photos of stars showing their age, their bellies, skinny legs, and less than ideally beautiful bodies, a form of abjection remarked by Julia Kristeva in her *Powers of Horror*. *Enquirer* stories routinely dealt with the ugly, forbidden, abject side of experience, outing celebrities, revealing the seamy side of their relationships, divorces, infidelities—all the ingredients of sin and scandal. As Kristeva writes, the abject is understood to be intertwined with the always fascinating ambiguities of sin (*Powers of Horror*, 113–32), where "victims of the abject are its fascinated victims—if not its submissive and willing ones" (9). Isn't that a nice description of an *Enquirer* reader, ashamed to buy the paper but unable to turn away?

pictures in hand, obtaining the usual quotes about how Harry's new love had changed his life would be a snap."[5] "Obtaining" would likely involve fashioning an "as-told-to-a-friend" story.

As celebrity stories were a staple of the *Enquirer,* many reporters dreaded being sent out on short notice to the West Coast, where for weeks, far from friends and family, they would be put under enormous pressure to troll for celebrity scandal. They were put up at the Chateau Marmont, the already famous hotel made more famous by John Belushi, who chose it for his final overdose in 1982. Considering that pressure, it's not surprising that some reporters resorted to desperate and dubious means. By the eighties the paper was a pariah to TV and film stars, with a few notable exceptions, so reporters, according to a carefully crafted legend, relied on a network of personal trainers, hotel doormen, maids, butlers, and ordinary people who worked in small jobs on TV and film sets. Pope often boasted about the *Enquirer's* "little people" network, and it was the core of his claim that his reporters got celebrities' stories "whether they talk to us or not." There was truth to Pope's claim, as many of the paper's best stories came from fired butlers and maids, who would also earn tens of thousands of dollars for their memoirs of celebrity service. In fact, $40,000 was about right for a resentful servant with a juicy inside story.

But sometimes the little people only seemed to talk. One of the tricks of some *Enquirer* reporters was to get a list of employees on TV or film sets and order up a series of small checks—$50 was a good amount—to be sent to their home addresses. The recipients would have no idea what the checks were for, but if they cashed them they immediately became a plausible source for an *Enquirer* story. If they denied cooperating, the *Enquirer* would have a canceled check as evidence of a transaction in information.

Despite the common public perception that the *Enquirer* was racy and traded in sexual scandal, a more careful reading verifies that romance in its pages was strictly sentimental. Romances, in the pages of the *Enquirer,* usually changed the lovers' lives. The lovers looked deeply into each other's eyes and held hands in public places. As a result, much of the celebrity "scandal" in the paper wasn't very scandalous and existed in the legal gray zone between harmless fiction and legally actionable lies.

Enquirer staffers learned other tricks for getting fabricated stories past research. One was the collection of a list of doctors who had lost their license to practice or who for other reasons—alcoholism or mental illness—were unable to practice any longer. However, they could be quoted and accurately cited in print as MDs. They had earned the degree, and it could not be rescinded. Over the years a list had been collected and shared of these desperate docs who would supply a backup quote—that this or that would cure this or that—for between $50 and $150. It's possible that practices like this are the origin of the term "money quote," used now even in mainstream journalism, which does not practice checkbook journalism, to denote the conclusive or central quotation in a story. The defrocked docs were known as the trained seals. It's possible that Pope didn't know about the trained seals, but it's a much better bet that he knew and winked at his enterprising journalists. He obviously tolerated many dubious and vicious practices in the newsroom, many of them fostered by the competition he encouraged between his own editors and reporters.

One of the most desperate attempts to get research's approval on a tape came from a freelancer's read-back tape. For a read-back the reporter read out the story over the phone, with a tape running, to the source, who then either approved it, disapproved it, or more commonly corrected it. In this case the source took a deep breath as he prepared to list a long litany of mistakes and problems, and said, "Okay . . ." The freelancer cut the tape right there, and submitted it to research. His stratagem failed.

There was no problem when there was a signed contract, when money changed hands. That situation gave the reporter carte blanche. Yet when a British reporter was sent to interview one of the young black men who had been shot by Bernard Goetz on the New York subway, the source had a decidedly East London way of phrasing his account. Sometimes Pope's British reporters unconsciously slipped Britishisms into their quotes or copy, like lorry for truck, or lift for elevator. *Enquirer* readers weren't likely to complain, and if they were sharp enough to notice, they might already be reading the paper as satire anyway.

So research's scrutiny did not mean a story was true, in the more ideal sense of the word, especially when the *Enquirer*'s checkbook journalism was taken into account. Once a contract was written for a source, no tape was required. Getting a story past research meant that it would likely stand up in court, as Pope's internal standard at that time came closer to the standard for testimony in court. By the time Pope added his research department, the *Enquirer* was coming to fit Foucault's definition of *truth* as "a system of ordered procedures for the production, regulation, distribution, circulation and operation of statements."[6] The methods of film studio and television publicists also fit Foucault's definition, though the outcome was different and routinely contradicted the *Enquirer*'s construction of truth. The *Enquirer* frequently debunked the self-serving cover stories studio flacks invented for their stars, although the paper was occasionally perfectly capable of running saccharine celebrity puff pieces. The paper also had its sacred cows, which boiled down to people Pope liked. One reporter once observed that Pope operated like the owner of a shoe shop that only sold shoes in his own size.

THIRTEEN

THE PEAK OF TABLOID: ELVIS

The issues of cultural abjectness and social transgression were very much alive in the *Enquirer*'s story on Elvis Presley's funeral in August 1977, which resulted in the highest sales for any issue of the *National Enquirer*—6.7 million—and was the benchmark record for any American tabloid. Spurred by the exclusive, pirated front-page head shot of Elvis in his coffin, sales that week might have gone even higher, according to Tom Kuncl, who, as executive editor, was on-the-ground commander of the *Enquirer*'s invasion of Memphis: "I was on the phone telling them to go to eight million—I think they ran out of paper. But it's still the all-time high."[1] Demand for the Elvis issue was so intense that *Enquirer* photo editor Vince Eckersley remembered hearing of a 7-Eleven robbery in Tennessee where "all they stole was the *Enquirer*s with the Elvis in the coffin on the front."[2] Tennessee's copies were sold out in forty-eight hours; one woman called up the Lantana offices and offered $50 for a copy. The *Enquirer* mailed her a copy for free, but when the Associated Press interviewed Iain Calder, he remembered her call and made use of it: AP's story noted the press-run sellout and added that copies were going for as much as $50.[3]

It became immediately clear that Pope had scored a bull's-eye and shot Cupid's arrow into the heartland's quivering center. The hardscrabble Elvis

150

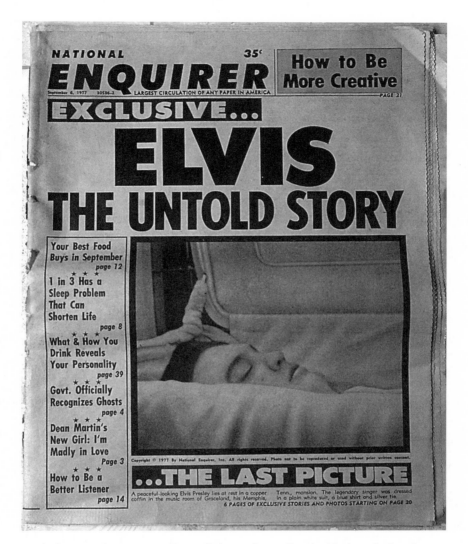

NATIONAL ENQUIRER 35¢

September 6, 1977 30536-2 LARGEST CIRCULATION OF ANY PAPER IN AMERICA

How to Be More Creative PAGE 27

EXCLUSIVE...

ELVIS THE UNTOLD STORY

Your Best Food Buys in September
page 12

★ ★ ★
1 in 3 Has a Sleep Problem That Can Shorten Life
page 8

★ ★ ★
What & How You Drink Reveals Your Personality
page 39

★ ★ ★
Govt. Officially Recognizes Ghosts
page 4

★ ★ ★
Dean Martin's New Girl: I'm Madly in Love
Page 3

★ ★ ★
How to Be a Better Listener
page 14

...THE LAST PICTURE

A peaceful-looking Elvis Presley lies at rest in a copper coffin in the music room of Graceland, his Memphis, Tenn., mansion. The legendary singer was dressed in a plain white suit, a blue shirt and silver tie.
6 PAGES OF EXCLUSIVE STORIES AND PHOTOS STARTING ON PAGE 20

Aside from its transgressive photo of Elvis in his coffin, the black-and-white layout of the *Enquirer*'s most famous cover seems tame compared to current lurid tabloids. (Staff photo by Chris Matula / *Palm Beach Post*)

story had everything: love, beauty, style, drama, talent, failure, pathos, bathos, fat, drugs, and music that would roll on and rock forever. But even at that point no one could imagine that the posthumous iconization of Elvis would build to such heights, topping everyone, Bogart, Gable, Harlow, James Dean, and even John Wayne and Marilyn Monroe. But somehow Pope was the first to understand, and he had a big role in making it happen by giving Elvis a smashing sendoff. After his *Weekly World News* began running the Elvis-is-alive story, Presley's fandom became ever more intensely interactive, and eventually the arrival of the Internet complemented the already ubiquitous impersonators with Web sites where fans could log their latest sightings—by the hundreds.

By 1977 the *Enquirer* was ready to flex some muscle. Its circulation was routinely running 5 million or more a week. From the Elvis peak, the *Enquirer* reached its highest consistent circulation in 1978 at about 5.7 million; by 1981 its circulation had fallen to 4.6 million and was still drifting downward. In 1982 Pope launched his massive "For Enquiring Minds" television advertising campaign, which cost him $30 million that year and rewarded him with an 11 percent boost in circulation, despite a 20-cent hike in the cover price to 65 cents, back into the 5 millions. In 1983 Pope told *Business Week,* in a rare moment of candor about his privately held paper, that revenue rose 54 percent in the year ending that March 31, the greatest increase for any U.S. magazine, including *TV Guide, Time,* and *People.* Net profit was "believed to be at least $15 million," *Business Week* reported in a story headlined "Now It Can Be Told! How the Tabloids Survived the Recession." Pope gloated in that interview, "Really the *Enquirer* is a cash cow. The recession didn't affect us at all."

The cultural merchandise the *Enquirer* purveyed ran counter to the normal business cycle, or at least was immune to it. Americans could dig deeper into their coin purses and pockets for tabloids, as they could for liquor, another cheap pleasure, whose sales remained steady or even increased on bad news from the economic sector. Since Pope survived on newsstand sales, fluctuations in advertising, which were closely influenced by the business cycle, hardly touched him at all. As far as steady circulation went, Pope could never consistently get much more than 5 million, and by his death in 1988 circulation was down to 4.3 million,[4] though his *Weekly World News* brought him another million, at very little expense. He was dogged by Rosenbloom's three clones, the *Globe,* the *Examiner,* and the *Sun,* and by Murdoch's *Star,* which shared the tabloid market. Had Pope remained alone in the field he had pioneered, his earlier goal of 20 million circulation, proclaimed to *Newsweek,* might not have seemed so grandiose.

Tabloid circulation, pegged to impulse buying and cover stories, was more volatile than that for most publications. Since the *Enquirer* was privately held, detailed financial data was not public, but Pope told *Forbes* in 1983 that revenue the year before had been $140 million.[5] *Business Week* also revealed in its interview with Pope that advertising accounted for only 12 percent of the *Enquirer*'s revenue, compared with more than 60 percent at *People* and *Time;* major advertisers stayed away in droves because of the paper's "editorial environment." Nevertheless, with that sort of gross revenue Pope could justify spending lavishly, incurring his operating expenses off the top of the paper's luxurious pretax income.

Pope's coverage of the Elvis funeral went full throttle. He chartered a Learjet between Lantana and Memphis several times that week in August

1977. Somehow, intuitively, Pope knew that the coffin picture was important—it was the masterstroke, in a sense the head of his victim, the very proof of his transgression, a savage symbol and ultimate proof of victory. No censorship, no boundaries of good taste, and no inner circle trying to bury their rock-and-roll king in privacy with dignity would encumber Pope's will. His coverage of the Elvis funeral was an invasion that stunned the nation's mainstream press, which also flocked to the slipping icon's funeral. Pope's style here, as always, was to make it perfectly clear to his reporters what he wanted. Theirs was not to reason why. "He didn't say don't come back without the picture," recalled Kuncl, "but he said, 'I'm expecting you to come back with it.' We had the chartered Learjet waiting on the runway for us to get the picture and rush it back." Kuncl continued, still enthusiastic in an interview more than twenty years later: "I bought every Minox camera in a three-state area. We were trying to sneak the casket shot. We brought forty people from all over the country. We rented the entire floor of a Holiday Inn. We were just grabbing everybody who knew anything and signing them to a contract. We had the ambulance drivers. We had Elvis's girlfriend, Ginger Alden. We had his stepmother. I think we had Uncle Vernon, too. We just had everybody tied to a contract. People who signed contracts we flew back to Lantana so they couldn't talk to anyone else."[6] The contracts were, of course, the *Enquirer's* much-criticized checkbook journalism. The contract for Ginger, Elvis's twenty-year-old fiancée, was reportedly for $105,000.[7] She had shared the eighty-one square feet of Elvis' emperor-sized bed that last night and found the King sprawled on his bathroom floor with his pajama bottoms around his ankles—probably already dead. The Alden interview—"Girl Elvis Was Going to Marry Tells Her Heartbreaking Story"—was the very core of the coverage.

The mainstream considered checkbook journalism shady: people would say things for money, and maybe even lie. But it wasn't illegal, and Pope practiced it openly.* The issue came to a head that week in Memphis. An undercover policeman infiltrated *Enquirer* reporters at the Holiday Inn. "We damn near got arrested for offering bribes," recalls Kuncl. But a contract for a story would hold up in court. A contract was not a bribe, and no arrest was made. Perhaps a fine line was involved, but Pope already knew a lot about fine lines and how to stay just on the right side.

In Kuncl's estimation, "it was a police beat story. A guy dies—how did he die? We had the benefit of forty good people fanned out all over town. And when the sun went down, the effort showed. Plus we had a lot of cash. I left Lantana with two bags, and it was parceled out pretty fast."[8] Kuncl figures that with the Learjet charter, plus helicopters, as well as all the contracts that were written with sources, the story cost Pope about $300,000: "A lot of money went down, a lot of ingenuity, and a lot of good tabloid reporting, old

---

* "The TV networks pay certain subjects for interviews," Pope commented to reporter Sid Kirchheimer. "What's unethical about that?" (Sid Kirchheimer, "Gigantic Smash!" *San Diego Union-Tribune,* February 22, 1987). Lorimar vice president Robert Crutchfield, who produced *Dallas,* said Pope offered him "a great deal of money over the years, especially when they wanted to know who shot J.R." ("Now the Story Can Be Told!" 145). Some sources were much cheaper; the trained seals, the paper's down-on-their luck or defrocked doctors, would give medical quotes for between $50 and $150. Val Virga remembered that when she was a green photo editor at her wit's end trying to find a picture on deadline, she approached Pope in his glass booth and asked him if he had any suggestions. (Pope generally wouldn't run a story without a picture.) "Well, did you try to grease his palm?" he inquired. "That was a defining moment," Virga recalled in an interview. "In those days no one would help you [in the newsroom], you were just thrown into the pool with the sharks. I was sitting there doing Journalism 101, and it was like, 'You mean I can pay people?'"

Chicago-style." Flying sources back to Lantana for an interlude at the beach-front Hawaiian didn't work with Ginger. Somehow she gave an interview to one of the Memphis dailies, and Pope reportedly reduced her payment to $35,000 because her story wasn't the exclusive that had been negotiated.[9]

The *Enquirer*'s power and panache stunned mainstream reporters working the funeral. Compared with the Fleet Streeters they encountered in great numbers in Memphis, America's mainstream press could be counted on to be high-minded, even on a pop story like Elvis. They had always condescended to the tabloid press as lightweights who made up stories about freaks and space aliens. But the specter of a horde of resourceful tabloid reporters with their twisted London accents traveling by Learjet with wads of cash in their pockets to pay for contracts and exclusives was certainly daunting. It was also a dazzling display from what a few years before had been perceived as a laughable gore-and-freak paper. Pope had nearly firmed up the formula for the supermarket tabloid, even if the shadow of the earlier, more turgid format continued to haunt him for years.

In retrospect the Elvis story seems a natural for the *Enquirer,* but this was far from obvious at the time. This was a turning point, the beginning of Elvis's elevation from a fat, fading celebrity to a beloved national, and eventually worldwide, fetish, for which the *Enquirer* deserves enormous credit. After the funeral Presley's image catapulted to the peak of the pop pantheon. But at the time, Presley's rebirth from the ashes was unforeseen. Yes, Elvis had been a giant, but by the mid-seventies, at age forty-two, he was looking very much like a has-been, maybe even a pathetic one. Word was leaking out that in some significant way Elvis was sick. "In past months we'd done several Elvis covers, and they didn't sell worth a shit," said Kuncl. "He weighed a ton and a half and he looked like shit. So it was a calculated risk really, and I'd have to credit the old man's intuition on that."[10]

The Elvis cover photo was a perfect example of what Pope was after when he would ask, What image—*even if they don't want to admit it*—does the American public want to see?[11] Later Pope ran coffin or death pictures of Bing Crosby, Steve McQueen, Rock Hudson, Christina Onassis, John Lennon, and Ted Bundy, all of them reprinted for the first time in the *Enquirer's* coffee-table book, *30 years of Unforgettable Images.* Kuncl often disagreed with Pope about which celebrities the *Enquirer* should cover: "I mean some of these were people were Sunset Boulevard, and he still thought they were hot shit. Pope had a list of names he wanted to see in there, and they were part of the formula, and they were the wrong part of the formula." Such reservations as Kuncl had, he did not discuss with Pope. Pope's executive editor carried out the will of his commander, and in his absence he acted for the commander. The judgment even in Pope's rare absence was never, "What should be done?" but "What would Pope want?" Now he wanted Elvis in his coffin, and this time he was right, right beyond anyone's wildest expectations.

In Memphis the *Enquirer* competed not only against the mainstream but also against other tabloids, and intramural tabloid journalism was a game of wits, rug pulling, and bare knuckles, which is what Kuncl meant by Chicago-style reporting. The contract with Ginger Alden was negotiated on the phone, but before the *Enquirer* could get over to Graceland to interview her, said Kuncl, "two guys from the *Star* went over there and tried to represent themselves as from the *Enquirer.* It was total war."[12] Passing oneself off as a reporter from a rival paper to steal an exclusive was an old trick.

Usually finding out the cause of death is merely a matter of waiting for the coroner's report, but Elvis's autopsy was a twisted tale, and the final toxicology report was not made public until October and was inconclusive at that. Stories circulated that people associated with the *Enquirer* were plotting to burglarize the medical examiner's office, that a secretary in Baptist Hospital had been offered $2,000 for the autopsy and the photos. In fact, no photos were taken at the autopsy, and the report itself, when it was finally written, was useless.[13] But early on Pope's reporters tracked down virtually everyone who was in the autopsy room, according to Kuncl. To the *Enquirer* the most useful person might be an insignificant orderly standing by, not the chief medical officer or the coroner making an official statement. "By the end of the night we knew just about everything there was to know except the final toxicology report," said Kuncl, "and we did know just from the gross autopsy that he'd gone out on drugs. And we calculatedly went ahead and said what we thought had happened, and we were pretty much on the money. 'Man Dies from Cheeseburgers and Dope.'" More than thirty years later no one has come up with a better story.

Pope got his casket picture, but it was a near thing, and a credit to the ingenuity and determination of his reporters. The picture was eventually shot by one of Elvis's distant cousins with a Minox supplied by Kuncl, who was passing the little spy cameras out to anyone willing who was entitled to file past the casket. "We tried everything," Kuncl remembered. "We had people dressed up like nuns. The efforts that failed were amazingly funny. People just chickened out. So a guy would get up on the line there and have his moment to pull the Minox out, and he'd look up and see Red and Sonny West standing there ready to kick the shit out of anyone who tried to take a picture, and he'd just keep on going." Red and Sonny were karate experts, relatives of Elvis and longtime sidekicks who'd recently been banished, probably precisely for their overzealousness in protecting Elvis, which had resulted in troubling lawsuits. They retaliated by cooperating on a best-selling tell-all book, ghosted by Murdoch's tabloid ace Steve Dunleavy,[14] an alternately tender and devastating look at their former boss and relative, published just a few weeks before. The overall import of *Elvis: What Happened?* was that Elvis, at heart a wonderful person, was heading over the edge.

The casket picture filled the *Enquirer's* cover and did its job. It echoed the gore of the *Enquirer's* earlier incarnation a decade earlier, when reportedly the only picture Pope ever turned away from was of a New York cop wearing a rubber glove, carrying a human head by the hair after a subway accident. Pope understood that there are human curiosities that can never be contained within the rules of good taste, and here in the supermarket-sanitized *Enquirer* he still trafficked in the abject. He still had no fear of crossing the border from good to bad taste, from good manners to bad, from press release to garbage. People may have recoiled from the picture of Elvis in his coffin, but they bought the paper in unprecedented numbers. "We took a lot of grief over that picture," Kuncl acknowledged. "Our defense was, and I think it was in the same week, the *Washington Post* ran a photo of a Buddhist monk burning himself to death. Take your choice: a guy in his coffin or a guy immolating himself, which one do you want for breakfast?"

That wasn't quite the end of the saga. A few years later two *Enquirer* reporters stole the negative of the picture from the tabloid's file and tried to sell it, in what could only be described as a lunatic scheme. Kuncl found the caper beyond comprehension: "We were in shock. It was just like unthinkable." The culprits were two British reporters, a younger one and a senior reporter whose salary, Kuncl estimated, was about $100,000 a year. "You can't imagine someone would throw all that away for . . . peanuts. I think they were going to get $10,000. They were going to print it on a t-shirt or something. The other part was how in the hell did anyone think they were going to get away with it?" The picture was copyrighted, and, said Kuncl: "We would have sued the shit out of anybody who did that. They would probably have ratted out whoever gave it to them to get their asses off the hook. We would have spared no expense."* In fact, the scheme was discovered when the younger reporter's girlfriend ratted him out. "She was pissed off about something and she dropped a dime on them," said Kuncl.

Motivation is perhaps the most bizarre part of that story, as Kuncl remembered it: "It was unbelievable who did it. It was a Brit—I used to call him the Vicar he was so straight. I did not believe he was involved until I went over to one of the bars he hung out in and I said, 'Until you tell me you did this, I

---

* Tabloid journalism has produced few, if any, star reporters. Australian Steve Dunleavy, who edited Murdoch's *Star* and later ran and reported for Murdoch's tabloid TV show *Current Affair* and served as top columnist for his *New York Post,* might qualify as one. According to John Cassidy's *New Yorker* piece "The Hell-Raiser" (September 11, 2001), Dunleavy is the model for the tabloid TV reporter Wayne Gale in Oliver Stone's *Natural Born Killers,* a fact that would support Dunleavy's candidacy. Mainstream journalism produced many stars, and most who come to mind—from H. L. Mencken and Ernie Pyle to Tom Wolfe, Gay Talese, David Halberstam, and Seymour Hersch—also moved on to write books. Significantly, there are no equivalents of the Pulitzer or Heywood Braun prizes in tabloid—*there are no prizes at all.* Tabloid authorship is complicated and cheapened by the fact that the story may be hyped, fabricated, or bought outright and was probably rewritten by someone else. In a real sense the possibly pseudonymous tabloid byline is a ruse, in that it seems to offer the authenticity of the mainstream journalist's certifying signature of authorship. The deceptively simple tabloid text is far more complicated than it seems.

refuse to believe it.' He said, 'I did it. God help me, I don't know why I did.'
The other guy was sort of a scoundrel, so that wasn't so hard to believe. They
arrested these guys and took them off in handcuffs."[15] The *Miami Herald* carried a story on the arrest of the two reporters, but Pope swore he would never
print the story. As Kuncl recalls it, the charges were eventually dropped or otherwise circumvented; the pair never went to jail.

Kuncl's theory is that it was a plot hatched in a bar "over a couple of pints
of Harp. For the one guy, I think he was just trying to be a friend to the other one. He was certainly blackballed all through the tabs. You're certainly not
going to trust a guy who does that." No one—not Kuncl, not the accountant
Chris Currie—can remember an instance of the *Enquirer* prosecuting a reporter, although one later robbed a bank elsewhere and did time for it, then
rejoined the tabloid community as a freelancer. Many *Enquirer* reporters, especially the British ones, seemed socially subversive in varying degrees. It
seemed that a working-class Brit, like the chauffeur played by Michael Caine
in *Alfie* (and more recently by Jude Law), just wasn't happy unless he had a
fiddle going against his boss. The stolen Elvis photo caper suggested that this
social subversiveness could reach the illogical degree of biting the hand that
feeds you, and it probably wasn't as unpredictable as Kuncl thought.*

---

* Stories have surfaced recently that the Elvis coffin photo was faked. Kuncl has died since
he was interviewed for this project, and Bob Stevens, the *Enquirer*'s chief airbrush maestro
during that era, was the sole fatality in 2001 of the anthrax attack on American Media's new
and now abandoned Boca Raton building. But former photo chief Val Virga, who coedited
the *Enquirer*'s coffee-table book, *30 Years,* saw the negative before that volume was published
in 2002. "The picture was definitely retouched, as all *Enquirer* pictures are retouched for
print publication—and Bob Stevens is the person who would have done it—but it was defi-

Kuncl was a loyal soldier, a rarity among Pope's employees. Despite his generous salaries and bursts of philanthropy, Pope often stimulated feelings of hostility in his staff, the result of his remoteness and the climate of fear he created. At the other end of the spectrum from Kuncl, for instance, was a resigning reporter who plotted to throw a pie in Pope's face at his last Friday party. The plan was thwarted at the last minute when a female reporter stole the pie and hid it in the ladies' room. There had been significant fear that Pope's security men would overreact and harm the reporter before they understood the attack was merely a prank. And Pope's reaction to such a public humiliation could hardly be predicted.

---

nitely not a fake," Virga said in an interview. Stevens, who had survived the winnowing of the Brits through the eighties, was such a virtuoso that he was renowned for somehow managing to play the opening notes of the "Star-Spangled Banner" on his wheezy little airbrush when he first cued up his instrument in the morning.

FOURTEEN

REPORTER AS GLADIATOR

In the seventies, as the *Enquirer* headed for its highest circulations, Pope was still experimenting with his formula and the boundaries of his new style of tabloid journalism. The paper became ever more diversified, sometimes even looking back to the old gore days. Pope sent a reporter to Uganda to write an eyewitness account of one of Field Marshal Idi Amin's imaginative mass executions. Amin had killed prisoners by crushing them with tanks, by disemboweling, beheading, and forcing them to kill other prisoners before being executed themselves. For the *National Enquirer* Amin executed seventeen prisoners by crushing their heads with a sledgehammer. That one certainly had a generous dollop of the old gore formula.

Pope revived stunt journalism—an old Hearst staple—sending, for example, wiry Australian reporter Brian Hogan into a small Kansas town dressed as a downed space alien, speaking in a down-under accent that might have seemed from outer space. Sometimes stunt journalism was dangerous: specialist Hogan had been threatened by a farmer with a shotgun and whacked with a lady's umbrella. Hogan also lived in a box on a city street in order to relate how he was treated. He boxed a kangaroo and lost. He visited Congress dressed as a sheik, presumably with a pocket full of oil money, and found the climate welcoming, even immediately after the Abscam scandal, the FBI sting in which five legislators, including a U.S. senator, were indicted in 1980 for taking bribes from wealthy Arabs. Hogan even dressed up as a gorilla and sat in a zoo cage to write about the view from the other side of the bars. His cover was blown on that one when a sharp-eyed little boy noticed his blue eyes and told his mother. Hogan also dressed up as a Soviet general and "infiltrated" an army post and the Pentagon.

Hearst had long ago perfected one variation of the stunt genre, notably with a group of female reporters known as the "sob sisters," famous for their tearjerkers. Sob sister Nellie Bly feigned madness to gain admission to an insane asylum so she could write about its horrors. Pope sent his reporters on similar missions. For a period of years there was a chance that one of the patients at the Betty Ford Clinic would be an *Enquirer* reporter looking for celebrities in rehab, a territory a Hearst sob sister would have known how to exploit.

Phil Brennan thought Pope was quite conscious about imitating Hearst: "I think he was trying to build his legend. That's why he wanted everyone to read *Citizen Hearst* and the biography of Joseph Pulitzer. It was made quite plain it was a good idea to read these books. He identified with them. He did many things just because he identified with Hearst and Pulitzer."[1] Unlike Hearst's stories, Pope's reports out of the Betty Ford Clinic did not encourage sympathy or tears; they were more a version of how low the mighty have fallen, getting up early, keeping to a tight schedule, sweeping out their own little rooms, going to endless Alcoholics Anonymous and Narcotics Anonymous meetings.

Stalking Jackie Kennedy became an *Enquirer* staple for a number of years, too, after she married Aristotle Onassis in 1968 and became Jackie O.

The jackpot was a cover paparazzi photo of Ari with his eyelids taped open in 1974, exposing a symptom of the myasthenia gravis that soon killed him. Yet the *Enquirer* never broke the real story, that Jackie and Ari's marriage was in name only. Nor did it disclose that Ari was still seeing his longtime lover, the beautiful Greek opera singer Maria Callas—and others.

Besides the celebrity stories, the rest of the *Enquirer* was made up by Pope's constantly tweaked formula, which included self-help pieces; quizzes; mazes; cute photos, especially of dogs and children; and accounts of good Samaritans and heroes, who were rewarded with the *Enquirer* Lifesaver Award. Pope instituted an Honest Person Award, to be given to good citizens who did things like returning a wallet full of money to its rightful owner.

And everyone, readers and reporters alike, loved a good way-out: Pope sent reporter Bob Timmy to Nepal to slog up to eighteen thousand feet in the Himalayas to find the Abominable Snowman, which he somehow failed to do.[2] There were those who thought if he'd sent a British instead of an American reporter the paper would have had at least a good footprint, as the Brits rarely came home totally empty-handed.

Pope sent reporter John Harris to find paradise, and somehow he, too, failed. The assignment must have been the best ever given any reporter. It took almost five months of traveling the world on a lavish expense account. Harris would almost be there in paradise, and then something would go wrong—a touch of pollution, too much noise, some blight on perfection, like an airport. "Every place had too many flies or something," said Iain Calder.[3] Harris listed some of his destinations in a recent blog account, "My Search for Utopia": "Madeira, the Azores, the Canaries, the Spanish Mediterranean islands, the Greek islands, the Channel islands (Guernsey, Jersey, and Sark), the Scottish isles of Mull and Gigha, Hawaii (Molokai), Tahiti, Moorea, Bora Bora, Fiji, Samoa, Bali, Sri Lanka, the Seychelles, Mauritius and other places too numerous to mention."[4]

Finally, Harris came to the end of his search for some reason (perhaps a phone call from his wife) and came home. When Pope read his story about finding paradise at last—in the Seychelles, by legend—he reputedly tossed it aside, saying, in his inimitable way, "Nah, that's not paradise." The story never ran. The story must have cost Pope a fortune and months of a good reporter's time. But from another angle, Pope hadn't wasted his money. The story of killing the paradise story made it an even better story, an *Enquirer* legend especially appealing to journalists accustomed to stingy managements and niggardly travel allowances. Pope could have written that story off as a recruiting expense. Harris, who had been working on a Cincinnati daily and supplementing his income freelancing for the *Enquirer,* eagerly came aboard the *Enquirer* full-time.

Pope once called a special editors' meeting because he wanted to use a submarine in a story, according to Iain Calder. "Find a way to use a submarine," he commanded. One editor, who was involved in stalking Caroline Kennedy in the Caribbean, did. He even suggested putting the *Enquirer* logo on the conning tower, so when the submarine surfaced the beleaguered celebs would know who had nailed them. But on reflection there seemed a serious danger, since Caroline was protected by the U.S. Secret Service. Couldn't they call in sub-killing planes to drop depth charges, someone wondered?[5] The idea of the paparazzi sub with the *Enquirer* logo—a rampant shark?—quietly died.

Another idea broached at an editors' meeting was that the *Enquirer* should buy an island and have its own country. "Wouldn't it be fun to have our own Enquirerland?" Pope asked. He was greeted with wooden smiles. He hired Ernest Hemingway's younger brother Leicester, an explorer and adventurer, to find an island for sale, which he did, in the Bahamas chain. Leicester was working it out with the United Nations when suddenly the project was killed—with Pope's silence. Calder said his theory was that Pope's wife, Lois, nixed it.[6]

When Frank Zahour went to work for the *Enquirer* in 1976, after six years with the *Chicago Tribune,* his first assignment was to fill in some information on how cattle prods were being used to control autistic kids at a school. Zahour obtained a cattle prod, and as part of his research he and the writer on the story, John Blackburn, went out into the parking lot and chased each other around zapping each other. Zahour immediately realized he was going to enjoy working for the *Enquirer:* "This was the kind of thing you could do that made the *Enquirer* a different breed of horse—the fun and involvement you had."[7]

Zahour had landed his job at the *Enquirer* through a tryout, like nearly everyone else who worked in editorial. He had flunked his earlier tryout as a writer. His reporting tryout was to tour several U.S. cities visiting three or four emergency rooms in each one with the same set of bogus symptoms, which he worked out in a conference with an MD: a head injury from a fall, including headache and nausea. It was a classic situation where an X-ray should be ordered, but as Zahour found out, most emergency room doctors didn't bother. In Tulsa he had to pay cash in advance to get treatment, and in a couple of other locations he had to go on welfare to get an exam and treatment. It was a typical *Enquirer* piece of the era—half stunt and half investigation—and, as Zahour said, "Everyone loved the story and I got the job."[8]

So Zahour worked through the late seventies, a rich time of continuing experimentation at the *Enquirer:*

> The format was some kind of social issue or romance on the front page, then the paper was jammed with UFOs, odd people, stories on how to get rich, how to start your own business. One feature was called Rags to Riches. The paper seemed to be a kind of blue-collar *Reader's Digest*. This was what Pope needed to get into the supermarkets. It was goodbye to "Boyfriend Grinds Up Girl-friend." For me the late seventies formula was vastly more interesting than the romance and celebrity stories which were on every page by the time I left [six years later].[9]

In October 1977, the *Enquirer* covered another funeral. Bing Crosby, who had been happily crooning to himself and in fine enough fettle to beat two Spanish golf pros on a course near Madrid, died so suddenly of a heart attack that his companions thought the seventy-four-year-old legend had tripped and fallen. Zahour was just hitting his stride as an *Enquirer* reporter when he was assigned to the funeral and sent to the West Coast with five or six other reporters. He looked on the assignment as a journey into tabloid's Heart of Darkness: "On many assignments there was no map, just a destination—mostly it was a fresh challenge, problem solving every time. You had to get there yourself, with whatever means of transport you could find, dream up, charter, snare, commandeer. That was the fun of it, and the pressure of it." Zahour was shadowing Crosby's widow, Kathryn Grant, at the Los Angeles airport, when she stepped into a cab: "I bolted past the people in line, grabbed the next cab, telling the driver, 'Follow that cab.' The driver smiled. 'Cool, man, just like the movies. No one has ever said that to me,' he said as he punched it. I didn't tell him I had never said that to anybody. And, yes, it was cool."[10]

Crosby had stipulated in his will that only his wife and seven children should attend his funeral. Kathryn had widened the list to include Bing's siblings as well as Bob Hope, Rosemary Clooney, and Phil Harris, but certainly no reporters or journalists were to be allowed. Zahour needed to think of an angle:

> I figured out no one would challenge a priest, so I grabbed the
> Yellow Pages and found a costume shop, no problem in LA, a
> city built on illusions. I rushed to the store in Sepulveda and
> asked what they had in the way of religious garb. The man at the
> counter offered me a full-dress red-and-black bishop's outfit.
> Well, I had a moment of fantasy there of myself strutting around
> in full bishop drag. But, no, too attention-getting. The man suggested just a priest's collar that I could wear with a dark suit.
> Back at the hotel I put on dark pants and suit coat and wire-rimmed glasses and slicked back my hair. The collar looked great.
> I walked around from room to room greeting my fellow reporters. We took the outfit for a test drive. On the elevator down
> some of Crosby's kids got on the elevator. One of my colleagues

motioned, suggesting I provide some solace for the family. But I thought that was going too far.[11]

Shortly before he was to be dropped off at the funeral in Culver City, Zahour hid his tape recorder in his coat pocket and taped the mike and cord along his arm: "Then I realized this was stupid, since I would look like a Secret Service guy talking to his sleeve, or aiming his sleeve at people during the eulogy. Too late to rip it off, so I made a mental note not to use it." When Zahour arrived, the site was jammed with reporters. Geraldo Rivera was covering the funeral for ABC:

> I step just behind some people who just exited from a limo, walking slowly, head down. Two or three reporters surround me, asking for comments. I know I must say nothing, lest I end up on the evening news. I remember Pope is a Catholic. I know he will love the story, but I am not so sure he will approve of one of his reporters being mistaken for a priest. I say nothing, slowly move into the chapel. I am in. I note everything, the casket, the flowers, the words of love and religion that send Bing Crosby to the great beyond. I turn to leave. I have what I need. I don't want to blow the thing.[12]

When he got to the door Zahour saw another *Enquirer* reporter, Gerry Hunt, a Brit dressed in a black tie, suit, and white shirt, acting as the doorman. Later Zahour found Hunt had insinuated himself in about the same way Zahour did, but from the back: "He is holding the door, sort of bowing to everyone as they leave. He smiles. I smile. I am struggling for composure as I walk by Hunt, and he says, 'Good evening, Father,' in that wonderful British accent. I must say he made an elegant doorman."

After turning down a request for an interview from a female reporter, Zahour went back to the hotel and filed his story. When he read the *Los Angeles Times* story the next morning, he found it lacking in details, details that he had noted and which would appear in the *Enquirer* story later in the week. He had scooped the hometown reporters. That morning Zahour also attended the burial, which was public, dressed normally, standing behind the brass rail with the other reporters. He noticed a female reporter eyeing him, the one who had tried to interview him the night before when he was dressed as a priest: "She can't take her eyes off me. It's one of those 'Have I seen this guy before?' looks. I just stay cool and stare ahead. I don't want to become her story."[13] Apparently that reporter never made the connection between the familiar-looking journalist and the priest at the funeral—or never wrote about it—but Frank's story became one of the *Enquirer* legends. It got better through repetition, including a version in which Geraldo Rivera sought an interview with Father Frank as he left the funeral and Frank scolded Geraldo for trying to invade the family's privacy.

Steve Coz came into the paper by way of a blind ad in a Boston paper, one way Pope recruited reporters, both with and without experience. Both kinds were paid the *Enquirer*'s starting rate, more than $50,000 a year from the late seventies well into the eighties. Coz was a few years out of Harvard, where he graduated cum laude, and surprisingly he found Ivy League company amid Pope's reporters. They were called the Whiz Kids and they had been recruited right out of college, many from Harvard and Yale. "There was a slew of people who came in and didn't make it," said Coz. "They told me about the Whiz Kid program, and they weren't too keen on it."[14] American journalism has a long tradition of being anti-intellectual, and Pope—in spite of his elite MIT education—fit right in. When he approved the Whiz Kid program he had stipulated "no journalism students." By the time Coz came on board, the Whiz Kids were down to a clique of four or five. Then in the early eighties the Ivy Leaguers gradually disappeared except Coz, who steadily rose in the editorial ranks.

Just out of Harvard, Coz had been drifting comfortably, an English major obviously in no hurry, traveling in Mexico and Central America, then to Houston and Nashville, where he stayed with a girlfriend who went to Vanderbilt. She went to Boston after graduation, and Coz followed. "I was in her apartment and doing some writing gigs and talking to some tech companies about writing manuals. I was scanning the writing ads in the *Boston Globe* when I saw one offering top dollar for a writing pro. I fired off a letter and within three days I got a phone call saying come to Florida for a six-week tryout. It was January and I said, 'This is pretty good.' So I came down for a vacation."[15]

Coz was put up in the Hawaiian, with its tiki bar, terrace, pool, and beach. Coz was paid a generous per diem, a consideration for a hand-to-mouth freelancer: "And not only were they putting me up, they were giving me money for food." The *Enquirer* had not been on Coz's map, but he warmed to the place: "When I met the people there and started doing the work, I said, 'Wow, this is just fabulous.' It was such a high-energy place. The people were just super talented. There was such a driving force in the building to get the story."

His first big break was in the stunt genre, which often served as a kind of initiation. Coz found himself transported from balmy Florida to Gary, Indiana, in the middle of freezing winter with $1,000 in $20 bills in his pocket to buy people's souls. Coz, graduate of a strict Catholic high school, might have wondered about his own soul, judging from the title of his introduction to the *Enquirer*'s coffee-table book, "I Did a Bad, Bad Thing," in which he recounted the assignment.

"I was flabbergasted," Coz recalled. "I was the only white guy on the street and I had this wad of bills in my pocket. I was in a tough neighborhood, though I think all the neighborhoods are tough there. I didn't know Gary was all black." To get out of the freezing cold, Coz ducked into a supermarket—until the manager threw him out. "I was hitting people up as they came out of the checkout line, asking them if they would sell their soul to the devil." Also in his pocket were contracts, drawn up on legal parchment: "We had the paper looking super legal. This guy said, 'Give me 20 bucks to sell my soul?' and I said, 'Yeah, yeah.' Then he called up his brother and sold his soul. Then he sold his mother's soul. He didn't even ask her."[16]

The man was called Goodson, and Coz used it in the lead of his fifteen-page file: "There were other tremendous anecdotes, and I remember my editor coming up to me and marching me in to Pope in his glass booth. My editor wanted to blow the story across pages 2 and 3. This was the first time I came to GP's attention."[17] Pope ultimately ran the story on three-quarters of page 3, which in tabloid is the lead page after the cover, which is ordinarily a photo and banner, with teasers.

In 1978 Pope briefly instigated one of the strangest practices in journalism, known by those who had to carry it out as gladiatorial journalism. To a lesser

degree Pope had always practiced it, setting his editors and reporters competing with one another, but this was so explicitly over the top. Pope decided that
his reporters weren't getting enough competition from the clone tabloids that
imitated his formula, so he sent two teams to New York to see who could get
the best and most stories. The penalties to the losers were unclear, but at the
very least they would be humiliated. Nor did it take much in this era of the
editorial bloodbaths to imagine the losing team would be fired en masse.

Team member Jay Gourley, already well known for sifting Henry Kissinger's garbage, wrote an account for *Washington Monthly* ("I Killed Gig
Young") that offers an inside story of how a tabloid story was hyped and re-
hyped. After a few initial days of stalemate, Gourley's group's winning streak
began by chance shortly after a teammate interviewed the aging Gig Young,
who a few hours later shot his young German wife of three weeks to death
and turned his pistol on himself. Maxed out in his role of outlaw reporter
functioning beyond the laws of socialization, Gourley heralded this event as
"the kind of senseless tragedy every good newsman prays for."[18] Whiz Kid
Steve Chao, a Harvard classics major who had interviewed Young, wrote the
story on the murder-suicide, making the most of his good luck.*

---

* After he left the *Enquirer,* Chao was employed by Rupert Murdoch, who appointed him
head of Fox News. Chao was also instrumental in inventing Fox's reality programming, including *Cops* and *America's Most Wanted.* Chao's post-*Enquirer* career is a perfect place to
contemplate the immense impact Pope had in the tabloidization of the whole culture. Judith
Regan, who went into publishing after working for Pope as an articles editor, was another
example of tabloid influence. Regan splashed publisher's row with her early picks—the ultra-
conservative motormouth Rush Limbaugh's and radio shock jock Howard Stern's books—
which defied conventional wisdom and became immediate best sellers. Regan continued
walking on the razor's edge of abject with books like porn star Jenna Jameson's until she fi-

Gourley's team, whose members had spent weeks psyching themselves for the big contest, found Chao's story "a little bland," according to Gourley: "The lead was something like, 'I'll never forget the pain in Gig Young's voice shortly before he murdered the woman he loved and turned the gun on himself.'"[19] So the team, without consulting Chao, hyped the file to read, "For the rest of my life I'll live with the pain that burns inside me when I ask myself, 'Could I have saved Gig Young in those last precious moments?'" Even that wasn't quite turgid enough, so the next round of revising came up with: "For the rest of my life I'll live with the pain of knowing I killed Gig Young."[20]

That seemed about as far as hype could go, but it wasn't good enough for Pope. Part of the trouble was that the dailies were all over the story, and the weekly *Enquirer*'s version wouldn't be out till after they'd had their day. So Pope dictated the story he wanted his reporters to find, the "inside story on why he did it," and he wanted the two teams to cooperate. That at least seemed to mean the story was big enough to transcend and end the short reign of gladiatorial journalism. The leaders of the two teams—Shelley Ross and Malcolm Balfour—put their heads together and decided that the inside story was "Gig Young foresaw his own death." The team noodled that idea around, recounted Gourley, until they found the fallacy: it wouldn't quite be wowy enough to foresee one's own suicide. So the story line was changed to "If they couldn't live together, they would die together."[21] Despite all the energy devot-

---

nally went too far and faltered with O. J. Simpson's book about how he would have killed Nicole, *if* he had. The backlash on that one was so intense that Murdoch ditched the "ill-conceived" project just as it was coming to full fruition and fired Regan a month later. But her long string of successes showed her deep understanding of the hidden power of the abject, which surely she honed at the *Enquirer*.

ed to it, the Gig Young story never jelled. When the reporters returned from New York, the Ross team was "disbanded," though its individual members remained employed, for the time being.

The milder form of gladiatorial journalism remained in effect: every week half a dozen articles editors, each with his or her circle of reporters, continued to routinely battle with each other, goaded on by Pope, who stood in the emperor's box, giving thumbs up or down to their projects. Pope spent a great deal of money and effort on the projects he killed, but he didn't see the process as a waste of money, energy, and time. It kept his gladiators sharp, edgy, and fit.

FIFTEEN

STAR WARS: HOLLYWOOD VERSUS THE *ENQUIRER*

By the mid-seventies the *National Enquirer* was routinely feeding on Hollywood's underbelly. The film factories manufactured the dreams and created leading ladies and men, and the *Enquirer* poked a hole and deflated the fantasies, revealing the warts, wrinkles, and sags in the idols, not to mention trumpeting their offscreen bad behavior. The idols were stalked and caught off guard in unglamorous private moments by the new legion of paparazzi supported by Pope's tabloids and their clones. Pope made it known that he would pay $250 for a story tip that panned out, significantly more for one that turned into a cover story—to journalists, to agents ratting out their rivals, or to simple civilian rodents. In at least one bizarre instance, the *Enquirer*'s source was the subject of the item as well. Before Tom Arnold married Roseanne Barr, he tipped off the paper on his girlfriend's activities, behind her back, because being her lover enhanced his status in Hollywood. Pope and his senior editors vigorously defended their paid anonymous sources as just as good as anyone else's anonymous sources. Of course, defending the anonymity of a paid source would have looked absurd in court, though it never came to that in the trivial world of gossip journalism.

While studio flacks constructed romances for their glamorous stable of stars, the *Enquirer* fed on the celebrities' infidelities, divorces, alcoholism, sui-

Pope kept his finger on the popular pulse. His exclusive cover featuring Elvis's coffin kicked off the rock-and-roll king's swift rise to iconic status after a long fall from grace. (Photo by Nick Borgert / *Palm Beach Post*)

cide attempts, and romantic peccadilloes. There seems little doubt that Pope enjoyed his paper's role as Hollywood's spoiler, but there's no doubt at all that his five million readers had a voracious appetite for the stories. Together Hollywood and the *Enquirer* created opposing binaries, the good and the bad, the ugly and the beautiful; and the American public, the consumers of Hollywood's product, seemed to relish the whole story. There's really little evidence that Pope's star bashing did much harm in the box office. Perhaps in the end the *Enquirer* served Hollywood by intensifying the public's interest in its product, but it infuriated the tarnished angels, and they plotted revenge.

The first salvo in the most decisive battle in the war between the *Enquirer* and the stars followed a seemingly inconsequential gossip item of some sixty-five words and four short sentences that ran in the first week of March

1976. The *Enquirer*'s editorial apparatus routinely assembled its gossip items and columns out of tips and leads too minor or weak for a full story and sometimes on almost nothing at all. After a libel suit that called fifteen witnesses and presented eight depositions, as well as a retraction published by the *Enquirer,* this one turned out to be definitely of the latter category: "At a Washington restaurant, a boisterous Burnett had a loud argument with another diner, Henry Kissinger. Then she traipsed around the place offering everyone a bite of her dessert. But Carol really raised eyebrows when she accidentally knocked a glass of wine over one diner and started giggling instead of apologizing. The guy wasn't amused and 'accidentally' spilled a glass of water over Carol's dress."[1]

Unfortunately for the *Enquirer* the item wasn't *complete* fiction, because there was a real city called Washington, a former secretary of state named Henry Kissinger, and a restaurant in the city where plausibly those elements might have combined with the real Carol Burnett. While most stars found it possible to ignore inconsequential items of this sort, however annoying, and while most of those items floated in a gray area where it was difficult to imagine grounds for a libel suit, Carol Burnett decided to sue, with a vengeance. Both her parents were alcoholics, she said, and she was practically a teetotaler; she deeply resented the insinuation that she was drunk. It seemed a libel suit highly unlikely to succeed. She was a public figure who under the prevailing case law would have to meet a tougher standard of damages where it seemed difficult to imagine any damages at all. In fact, in court she could show only $250 in monetary damages. Moreover, she would have to prove actual malice on the part of the *Enquirer,* or a reckless disregard for the truth.

Up to this point the *Enquirer* had never had a libel suit come to trial. For nearly three decades the paper had settled its libel suits out of court, often after a great deal of costly pretrial maneuvering that wore down its adversaries. Burnett claimed that that sort of maneuvering had cost her $200,000 in the five years before the trial, but she didn't back off. The *Enquirer* also failed in its attempts to get the lawsuit dismissed, in part because two restaurant employees testified that they had told the *Enquirer* before publication that the story was untrue.[2] Possibly there had been a real tip from Pope's much-touted network of "little people" who were the substance of Pope's boast that "we'll get the story whether [the celebrities] talk to us or not." The Burnett situation suggested that the supposedly hundreds-strong little-people network could also serve as a front for fabrication. But whatever happened between Kissinger and Burnett (a smile and a kind word?) needed to be hyped. That was the tabloid formula, reality served up double or triple strength.

The outcome of the jury trial after five years and the kind of play it got in the media seemed to suggest that the tide of opinion was running against the *Enquirer,* even as its circulation was holding strong at about five million. Was American culture schizophrenic, totally fragmented into subcultures, or just hypocritical? At any rate, in the long run-up to the Burnett trial a posse of Hollywood celebrities gathered and galloped behind her. In addition to Burnett's $10 million suit, Ed McMahon, Rudy Vallee, Rory Calhoun, Shirley Jones and her husband Marty Ingels, Phil Silvers, and Paul Lynde were coming at the paper with lawsuits totaling another $52 million.[3] Rory Calhoun was suing over a story that he had cancer, claiming mortal damage to his career, since producers of long film projects are loath to sign on actors with potentially fatal illnesses.

"They told a lie," Calhoun told the *New York Times.* "I don't have cancer, and I hate their guts. I even told them they could have a doctor check me out, but they didn't give retractions. I figure it will be five to eight years before I get to court, but I have a war chest just for this purpose, and I won't drop out."[4]

Raquel Welch was poised to sue after she was savaged in an *Enquirer* story headlined "Pushing 40 and Shunned by Hollywood, Raquel Welch Weds Out of Desperation." Her agent complained that the *Enquirer* ran two negative stories on her after being outbid by Murdoch's *Star* for photos of her wedding. (Welch managed to hold her career and her figure together long after forty and was still making the gossip magazines at sixty-six in 2007.) *Enquirer* reporters did threaten stars with negative stories for failing to cooperate, most memorably when a young green reporter made the mistake of doing so in writing to Michael Landon, of TV's beloved series *Little House on the Prairie.* Landon showed the letter to the Associated Press, which put the story on the national wires. Pope summarily fired the reporter, who went right on to write a best-selling book about Elvis Presley.

The celebrity libel posse's hope was to put Pope out of business, just as celebrities had ganged up on the gossip rag *Confidential,* the scourge of Hollywood in the fifties. Maureen O'Hara had sued the magazine over a story that she behaved indecorously in a movie theater, and Robert Mitchum followed suit for a story that he covered himself with ketchup at a party, called himself a hamburger or hotdog, and asked a woman to eat him. After *Confidential* was raked by the celebrity broadsides, the magazine backed down, cleaned up its format, and eventually foundered and sank to an inglorious end. The group lined up behind Burnett hoped to do as much to the *Enquirer,* although *Confidential*'s lack of sexual decorum had been a factor in its demise: *Confidential* was *dirty.* Since then American culture had been through a sexual revolution, and a close reading of the supermarket version of the *Enquirer* confirmed that its pages were far less explicit than a mainstream bodice ripper. When the *Enquirer* wrote romance, even illicit lovers did little more than hold hands and gaze into each other's eyes.

Nevertheless, the celebrity posse's goal seemed within the realm of possibility. "It is apparent that many of the celebrities involved feel a spiritual commitment to fight the *Enquirer*," the *New York Times* reported (or editorialized), "no matter what the emotional or financial cost."[5] The *Times* explained that a "wave of revulsion" had spread through Hollywood following callous stories that gleefully spotlighted Steve McQueen's death agonies from lung cancer, or cruelly blamed Mary Tyler Moore for her son's suicide in a story headlined "Too Busy to Give Him Love He Craved—Son Killed Himself."

When the shockingly enfeebled Steve McQueen found himself stalked by Pope's reporters as he sought last-resort alternative therapy for his lung cancer in Mexico, he decided to break his own story. He did so in a halting, raspy voice as he gasped for breath, speaking to his public through the mainstream media. Haydn Cameron, who was fielding publicity for the *Enquirer*, seemed to regard the situation as a spirited game: "They knew the *Enquirer* was going to publish, and they scooped us!" he crowed to the *Times*. Likewise, he defended the cruel story on Moore's son's suicide: "We understand we were right on that story, too. Factually correct. Facts are facts." Grant Tinker, Moore's ex-husband and the boy's stepfather, proclaimed that there would be no lawsuit: "We have nothing to sue them about in a court of law, only in the court of decency."

Marty Ingels, a former actor turned agent and manager and married to actress Shirley Jones, unburdened his heart to the press. He told how he had studied libel law and noted that California libel statutes made it easier for stars to sue. Under federal law they needed to prove a conspiracy against them, but in California the standard was lower; they needed only to prove "actual malice." Ingels said he was suing after the *Enquirer* "accused me of everything from sleeping with a lamp to being Jack the Ripper. They said I had the most active casting couch in Hollywood. They said I was stealing a) Shirley's children, b) her money, and c) her house. They said Shirley was too drunk to go to work, so they had to close down the set of her television series every afternoon."[6]

Carroll O'Connor, who played TV's Archie Bunker, complained about the *Enquirer*'s negative research. He said that Pope sent reporters to Rome to find the natural parents of his adopted son and combed his grade-school records looking for dirt. He also complained that *Enquirer* reporters often pretended to be from prestigious mainstream publications. He cited a story on his son written by an *Enquirer* reporter pretending to be from a British women's magazine.* She said she was doing a story on women and charity work, he claimed, but actually she was composing a maudlin file on how his son was dying from cancer. O'Connor also accused the *Enquirer* of offering two secretaries at his production company thousands of dollars to spy on him and disclose his salary.

---

* This was a common practice at the *Enquirer*, although eventually, under pressure, Pope required his staff reporters to correctly identify themselves when working stories. However, this decree did not apply to freelancers. Likewise, in Florida secretly taping a source without permission was a felony, but in many other states a freelancer could do so legally. Certain staffers were stationed in different locations, including California, Washington, and New York, and whatever legal loopholes geography permitted, the *Enquirer* exploited.

O'Connor's lawyers counseled him against suing over several *Enquirer* stories, but he still felt like mooning a chartered helicopter of chopperazzis taking photos over his Malibu house. "Can you imagine a shot of your behind in the *Enquirer*?" his wife reportedly hissed, dragging him back. "That's just what they want!"[7]

There can be little doubt that many of the *Enquirer* stories were heavy-handed and clumsy, often crossing over to the callous and cruel. How much did this have to do with Pope's personality, the lack of humor, finesse, and general social skills that were so often observed in his own editorial offices? Val Virga, who rose from an editorial assistant to head the photo department in her many years of serving the *Enquirer,* used the word *schadenfreude* to describe Pope's attitude: gleeful delight in other's misfortunes. "That sums Pope up," she said. Humor or irony that would soften or temper negative stories was generally ground out by the merciless tabloid prose machine Pope had fashioned. The Burnett item that went so horribly awry was a perfect example of *Enquirer* prose at its worst. No wonder the stars hated the paper. Only rarely was there a tempering flash of cosmic irony, as in the unglamorous portrait of Donald Trump's life in Palm Beach (seen through the eyes of a maid he fired), which consisted of sequestering himself in his Mar-a-Lago bedroom wearing wrinkled shirts or pajamas and talking on the phone all day while he lived on tinned oysters and diet cola.

The trial of Burnett's libel suit against the *Enquirer* opened in Los Angeles on March 12, 1981, the fifth anniversary of the publication of the offending item.

"It's been like a five-year-old toothache," Burnett told a reporter. "I'm very relieved that we've finally gotten it into court. I feel like 'Rocky' in the movie. I've stayed the course."[8]

The *New York Times* noted that "Miss Burnett has become a symbol for a growing group of entertainment figures who have sued the *Enquirer* in recent years in what they contend is a battle against sensational journalism" and reported that the *Enquirer* was defending itself on First Amendment grounds, freedom of the press.[9] "Carol Burnett did not suffer from the story," the *Enquirer*'s lawyer informed the press. Generoso Pope was on the list of prospective witnesses, but in the pretrial maneuvering he was removed as a defendant, along with a reporter and Iain Calder, the executive editor. The judge refused, once again, a motion to dismiss the lawsuit. Pool reporters from radio and television were allowed into the courtroom, and the trial was eagerly attended and widely covered by the mainstream press. The trial of sensational journalism was itself a sensation.

Pope's lawyers called no witnesses at all during the seven-day trial. One of the key issues was whether the *Enquirer* was a magazine or a newspaper, a crucial distinction because the retraction Pope had published, which Burnett called a "bouquet of crabgrass," would carry weight if it was deemed a newspaper, but not if it was ruled a magazine. The judge decided that the *Enquirer*, which had always considered itself a newspaper and was still published in black and white at the time of the offending item, was a magazine because it was stapled, a ruling that was later called puzzling, even perverse.

Enquirer reporter Steve Tinney revealed in a deposition that, although his byline appeared on the article, he had not trusted the source, and the item had in fact been written by a senior editor. This was an example of how tabloid bylines did not signify the same authenticity as bylines in the mainstream press and often were, as in this case, something of a ruse. Greg Lyon, another reporter, testified that he'd been asked to check the item's accuracy an hour before deadline but had been unable to do so to his own satisfaction.[10] He said a senior editor had pressured him to give approval. Such testimony indicated why *Enquirer* stories usually came out the way Pope and his senior editors wanted them.

During the trial, on his *Late Show* Johnny Carson lit into the *Enquirer,* which had published stories about his marital problems. He later dared the paper to come after him for slander. "I'm available," he taunted. As a result of his outburst, the judge dismissed two jurors who disclosed that they had watched the program.

The jury deliberated for three days.

"It's like waiting to have my children," Burnett told reporters.

"It's like waiting for my draft notice," said William Masterson, who presented the *Enquirer*'s case.

On the fourth day the jury decided in Burnett's favor and awarded $1.3 million in punitive damages and $300,000 in general damages.

"The verdict is an affront to the First Amendment and on appeal it cannot stand," the *Enquirer*'s lawyer protested. "This is almost the equivalent of capital punishment for a corporation." The amount of the damages was thought to be half the net worth of the *Enquirer.*

Burnett smiled, then choked back tears. Her producer husband, Joseph Hamilton, said, "I don't think this decision will hurt good journalism; it will hurt bad journalism, yellow journalism." Burnett said she would give some of her award to charity.

For a while it seemed that the mainstream press agreed with Hamilton. The *New York Times* sensed "a lack of outrage" in publishing circles after the verdict: "According to journalists and lawyers specializing in First Amendment cases, the lack of outrage stems primarily from a deep ambivalence about the *Enquirer* and its methods. . . . Many journalists say they cannot be comfortable riding in the same First Amendment boat with the *Enquirer*. Reg Murphy, editor of the *San Francisco Examiner,* has called the *Enquirer* 'a disgrace to journalism' that should not be defended because it 'has not played with the same rules with everybody else in the country.' "[11]

But the size of the award came very much to concern the nation's press, which might eventually be sinking in the same boat with the *Enquirer* after all. The Supreme Court presided over by Warren Burger had been decidedly unfriendly to the press on First Amendment issues, and it was possible that the Burnett case would end up on the steps of the high court. Experts noted that while the Burnett case by itself would not set much of a precedent, the appeals process, which the *Enquirer* immediately began, would. But, after noting that the higher court should reduce the damages award, the *New York Times* nevertheless sermonized in an editorial: "The verdict is no blow to a free press. It posts a warning for extra care where that warning is most needed, in the gossip sheets that thrive on tarnished images of celebrities." The editorial ended: "Provided only that her financial award is not left at a prohibitive level, Carol Burnett's vindication does not imperil the Bill of Rights any more than it does the *Enquirer*."[12] That might have been wishful thinking. A few days later the paper quoted Burke Marshall, a former assistant attorney general then teaching at Yale Law School: "It is dangerous to let juries award damages because a publication is so irritating, nasty and offensive."[13]

A few days later, James Goodale, general counsel of the *New York Times,* parsed out the implications of the Burnett case in an op-ed piece: "First, did the 1976 gossip column item ruin Carol Burnett? No one's career seems to be burning brighter, and no comedienne seems more popular with the public." He suggested that the $1.3 million punitive damages awarded by the jury was intended to put the *Enquirer* out of business, and that sent a chill through all the press. The punitive award, said Goodale, "threatens the First Amendment, and it hangs like a dark cloud over the press."[14]

In May an appeals judge cut Burnett's award in half, to $800,000, and denied the *Enquirer* a new trial. Superior Court Judge Peter Smith said that the court had the distinct impression that the defendants had no remorse and noted that the journalist "who started this whole travesty" had been promoted to gossip columnist. "This defendant engages in a form of legalized pandering intended to appeal to the readers' morbid curiosity," he added. While he believed the original award was "clearly excessive," Smith said, "For the *National Enquirer* to contend it was not guilty of actual malice and that the article was not libelous borders on absurdity."[15]

In June Burnett said that she would donate $100,000 of her award to the undergraduate journalism program at the University of Hawaii and $100,000 to the graduate program in journalism at the University of California at Berkeley.[16]

Two years later, in July 1983, the state court of appeals gave Burnett the choice of accepting another cut in her award, to $200,000, or undergoing a new trial. She took the cut. One of the three-judge panel, Lester Roth, wrote, "We have no doubt the conduct was reprehensible and was undertaken with the kind of improper motive which supports the imposition of punitive damages."[17]

The court battle went on one more stage until, in October 1983, the California Supreme Court denied without comment petitions from both Burnett and the *Enquirer* for review of the case. The lawsuit would not after all go to the U.S. Supreme Court.

By this time Burnett's celebrity posse had melted away, except for Shirley Jones and her husband, Marty Ingels, who were still suing for $20 million over a 1979 article saying Jones was too drunk to go to work on her TV series because Ingels had driven her to drink. They settled in April 1984 for an undisclosed amount after a pretrial conference with a Los Angeles Superior Court judge who was to decide the amount of the settlement. An unusual part of the settlement was a requirement that the *Enquirer* publish a detailed, five-paragraph retraction, which would then belong to Ingels and Jones to publish wherever and whenever they wanted. Ingels said they would republish the retraction as paid ads in *Daily Variety*, the *Hollywood Reporter*, the *New York Times*, the *Los Angeles Times*, the *Washington Post*, and the *Chicago Tribune*. Robert Sack, a First Amendment lawyer, told the *New York Times* he had never before heard of such a provision in a libel settlement.[18]

SIXTEEN

WACKY WORLD NEWS (TABLOID II)

By 1979 it became obvious that Pope had to move the *Enquirer* into color. It was the technology of the time, and even more compelling, Murdoch was employing color in the *Star,* whose vivid covers were upstaging the *Enquirer* on the news racks. Color, it was also expected, would boost the *Enquirer's* circulation and attract classy advertising—expectations that were never clearly realized. Rather, color was becoming necessary for the *Enquirer* merely to hold its leading place in the rapidly changing milieu of tabloid journalism. Yet the masterstroke Pope was yearning for turned up in a serendipitous but related development, in his sudden creation of a new cash-cow tabloid.

Characteristically, Pope sought to build his own color plant nearby in the suburban sprawl heading toward the Everglades northwest of Lantana, rather than contract out his color printing, as was becoming standard in the industry. Color plants were immensely more complicated than the black-and-white presses Pope owned south of Lantana near Pompano. The proposed new plant ran into neighborhood opposition in hearings, as there were serious pollution issues with the chemicals involved. Rafe Klinger, who was to become a writer and columnist for the *Weekly World News,* covered the story for the *Palm Beach Post.* "Pope got fed up. He was going to bring a little industry there and nobody wanted it, so he would farm out the printing," Klinger said.[1]

Rather than sell the old-fashioned monochrome presses and write off his loses against taxes, Pope had a stunning idea. He would start a second weekly tabloid from scratch, to be printed on the presses where the *Enquirer* was currently printed. To head the operation, he pirated Phil Bunton, a Scottish-born Fleet-Streeter, who was currently working for Murdoch on his recently acquired *New York Post*. Klinger, who was already freelancing for the *Enquirer*, got in on the ground floor, as the third person Bunton hired. Klinger's starting salary—$28,000—was about half of the *Enquirer's* starting salary, but it was more than twice what Klinger was making on the *Post*. "Within two or three years, I was making over $50,000," Klinger recalled.

As to what the new paper was to be, Pope was vague, according to Klinger. "The new startup was to be more like the old *Enquirer*," he said. "It was going to be, like, bizarre news. Someone actually said it would be like a bizarre, wild *Time* magazine." Over a period of several months a method and a formula were worked out. Klinger was hired in late April 1979. The first issue of the *Weekly World News* wouldn't come out until six months later, in October, when the presses became available after the *Enquirer* switched over to color.

Bunton had been tempted to the United States from London to work on Rupert Murdoch's startup of the *Star* in 1973. "We came over with the idea that we were going to teach the Americans to do tabloid, and then go back to Britain. We were sort of the Peace Corps for tabloids."[2] Bunton stayed on and was working on the *New York Post,* then also owned by Murdoch, when Pope asked him to make a proposal for the new tabloid. "Pope asked for proposals from various people. The general idea was that it would be a kind of retro tabloid. My idea was that it should be a cross between *Time* magazine and the

National Enquirer. I'm embarrassed to say that, because it ended up being nothing of the sort. But Pope liked my idea," Bunton recalled.

Bunton's involvement with the *Weekly World News* represented yet another influx of British tabloid expertise and influence. To a significant degree, Pope gave Bunton independence, so the second tabloid evolved differently. Pope obviously realized that his black-and-white paper couldn't be merely a monochromatic shadow of the *Enquirer.* This fork in the road of tabloid history is another point to study and remark upon the way Pope worked, to reiterate that he was not a man of ideas or theories. He saw a practical opportunity in the idled presses, but he didn't have much of a concept; he needed to pick other people's brains, to continue his catalytic role, whether he consciously understood it as such or not. What little concept there was, by Bunton's account, quickly evaporated.

Nor did Pope have time or energy to devote to a new tabloid: he had all ten fingers in his *Enquirer* pie, and he obviously wanted and enjoyed it that way. He loved the daily operation of his premier tabloid and did not want to back off and become a remote media mogul. It was a significant difference between Pope and the moguls after whom he so self-consciously modeled himself. Late in life Pulitzer roamed the world in his yacht, and during the landmark libel lawsuit brought against him by President Theodore Roosevelt, the court discovered that he had been in the editorial offices of his *New York World* only twice in eighteen years. Hearst stayed in touch with his editors, but by telephone. Dinners at San Simeon in California did not begin until Hearst had finished discussing the lineup of front-page stories with his editors in New York. But Pope reveled in every editorial detail of his leading paper six days a week. He was the ultimate micromanager.

So the *Weekly World News* offices were set up a few blocks from the *Enquirer.* "Pope wanted us to have total freedom," said Bunton. "He said, 'I don't want you contaminated by the paranoia in the Lantana building.' But after three or four months he moved us into the Lantana building, and we became *Enquirer*-ized."

But at this stage Pope was true to his word. "Phil organized everything and he taught everyone how to do everything," recalled Klinger. "Phil was one of the few journalists I ever worked for who really knew everything editorial himself. Phil designed the paper, set it up, and he trained everybody how to do it. I learned a lot from him. Phil is really a top journalist as far as I'm concerned."

Initially Bunton hired three other reporters, one from the *Fort Lauderdale Sun-Sentinel,* one from a New Hampshire daily, and another, a woman, from the *Palm Beach Post.* He hired two clippers and subscribed to 150 to 200 dailies and magazines throughout the country. The clippers' job, according to Klinger, was to spend the day scouring these publications for stories with some sort of bizarre or unusual angle, including crimes, hype-able stories about killer bees and such, and wild medical or health stories. Those early stories were hyped rather than made up. Of course even mainstream journalism hypes stories, sometimes by merely focusing them so intensely, so this was a matter of degree. The paper gleaned its way-outs from the mainstream press, often published as shorts in the back pages, where stories of the Loch Ness monster, Bigfoot, and UFOs ran. "We would redo the stories and expand them, most of them from the mainstream," said Klinger. "We made calls and spoke to sources, though it's possible some sources might not have been as reliable or as acceptable." The paper was taking minute footnotes to American journalism, often two- and three-paragraph fillers, and making them its major focus. But the new tabloid was not as yet fictionalizing.

"Ninety-five to 99 percent of our stories were done that way, in a more or less professional manner," said Klinger. "We would certainly hype them as much as we could. We made them as melodramatic as possible—it was always the highway of horror, or the tower of terror. But that's the way the paper was run, off the clippers."[3]

Bunton's method makes it easy to understand tabloid journalism not as something separate from the mainstream but as part of a continuum. Bunton harvested his raw material from the mainstream, then he tweaked, or refined, it into something more. If news were to be regarded as an addictive substance, Bunton and his crew were like the laboratory workers who refined the raw cocaine leaves or poppy sap into fine white powder.

It's tempting to carry that metaphor further. Distilled and heavily processed substances—from heroin and cocaine to alcohol and sugar—seem always to be addictive, and thus they enter the realm of the dangerous. And dangerous consumables in turn enter the realm of the abject, at least insofar as they can be abused. So the outlaw status of tabloid editors and journalists can be explained in those terms: they are selling a drug, they are the pushers of the media.

By August 1979 the modus operandi was smoothed out. "We would come every day and work ten hours," said Klinger. "After five [o'clock] we would go out and bring beer to the office. Then we'd go out to the Nostalgia at night." The Nostalgia at the time was a sleepy bar on Dixie Highway in Lantana where, by the subtropical blazing afternoons, a few serious drinkers would already be ensconced—usually retirees with time on their hands and probably nostalgia in their hearts. The bar was aptly named. Through the summer Bunton was having his crew write stories, put together issues, and eventually turn out a complete issue every week. Klinger found it strange: "I would do stories, call up people and tell them I worked for the *Weekly World News,* which didn't even exist." The stories and pages were set up and dummied in issues that were running about forty pages, though they were never plated, as they would have been for a real press run. By October, Klinger recalled, there were already nine issues: "So the first month or two of publishing turned out to be kind of easy, because we just started cannibalizing those issues. We'd take stories and freshen them up. We did use a lot of that material." The *Weekly World News,* relying on Pope's own supermarket racks, was an instant success. Incredibly, the first issue sold about 120,000 copies, establishing profitability from day one, with its skeleton crew and offices tucked in a shaded corner of the *Enquirer* building.

"Pope pretty much left the *Weekly World News* on its own," said Klinger, "as he was mainly interested in the *Enquirer.*" Nevertheless, Pope insisted on having every page brought in for his approval and "would make a change or two here and there. Every once in a while he would kill a front-page story." But this was nothing, an afternoon routine of an hour or two, compared with his obsessive devotion to the *Enquirer.* The *Weekly Worlds News's* trajectory went nearly straight up. Relatively soon the circulation reached one million and Pope gave its reporters and editors salary parity with the *Enquirer's* staff. Said Klinger:

> That first issue sold 120,000, and from then on it basically went steadily up. You'd have dips. If it was selling 250,000 it might

dip to 230,000, but all of a sudden it would go to 280,000 or 290,000. It was basically upward with a slight spike downward for a week or so. It was like finding gold; you couldn't lose. Until finally we had an issue that sold 1.1 million, and then several that sold 1 million. And we had been averaging 990,000 for at least a year. Considering this cost nothing, with a small staff, so naturally Pope loved it.[4]

So the *Weekly World News* came as the surprise bonus when the *Enquirer* went to color. The *Enquirer* never topped its 1977 peak of 6.7 million and was leveling off in the 5 millions for the early eighties, which still left it the nation's largest newspaper, as Pope continued to boast. But he was gaining circulation on another front with the *Weekly World News* with very little effort or expense.

Klinger summed it up: "Color for the *Enquirer* never actually raised circulation. And it never got real good advertising, which I think was another idea. While the *Enquirer* held its own and did okay, the *Weekly World News* turned out to be the masterstroke. Pope asked himself, 'What do I do with these useless presses? I can't sell them. If I sell them [at a loss] I'll just have to take a tax write-off. So we'll have a cheap paper and we'll start distributing it,' and whammo, it's making a huge, huge profit, and it's growing like wildfire."[5]

Together the *Weekly World News* and the *Enquirer* covered what was to be the full spectrum of supermarket tabloid journalism. The *News* soon spawned an imitator, the *Sun,* another Mike Rosenbloom clone, which became third in his lineup with the *Globe* and *Examiner*. The *Enquirer, Globe,* and *Star* competed for celebrity gossip and scandal, while the *Sun* and the

News worked the wackiest and weirdest terrain, with the *Examiner* falling somewhere in between. The *News,* followed by the *Sun,* moved into ever more imaginative topography, stretching plausibility to its furthest limits and eventually moving into the realm of totally fictionalized stories. For this they were most often quoted—with gentle ridicule or sarcasm—by the mainstream press. They read very well as satire.

The *News* was first to complete the posthumous story of Elvis Presley, already elevated to pop icon by the *Enquirer*'s reportage of his funeral. Significantly, Elvis's earthly afterlife wasn't a tabloid idea—original ideas weren't really what tabloids specialized in. Their specialty was probing and finding popular culture's mother lode and repackaging it in tabloid form. The Elvis afterlife story came rather offhandedly, according to Rafe Klinger. "It was deadline day, and Eddie Klontz [then managing editor] and Joe West [executive editor] were devoid of an idea for a good front page," Klinger remembered. "Then [reporter] Dick Donovan asked whether they had seen this story on TV the night before. It was about a woman who claimed Elvis was alive. She had written a book she was promoting." Donovan had taped the show, and, as Klinger remembered the incident, another reporter listened to the tape, called the author, and wrote the story. "We didn't even think it was a very special story, but Joe and Eddie put it on the front page and the issue turned out to be our top seller—1.1 million. It wasn't like, 'This is great, we're going to run with it.' They thought they were taking a chance with it."

Months after the success of the first Elvis-is-alive story, *News* reporter Sue Jamison remembered writing a story about a woman who claimed to have lived with Elvis for six weeks. That woman, too, had written a book, and passed a lie detector test arranged by the *Weekly World News* (tabloid-administered lie detector tests became common, and they always came out the way the editors wanted). "Elvis told her not to tell anyone, that he was in hiding," recalled Jamison.[6] It was clear that sighting stories were to be repeated, as a genre, and it was through the Wacky World News that Elvis sightings became a game that continues to this day, with numerous Internet sites where fans can log the details of their latest encounter with their cult icon.*

Other tabloids chimed in with made-up Elvis stories. One of the most interesting was that Elvis and the Beatles had once secretly jammed together and made a tape. The story bounced from tabloid to tabloid, even crossing the Atlantic to the British tabloids, then back again to the United States. As it traveled, the story picked up new details with each telling, and the various independently published versions added a dimension of veracity. The Elvis/

---

* The great body of Elvis material on the Web is extremely short on facts. It might be a natural assumption that current fans would want to fill in their initial sketchy picture of Elvis, since they were unlikely to be old enough to have caught him the first time around, but this is not the case. A surfer can move from Web site to Web site looking for even so elementary a fact as the actual date of his death—August 16—before finding it, and then only in the context of a numerology study that supports the tortured reasoning that Elvis is alive. Elvis has been cut off from the mooring of actual biography in this extreme manifestation of celebrity cult and fetish. This supports John Fiske's observation in *Power Plays, Power Works* that tabloid culture offers its readers an alternative world and can be understood as a form of resistance to mainstream culture. Fiske's alternative world is an interesting way of thinking about how tabloids compete on newsstands with mainstream newspapers that cover local, national, and world news of the day, or of the *Enquirer* competing with the *Wall Street Journal* for the title of the nation's leading newspaper, the former nuts-and-bolts practical finance and the latter shading off into fantasy and the cult of celebrity, thus performing as the extremes of a polarity.

Beatles tape perfectly fit Norman Mailer's definition of a *factoid:* a fact that existed solely in the pages of the press. It also came close to fitting Jean Baudrillard's conception of hyperreality, where images and signifiers in their endless replication in the media become completely cut off from reality and continue to live and multiply independently.

In the early days the *Weekly World News* didn't need to make up UFO stories; the writers could find plenty of them. "I found this psychology professor out in Wyoming or Montana who was investigating UFO phenomena," Klinger recalled. "He would give me a lot of people who would claim to be abducted by UFOs, and I would interview them and write the stories." No doubt many UFO stories were hoaxes, many of them put over by tabloid journalists, but were they all? One *News* reporter said she didn't know whether UFOs were real or not, but she did believe that the person she interviewed believed he had been abducted. The *Weekly World News* worked a paranormal territory only a little to the left of Scully and Mulder in *The X-Files*, and one could well wonder whether that long-running TV series would have been possible had not the tabloids tilled and seeded the paranormal soil beforehand.

By the late eighties the *News* was fabricating many of its stories, because a new editor, Eddie Klontz, according to Klinger, preferred top-of-the-headers, as fictionalized stories with no basis in reality—no clip from the mainstream— were known in tabloid slang. The paper alternated sourced stories and top-of-the-headers, blurring the line between fiction and reality. Blurring that line was part of the craft of tabloid, and one of the complications of the tabloid text. In the eighties tabloid reporters and editors often went on talk shows and proved expert at fogging up any preconceived notions of differences between the tabloid and mainstream press. Tabloid writers enjoyed playing a kind of gotcha game with each other, striving to write stories that would fool even their cohorts, who would be teased into asking, "Did that really happen?" They made up the sources as well as the stories, and their bylines, too, were often parodies (Bill Stern, Steve Czynch, Cash Royale, Vance Lipscombe, Henri Boujean, and of course, most famously, *Weekly World News* My America columnist Ed Anger).

Klinger opened a line of communication between the *News* and the Chinese news agency Xin Wa. Some stories he got from the Chinese were like Ripley's Believe It or Not—for instance, the two-headed man, with pictures. "He had a second face growing out of the side of his head," said Klinger. The Chinese also sold the *News* the story of a 142-year-old man who was getting younger and growing a third set of teeth. The *News* paid $200 for these stories. "It was damned cheap for us but was big money for China," observed Klinger. "The funny thing was that at that time China was closed to the West, but they were doing business with me every week."

Also from the Chinese came pictures of an isolated pocket of people with thick hair growing all over their bodies. The Chinese claimed these people also had psychic powers. Klinger tailored that story into "The Wolf People of China." Another was "The Valley of the White Animals." This packet included pictures of a white deer and a white squirrel, not albinos, and the claim that they all came from the same valley. Klinger believes the Chinese caught on to how the *Weekly World News* worked. "They were confused at first, but I think they were eventually faking it. I'm not sure they didn't spray paint those animals themselves."

The *News* also got kill files from the *Enquirer;* these files contained stories that had been worked to completion but were found lacking, with "Kill—GP" scrawled on them. In many ways the standards, and certainly the standards of plausibility, were lower at the *News*. But often those kill files were better than the stories that ran in the *Enquirer,* according to Klinger. Most *Enquirer* stories were chosen by Pope from leads submitted by reporters and freelancers. If the completed story did not fulfill the lead literally, Pope would usually kill it. Klinger explained:

> GP was very exacting when he would accept a file. If you submitted a lead that a hero wearing red pants saves a school bus full of children and then it turned out the man was wearing green pants, he would put "Kill—GP." This is how he was. You couldn't have anything off-lead. He had a system set up where you got a lead through and the story had better be on-lead. We'd get all these kill files, and some of them were great stories. Some of them were even better than the lead. They had a twist in them that turned out for the better. All this was done by *Enquirer* reporters. We would rewrite them and put them in our paper.[7]

Once in a while in those early days the *Enquirer* and the *News* would work the same story, though the *News,* working on the proverbial shoestring, had no budget for travel. Bunton recalled an instance when both papers covered some kind of natural disaster in the South: "The *Enquirer* had sent ten reporters and we had worked the story by phone, but Pope liked our story better, and he made that clear. Sometimes he used the *News* as a whipping boy for the *Enquirer*." Pope never had a problem with his reporters competing with each other. On the contrary, he loved and fostered competition to the point that the *Enquirer* plant was like an aquarium of journalistic sharks and stingrays.

The *News* and its staff remained a separate, break-off colony in its corner of the Lantana building. *News* reporters and staff were invited to the Friday afternoon buffet and open bar of the era, but they remained segregated there. Said Bunton, "We always stayed together in one corner of the room." He remembers a defining moment the Friday afternoon that John Wayne "died." The *News,* in Pope's mind, had become the fun paper, and its staff had more personal latitude. *News* staffers not only had permission to laugh; they even felt a pressure to be wacky, to perform the zany role Pope was expecting of them. However, on this Friday their laughter annoyed Pope, and he sent someone to talk to them. "This person said, 'Enjoy yourselves, but stop laughing. John Wayne is dying,'" Bunton recalled. "Well, we didn't stop laughing and this person kept looking at us, and I realized this poor guy's job probably hinged on shutting us up. I'll always remember it as the night John Wayne died—only he didn't die. He lived for another two years."[8]

SEVENTEEN

ANGER AS SATIRE

One of the most memorable creations of the *Weekly World News* was the radically conservative columnist Ed Anger. The column was written during Pope's lifetime by Rafe Klinger. Ed Anger is also a good place to examine the motivations and politics so widely discussed in academic readings of tabloid culture. Klinger wrote his first Ed Anger column within four months of the *Weekly World News* startup. He had been nagging Phil Bunton, who didn't think it was right for the paper. Bunton finally told him to write a few samples and he would run a couple for two weeks to see what happened.

Ed's first column was about suicide and what a pity it was that brave firemen and cops had to risk their lives going out on ledges and bridges for crybabies and cowards who didn't have the guts to face this tough life. Ed suggested building towers outside every major city where the crybabies could jump without putting brave cops and firemen at risk. "We got a lot of mail, incredible letters—from people who had attempted suicide, people with relatives who had," Klinger remembered. This sudden, unexpected strong reaction floored Klinger, Bunton, and everyone on the *News*.

The persona of Ed was developed from a real-life prototype. Klinger had just done a story about a right-wing preacher in Florida who was claiming that Fidel Castro and the Commies were going to invade the United States from Cuba:

> This guy was one of those wacko Bible belt preachers, a wild, wild, over-the-top guy. I interviewed him and wrote the story. I was laughing the whole time. I thought, "Why don't we have a column on politics and social phenomena with a guy who is over the top and has all these wacky ideas?" I thought conservative ideas were pretty zany. Naïve me, I thought it was satire. I came up with the name Anger because I realized these fire-and-brimstone preachers were always angry, they were screaming things from the pulpit. I thought, "I'll have to write things angrily."[1]

The column was named My America, by Ed Anger (the Ed came from Klinger's uncle). The column became a hit, and Pope once told Klinger he thought people bought the paper just to read My America, just as people had once bought papers to read Walter Winchell. "He said, 'I know that people buy the *Weekly World News* to read Ed Anger.' I think GP got a kick out of the column, though he never otherwise talked to me about it. I think Pope admired the fact that out of nowhere, out of someone's imagination, came some sort of unique fluke sort of thing, which is what Ed Anger was," said Klinger. So Klinger became one of Pope's favorites, and Pope often asked about him during Friday's afternoon social, where Klinger didn't have a problem performing to Pope's expectations. Klinger had a natural streak of zaniness.

Ed Anger continued to be written, often halfheartedly, by other writers after a rancorous lawsuit over ownership of the column following Klinger's firing in 1989, soon after Pope's death. The corporation won over individual authorship, in a court decision that undermined tabloid authorship, which had never been taken very seriously anyway.* Klinger's original formula was followed rigorously for years, underscoring the problem of the late-stage tabloids: there were only so many variations, and after a while the column seemed a perfunctory imitation of the original. Subsequent writers didn't have Klinger's original touch, the sense and backstory of the character he had created. Klinger was hard to imitate.

---

* The byline in mainstream journalism is still tied to modernist concepts of authorship and intellectual property, while the tabloid byline and story are better understood within postmodern concepts of the death of the author, variously treated by Jacques Derrida, Michel Foucault, Roland Barthes, and others. Formulaic tabloid stories—vampires, Atlantis, the Bermuda Triangle, the Loch Ness monster, killer bees—are clearly palimpsests, overwritten again and again like folktales, and their authors are closer to ancient concepts of shamans and mediators. The rise of tabloid journalism in the seventies and eighties was contemporary with a particularly fertile period for postmodern thinkers, and their conceptualization and analysis of language, semiotics, and images work very well in understanding tabloid culture—for instance, Jean Baudrillard's treatment of images floating free of their signifiers to proliferate independently in media hyperreality—or in applying concepts of postmodern depthlessness fruitfully to tabloid culture.

Fredric Jameson's belief, as stated in "The Cultural Logic of Late Capitalism," that "culture analysis always involves a buried or repressed theory of historical periodization" (559) supports a link between tabloids and postmodern theory, though he leaves tabloids outside his "periodizing hypothesis" of postmodernism "with its degraded landscape of schlock and kitsch, of TV series and *Reader's Digest* culture, of advertising and motels, of the late show and the grade-B Hollywood film, of so-called paraliterature, with its airport paperback categories of the gothic and the romance, the popular biography, the murder mystery, and the science fiction or fantasy novel" (558). We know Pope used the *Reader's Digest* as a model, and his tabloids certainly fit into Jameson's list of schlock and kitsch, though Jameson somehow failed to observe the rapidly rising tabloid culture of the supermarket.

But Ed Anger was hot while Klinger wrote him (he was often read over the air by radio journalists), and it had something to do with his connection with the complex psyche of his originator. Jovial, curly-haired Klinger was a Jewish liberal, and temperamentally a fundamentally gentle man, though he was always thrumming with a high level of energy. Klinger once had a fight with a fellow *News* editor in the parking lot after work and quickly pinned his opponent. No one was hurt. Klinger was a former college wrestler, and his stocky frame was well muscled. He often jogged on the beach after work or played paddleball on the Hawaiian beachfront. Klinger's father was the former director of the American Jewish Congress, the foremost Jewish organization in the civil rights movement of the sixties. Klinger said his father attended rallies with Black Muslims Elijah Mohammed and Malcolm X in Chicago and helped organize the counterdemonstration when the neo-Nazis marched in Skokie in the Chicago suburbs. "The American Jewish Congress was a very aggressive organization for civil rights," said Klinger. "My father knew and worked with Ralph Bunche and Whitney Young and the NAACP people. I was never even exposed to right-wing thinking."[2]

Initially Klinger had a hard time writing the columns: "It was very foreign for me to do it. It would take a long time. I would pick a controversy and then I would take an opposite stand to whatever my personal stand would be, exactly an opposite stand. Then I would try to work myself into a state of anger and I would write angrily." After two years Klinger worked out a formula for the column. It would usually start out with Ed writing, "I'm madder than" something like but other than a wet hen, which varied greatly, maybe madder than "Batman with a run in his tights," or maybe just "pig-biting mad." Exuberantly elaborating his vocabulary was part of the fun. Ed was flagrantly politically incorrect: Arabs were towelheads and Hispanics were Chilipepperese. Feminists were women's libbers and women belonged in the home. Ed liked Vanna White because Vanna, whom the *Enquirer* had turned into a celebrity, was the ultimate helpmate to a man.* San Francisco was San Fransissico. Vegetarians were Broccoli Bruces. Ed's biography was fleshed out. He was a war hero. He had a daughter named Sarah Lee, whom he called "my little cupcake," and a wife, Thelma Jean. Jimbo was his son. Ed believed Americans shouldn't let Pizza Hut and McDonald's open franchises in Russia and China because junk food was what made Americans, who were stronger and smarter, great.

"The Angers sounded kind of southern, but I never thought of Ed as a redneck," said Klinger. "I always though of Ed as the ultimate protector of the Bill of Rights. His bible was the Constitution. That was my philosophy behind Ed. In spite of the fact he sounded conservative, he believed in freedom of speech, and used it all the time. Ed wouldn't be for censorship, but he was a great critic of changing times. He was an upholder of traditional American values."

As Klinger wrote Ed there was a deliberate double edge: "I tried to write things that were outrageously insulting to everybody. Half the people thought Ed was the funniest thing on Earth, like a *Saturday Night Live* skit. Others would say, 'Right on, Ed,' and some would write, 'Ed, you're getting soft, you

---

* Pope himself appeared to feel something special for Vanna White, and this was reflected in both his tabloids. In an interview, Steve Coz said he believed the *Enquirer* created her as a celebrity by constantly covering her: "Vanna White was a nobody, a letter turner on a show with decent ratings [*Wheel of Fortune*]. People wouldn't know her name if the tabloids hadn't kept pounding her on page one. They had the ability to create a soap opera about someone."

haven't gone far enough.' I was getting letters from sixty-year-old people in the Midwest who were saying, 'You're standing up for what I believe in,' and then from college girls inviting me to come out and stay with them." Ed Anger had somehow managed to appeal to nearly everyone: "Ed was accepted by all political spectrums of political life. Conservatives took him seriously and liberals thought he was funny. I struck a line where some people read him seriously and others thought he was a joke."[3]

Nearly all *Weekly World News* writers were former mainstream journalists, like Klinger, and most of what they wrote could be read as satire, too—of the jobs they used to have, of their former selves. Because Ed Anger was a personality, an editorialist, he got letters, which made the interaction with his readers more explicit than in the rest of the paper's editorial content.

"The popularity of Ed was always a surprise to me, and it was a shock to everyone else," Klinger said. "*Enquirer* reporters traveling all over the country were telling me that people were asking about Ed Anger."

Though Pope generally kept his hands off the *News,* he was always watching. Klinger recalls he did kill one Ed Anger column:

> In the seven years I was writing the column in Pope's lifetime, he only killed one column. It was during the time of the airline hijackings. Ed wrote that they ought to hand out guns as passengers got on planes, then we'd see what the hijackers feel like doing. I had to rewrite the column. Really it was kind of a takeoff on one of the earliest Ed Angers I did, which was even a bit wilder. I said that American cities were so dangerous instead of controlling guns, we should have gun vending machines in subway

stations, and instead of food stamps we should have gun stamps so poor people could buy guns and ammo.[4]

Pope met with the *News* staff only twice, according to Klinger, and that was to deliver his standard rap about how he wanted stories that women hanging out clothes in the backyard remarked to each other about over the fence. "One woman turns to the other and she says, 'Did you hear about this story?'" Klinger remembered Pope telling the staff. "He said every paper should have two or three of those stories." Backyard fences, kitchen tables, husbands and wives seemed always on Pope's mind when he talked about his paper. Pope truly did want to know, as he asked in his editorial meetings, what America was thinking. He couldn't do much direct research himself, given his strangely cloistered life, but there was one place where he did, according to Steve Coz. As a creature of habit, Pope had his hair cut at a local barbershop near the *Enquirer,* at the corner of Dixie Highway and Ocean Avenue, though sometimes the barber came to him at the office. "He always asked the barber—Dave was his name, I think—what everyone was talking about," said Coz. "He always wanted to know what the average Joe was talking about."[5] Val Virga remembered that Pope had his mission statement, several pages long, committed to paper: "He quoted Hearst. He quoted Pulitzer. He said, 'If you want to know what to put on the cover, just go down to the bar, to the barber, to the beauty shop and just listen to what people are talking about.' He wasn't telling you what to do. He was following cultural trends."[6]

Klinger had one other talk with Pope, in the late hours of the yearly Christmas party, when the then teenage Paul Pope invited everyone over to the Manalapan house on the beach, almost surely against his parents' wishes. "I'm sure Lois was livid," said Klinger, "and I'm sure GP didn't want to do it either, but they were committed and they wanted to be gracious, and they were very gracious." Pope gave a tour, showing off the windshield washers on the big picture window in the living room overlooking the ocean, which cleaned off the salt spray when the Atlantic was rough, and took them to the basement-level garage, where he kept a big white Rolls Royce he hardly ever drove.

On the couch drinking Scotches, the small group with Pope was getting buzzed and waxed nostalgic about the old days in New York. Klinger thought Pope was talking about "his tremendous fondness for old-time journalism." Pope also, once again, shared his ideas about what made the *Enquirer* a success. It was about the formula. "That was his theory: you cover the factors. It was an engineer's answer," Klinger remembered. It's possible Pope's engineer's education had more effect on him than was readily obvious. Klinger always thought he saw a scientist in Pope, but he also saw something else: "I personally thought Pope was bullshitting himself. He had the magic touch; he had a good feeling for what the common man thought. His favorite TV show was *Hogan's Heroes*. What made him laugh made the average American laugh. What he found interesting was what the average American found interesting. He was way too smart to have this kind of sensibility—but he wasn't an intellectual. He also believed in spending money to make money." Klinger also thought Pope had luck, that the *Enquirer* was "a lucky phenomenon"—like the *News*'s Elvis-is-alive story, and famous Ed Anger himself.

EIGHTEEN

SECOND PEAK
(TWO GARDENERS' STORIES)

There was nothing architecturally distinguished about the building Pope put up off Dixie Highway to house his paper. The *Enquirer*'s one-story, flat-roofed building was low profile, largely hidden from view by high hedges. The utilitarian structure was sprawling and comfortable and had a great deal of glass, offering views from inside of many varieties of flowering plants, shrubs, trees, and happy squirrels and birds. The modest building harmonized nicely with the neighborhood's small, lower-middle-class homes, most of them one-story cinderblock bungalows built during Florida's second land boom in the fifties. Across from the *Enquirer*'s parking lot, in the shadow of the Lantana water tower, was a red-dirt baseball diamond, used by the local Little Leaguers that Pope sponsored in his early days in the building. Unlike the grand multistoried buildings that housed Hearst's and Pulitzer's newspapers, the *Enquirer* had a modest, suburban middle-class ambience. Like the bungalow dwellers around him, Pope loved and cared for his lawn. Pope and his tabloids were just like them, and he was a modest man of the people.

Pope obviously didn't care much about architecture. But he was particularly fussy and proprietary about the gardens spread across seven campuslike acres, and this was where he focused his pride. His character was revealed as surely amid the lawns, leaves, and flowers as in the editorial offices. If nature could be controlled, Pope would control it, and he was as obsessive in the garden as in the office. A sign visible from the highway announced the presence of the *Enquirer,* itself invisible within its bower, and flashed the temperature. If the temperature reading Pope heard on the radio in his short drive across the Intracoastal to work was different from the sign's digital figure, he had someone on it within minutes. The sign had to be right.

The hedges had to be trimmed by hand, one branch at a time, with inch-and-a-half shears: Pope thought they looked more natural that way. "As a result it took three gardeners three days to do what could have been done with a power trimmer in a matter of hours," according to Mike Harris, Pope's last head gardener. The hedge's height had to be exact, so the gardeners kept a length of polyvinyl pipe to measure with. Likewise the lawns had to be mowed to three and a half inches. The use of power tools was forbidden in the garden after 9:00 a.m. so that the editors, writers, and reporters could concentrate— though the gardeners blasted the parking lots with the leaf blowers at 7:00 a.m. with no regard for the neighbors' comfort. But then wasn't the noise of landscaping power tools a comforting sound in suburbia anyway? Nor did Lantana people sleep late on workdays.

Heads rolled in the garden as surely as they did in the editorial offices. Gardeners didn't last long, especially head gardeners. The closer employees got to dealing directly with Pope, the less their job security. To recruit Harris, Pope hired the New York–based executive search firm Korn/Ferry International. When Harris was first approached, he said, "I'm not a gardener; I'm a landscaper." When Harris found out what kind of money Pope was paying, he said, "Okay, for that kind of money I'll be a gardener."[1]

Harris managed to charm Pope during his first interview, when he was called out to the Manalapan house on the beach for a consultation: "Pope asked how come he could see his neighbors now when he couldn't five years ago. I explained that his Australian pines had grown up and were shading out the sea grapes, which were dropping their leaves." Harris also noticed that Pope wasn't taking full advantage of the landscaping possibilities of Florida's subtropical climate, but fortunately he kept his mouth shut about that. "Pope didn't like palm trees. He liked things to look like they did in New York, shrubby." Harris was an expert on palm trees.

When Harris got back to the grounds, office manager Joe Chin told him that if he didn't screw up, he had a job for life. Chin said Pope had called him and told him to do whatever Mike said to do. Chin said Pope had never said such a thing about anyone within his hearing. "That's really good," Chin told Harris, "and it's good for me because I hired you."[2]

Naturally those orders about doing what Mike said applied to everyone but Pope himself. He always ordered two thousand pounds of a nitrogen-based fertilizer to be put down in March. "It rained a lot in March, and we would get lots of fungus; then we'd be putting fungicides in all summer," Harris recalled. When he and Chin discussed telling Pope he should hold off on the fertilizer till after the rains, the office manager asked him, "Do you like working here?" Harris bit his tongue. Later when Pope sent him to a horticulture seminar, Harris's view on fungicides was confirmed, but he did not tell Pope. Pope also liked to water the lawns, at home and on the grounds, in the late afternoon. Harris knew that was the worst time. "The grass would be wet all night and fungus would set in." But Harris preferred to fight fungus rather than tell Pope how to prevent it. He said he did come to wonder why Pope was paying for his expertise if Pope just wanted someone to follow his orders. Sometimes Harris felt a straight laborer might have done the job as well.

Once Pope was convinced that the gardener who mowed his lawn at home was not keeping to the prescribed three and a half inches. "So I went out to his house and crawled on my belly from the porch to the seawall measuring the grass every six inches with Pope's specially marked ruler," Harris recalled. This was the kind of humiliation on the cross of Pope's obsessiveness and willfulness that nearly everyone who worked in direct contact with him experienced at some time or another. There was an often repeated saying at the *Enquirer* that you left your ego on the doorstep when you entered the building. Pope demanded obedience at all times, and many found this humiliating, especially the many free spirits of journalism. The conflict between a boss who exerted such authority and an instinctively transgressive staff exerted a constant tension.

One day Pope called the gardeners about a weed he saw from his office window. The crew went out and weeded all morning. The next day Pope called again and said the weed was still there. The gardeners went over the territory again. The third day Pope called the office manager and asked if the gardeners were playing games with him. They went out again and looked and looked and couldn't find a single weed. Then a location was called in. "It was at the base of a silk oak," said Harris. "We went and looked. It was a yellow bougainvillea we had planted on Pope's orders, grown to about a foot and a half tall." They ripped it out and did not remind Pope that the offending botanical was not a weed but a species he had personally ordered them to plant. In the garden as well as in the newsroom, the correct procedure when Pope gave contradictory orders was to follow his most recent demand. The garden was, to use a scientific term, a homology to the editorial offices; both operated by the same principles: submit to Pope's often self-contradictory, always authoritarian personality.

Pope never put on a front, certainly not to his employees. He wore a Timex watch and never bothered to dress well, any more than he ever bothered to explain his editorial tactics to his staffers. Their job was to carry out orders. That made the discourse that nevertheless went on between Pope and his journalists even more interesting and complex. On the matter of covering the British royals, Pope could go from strongly against to strongly pro without anything much in the way of perceptible discussion. When British reporters tried to float stories about Britain's royal family, a staple of tabloid journalism across the pond, Pope waved them away. "Americans don't care about kings and princesses," he would say. However, after the Brits slipped some prince-and-princess stories through, perhaps by way of Princess Grace of Monaco and her daughters, Stephanie and Caroline, Pope saw that Americans *were* interested. Grace's pretty, lively daughters were staples of what passed for tabloid culture in Europe. There would be stories in Spain's *Hola!* or France's *Paris Match* about their romantic antics nearly every week. But discussion of matters like this was clearly beneath Pope's tolerance. Pope always conformed to the most rigid construction of masculine leadership, where to take suggestions from lesser creatures would be inappropriate.

So coverage of British royalty tabloid-style was brought to the *Enquirer* and then to the whole nation courtesy of the *Enquirer*'s British reporters. When Diana Spencer became Princess Di with her marriage to Prince Charles in 1981, the *Enquirer* covered the fairy-tale wedding, then moved on to extend coverage to Sarah Ferguson, the Duchess of York, and her royal husband, Prince Andrew. Pope's initial tabloid coverage of Randy Andy, Fergie, Charles, and Di had a role in catapulting Di to international celebrity on the monumental scale the world saw upon her death in a Paris car crash in 1997. The divorced Di, on the outs with Buckingham Palace, transcended even the homage owed to her as a British royal. It was also clear that she in turn was helping push the royals into the celebrity category long established for film, TV, and music stars. As they were elevated to stand beside the new royals of celebrity culture, the princes, princesses, and duchesses of the old feudalism were elevated to a new importance in the eyes of Americans. We didn't care about royals in politics, but as celebrities they caught our interest. Americans, against the prevailing journalistic wisdom, eagerly tuned in to the royal British soap opera brought to them by the *Enquirer*'s British reporters.

When Steve Coz rose to become an articles editor, or AE, he would come in, like many of Pope's editing cadre, on Saturday mornings, especially if he had an important story working. Like Tom Kuncl, he was intrigued with Pope's habitual attire for these sessions. He noted the slippers and the mystery of the shorts/bathing suit/pajama bottoms: "They were threadbare and knee-length, and the shirt looked like it had been washed with all the colors." Coz talked with Pope about several stories and, significantly, noted that the boss's editorial concerns and judgments were always based on the reader. "It was really very simple," said Coz. "Every single aspect of what he was doing was for the reader."

The most telling conference Coz remembered was over the gory death of actor Vic Morrow and two children, who were chopped to bits when a helicopter went out of control shooting a stunt sequence in a combat scene for the *Twilight Zone* movie. Coz spent forty-five minutes with Pope patiently reconciling the story with the photos and working out a theory as to how all the body parts ended up where they were. Pope could be unnervingly literal about details: "Pope didn't understand how half his body could be here and the other half ten feet away. I put the story together and he reread it and still didn't understand. Then I figured out that one, and I got another set of questions. It was always him saying, 'If the readers read this, they're not going to understand how the body parts ended up in different places.' It's very specific to the reader, which I think was what he brought to journalism."[3]

The second-highest-selling issue of the *Enquirer* involved the death of Princess Grace, the beauty from Philadelphia remembered for starring as Alfred Hitchcock's favorite icy blonde in *To Catch a Thief, Rear Window,* and *Dial M for Murder.* In 1956 Grace Kelly had ended her film career at a peak, after working with such leading men as Cary Grant, Gary Cooper, James Stewart, William Holden, and Clark Gable, to marry her real Prince Charming, Prince Rainier of Monaco—whom she met while filming *To Catch a Thief* on the prince's turf—and to enter, at least in the eyes of much of her public, a real-life fairy-tale world. At the age of fifty-two, on September 14, 1982, she died after she apparently suffered a stroke the day before while driving on a winding mountain road, arguing with her daughter Stephanie, seventeen. Grace's Rover veered off the road and careened down a forty-five-foot embankment. Stephanie escaped with minor bruises, but Grace died in the hospital. Closer scrutiny confirmed that she was not living in a fairy tale, and for years stories persisted that the stroke had been brought on by her fierce argument with Stephanie over her plans to marry Paul Belmondo, son of the famous French actor Jean-Paul Belmondo, who starred in Jean-Luc Godard's *Breathless* with Jean Seberg.

Through a fortunate coincidence the *Enquirer* got an early beat on the story, and Pope moved decisively to capitalize on his lead time of several hours before the other tabloid jackals closed in. Coz, as a story editor, was supervising freelancer Martin Dunn, who was in Philadelphia with a Kelly relative, an aunt, working a story on Grace that had nothing to do with the accident. Reports had come over the wires, either rumors or deliberate distracters floated by the palace in Monaco, that Grace had broken her leg in an auto accident. A very senior editor, Charlie Parmiter, was working the broken-leg lead that had come over the wires, but Dunn called Coz and told him Grace was dead: "I'm sitting here with the aunt," Dunn told Coz, "and she's just got a call from the palace and she's crumpled in tears."

Coz believed him. However, in the volatile and competitive newsroom of the *Enquirer,* the relatively green Coz was rebuffed: "Parmiter went crazy; he was screaming, 'It's not true!' and stood there raving at me."[4]

Coz told Dunn to go out and buy some flowers and get back into the aunt's apartment: "She let him back in, and he sat there through the whole thing while she was communicating with the palace about how they were going to announce Grace was dead. Then Parmiter realized the information was rock solid and went storming in and told the executive editor. That's when GP got involved, and that's when the private plane went over."

Pope acted decisively, sending twelve reporters to Monaco in a Learjet. A second wave arrived by commercial jet, including a reporter with $50,000 cash in his backpack. The *Enquirer* hounds, first on the scene, found the last person to see Grace, a gardener who had seen the crash in front of his house.

He had run down to help and talked to her as she lay dying. "They nailed the gardener and took him away and babysat him," said Coz, citing the standard *Enquirer* practice.

The gardener's story, it turned out, was a world exclusive. "The picture for that time was of the gardener pointing to a spot in the road [where Grace had veered off]," Coz recalled. "Our cover was a beautiful picture of her with a black background—I think that was the first time we used the black background."

This became the *Enquirer*'s second-biggest seller at 6,640,000 and reflected the speed and ingenuity of Pope's reporters, as well as his judgment, support, and wealth.[5] Coz estimated that Pope spent $300,000 to $400,000 covering the story. "Those were eighties dollars," said Coz. "What would that be now? Maybe a million and a half?" Obviously the outlay was worth it. "Pope knew this was about an icon, what everyone would be talking about, that this transcended news, which was the way everyone else was thinking about it," said Coz. "It was nice to have a guy so rich that he doesn't care about money."

Grace's death would have been noted as news in any cultural climate, but the degree to which tabloid culture was infiltrating other media could be remarked in how the mainstream media would cover Grace's death, and how close this news about her death would move to the front of the lineup. The day of Grace's death coincided with the debut of *USA Today*, which, after an intense debate in the newsroom, would play her death as its lead story. As America's first truly national paper, *USA Today* would steal many tabloid tricks, both in the writing and presentation of stories—punchy, bulleted, in short form—and in their substance. September 14, 1982, when Grace died, would mark a significant connection between tabloid and mainstream culture. McPaper, as *USA Today* would soon be nicknamed, was seeking a truly mass circulation, and in that realm the *Enquirer* was the leader in print culture.

The obvious traditional hard-news choice for the lead story that September 15 was the violent death of Lebanese president-elect Bashir Gemayel after a TNT explosion toppled two floors of concrete atop him, dashing hopes for ending Lebanon's civil war. But *USA Today*'s new managing editor, Nancy Woodhull, argued, "More readers will want to know about Princess Grace."[6] She was the only editor on the editorial floor of the new paper's offices in McLean, Virginia, who wanted to play Grace as the lead, but chairman Al Neuharth's unconventional vision for the new paper backed her up 100 percent. *More* readers was the operational word: *more* weighed heavier than *consequential* or *important. USA Today* reduced Gemayel to a brief, while the *New York Times,* the *Los Angeles Times,* and the *Washington Post* led with his death.

By the mid-eighties Pope had stabilized the *Enquirer*'s formula, and the bloodbath firings were over. There was no lawsuit equivalent to Carol Burnett's, though libel suits were still a cost of doing business. Small nuisance suits were settled out of court, and the threat of the scorpion defense proved enough to hold off the big cases.* There were, to be sure, subtle changes of method, but

---

* The obvious lesson of the Burnett libel suit was that it wasn't worth suing the *Enquirer* because even if you won, you lost. Vincent Chieffo, a veteran Los Angeles entertainment lawyer christened the tactic "the scorpion defense: You don't attack a scorpion because you're going to get stung" ("Now the Story Can Be Told! How Tabloids Survived the Recession," *Business Week,* 7 November 1983).

the *Enquirer* sailed more or less smoothly through reasonably charted waters. Circulation was relatively stable, though the trajectory still floated slowly down, and the best explanation for that was the leaking of tabloid fare into the mainstream. It would take Pope's Enquiring Minds advertising campaign to keep the *Enquirer*'s numbers up, but the paper was still a cash cow. His ad campaign apparently benefited his clone-like competitors and the *Star,* too. After the *Star* began running ads, Pope noticed that the *Enquirer*'s circulation went up as well. Apparently readers of supermarket tabloids had rather indiscriminate tastes, and the ads boosted the voracious appetite for all the tabloids. But the *Enquirer*'s place at the top of the racks and its lead in the market were maintained, and all his life the *Star* ran a distant second place, a million or more behind the *Enquirer* in circulation. Pope was like a homeowner who had built his house with his own hands—there was no mortgage on the *Enquirer,* no debt whatsoever. Yet it was abundantly clear that the steep growth of the seventies was over.

Pope was mellowing; there were fewer impulsive firings. In fact, in the eighties Pope instituted a practice that seemed to avert editorial firings altogether and was based entirely on performance. Computers were now tracking reporters' productivity, so when a reporter's "numbers" were down, he or she was put on "thirty days." A reporter who didn't improve within a month would be fired. In practice, reporters always improved, usually with a burst of frenetic energy. They were in a spot, in danger of losing the best-paying journalistic job in the nation, and facing the fact that, marked with tabloid's stain, they would likely be unemployable in the mainstream. They would have no choice but to enter the whirlpool of the Tabloid Triangle, where many sank, eventually, out of sight.

An alcoholic writer on the *Weekly World News* was the rare exception to the success of the thirty-days program. He was a spectacular alcoholic among a tribe of alcoholic journalists. Drinking and drugging went on nightly at a rowdy pace in the Lantana bars. On Friday afternoons reporters even drank martinis out of paper cups in the back row of the *Enquirer* newsroom, getting a head start. The really wild ones would leave lines of cocaine for each other on the tops of the toilet cisterns in the men's room. Pope sent the *News* writer to rehab for a month. On his return he hung out at the Hawaiian tiki bar sadly drinking club soda for a few weeks, where anyone who knew about rehabilitation knew he'd soon be drunk again. One day, coming back from lunch drunk, he weaved into Lois Pope in the hallway. He was gone the next day. In the next few months he sadly and determinedly drank himself to death.

Princess Grace's death marked one major intersection of tabloid and mainstream journalism. Gary Hart's swan dive from the presidential primaries in 1987 marked an even closer conjunction, more important because, anomalously for the *Enquirer,* it involved politics, or seemed to. That spring the *Miami Herald* and the *Washington Post* were writing stories about the Colorado senator's womanizing—and staking out his Washington digs in true tabloid fashion. Both papers were carving nicks into the candidate's hide, but the final slash was delivered by the *National Enquirer.* The *Enquirer*'s interest in the story in turn marked a movement toward the mainstream by the nation's leading tabloid. The *Enquirer* had never been concerned with politics per se, though, significantly, executive editor Iain Calder said he saw the Hart scandal purely as a celebrity story. Perspectives had changed since the days when a priapic president like Jack Kennedy would be accorded silence and a sportsman's knowing wink from the press. Presidents had always been in the spotlight by virtue of their power, but this was the limelight that bathed glamorous celebrities who were not powerful in political terms. It was a considerable cultural change that seemed to revoke the privileges of both power and gender. Presidents, as we would eventually see with Bill Clinton, were coming to be valued for their entertainment value as well.

The end of Hart's candidacy came in the form of photos of the monkey business aboard a yacht of that name: Donna Rice wearing her *Monkey Business* T-shirt sitting in Hart's lap. No one could have any doubts about what was going on: the private photo completely contradicted Hart's unimaginative story that Donna was "only a friend." Other photos, which the *Enquirer* ran inside, also taken by one of the other women on the trip, showed the senator clowning in a Bahamas nightclub, grinning maniacally and holding maracas. The days of allowing presidential candidates a private life seemed over.

Fearing that the story wouldn't hold for the few days before its next edition, the *Enquirer* released the news in the form of a taped interview with Calder. Pope was also worried that the money he had paid for the photos would become a distracting issue. Calder, who negotiated the deal with the woman's lawyer, still refuses to name the amount, but other sources suggested it was between $25,000 and $50,000[7] or a package that included photos and the story for $75,000.[8] Pope was surprised at the amount, whatever it was. "That's a lot of money," he told Calder, who quickly reassured him that the photos were worth twice the amount. It *was* a lot of money for the time, but the photos proved definitely worth it for establishing another tabloid benchmark. To the straitlaced Pope it was also incredible that a man in Hart's position would pose for such photos. "What an idiot," he muttered, when he saw the photos.[9] Hart, knowing how thoroughly he was skewered, bowed out of the presidential race before the issue hit the stands.

Here, of course, the *Enquirer* seemed to be engaged in politics, more deeply and efficiently than the *Miami Herald* and the *Washington Post* (which would not, however, pay for stories). The *Enquirer* had reportedly passed on the *Monkey Business* photos weeks earlier: the trip had been in March, but the *Enquirer* didn't run the pictures until June 2. But after the *Herald* and *Post* started covering the candidate, the issues seemed to be girl-chasing and marital infidelity, and Hart was suddenly caught in the crosshairs of tabloid journalism. Calder insisted that the *Enquirer* ran the photos because the paper came to see Hart as a celebrity and covered him as such.

The *Enquirer*'s story probably significantly altered the course of American politics, even though it's not likely either Pope or Calder had particularly strong feelings against Hart. Hart seemed a strong candidate politically, much stronger than Michael Dukakis, who eventually won the Democratic nomination. George H. W. Bush was elected, and Calder muses in his memoir about who would have won in 2000 had the senior Bush not won in 1988: "Certainly not Dubya."[10] Here and elsewhere in his book Calder delights in the power of the *Enquirer* and is little troubled by its lack of a political rationale. Calder seemed happy to let the *Enquirer* function as a journalistic loose cannon, with its considerable power left unfocused.

In withdrawing from the race at a Denver press conference, Hart lambasted the press, including the mainstream for its newly acquired tabloid ways: "We are all going to have to seriously question the system for selecting our national leaders that reduces the press of this nation to hunters and presidential candidates to being hunted, that has reporters in bushes, false and inaccurate stories printed, photographers peeking in our windows, swarms of helicopters hovering over our roof, and my very strong wife reduced to tears because she can't even get in her own house at night without being harassed."[11]

NINETEEN

SUDDEN DEATH, IRONICALLY

Pope never let down. He worked obsessively. Clearly this was what he considered the ideal life—performing the boss totally, sedentarily, smoking three packs of cigarettes a day. It was too good to miss even a few days for recreation. For all the medical stories the *Enquirer* ran, Pope didn't trust doctors. He didn't have his first physical exam until he was forty-five.[1] And his editors knew better than to propose a story on the dangers of smoking. Months before his fatal heart attack Pope was diagnosed at the hospital that was also his favorite charity, JFK Medical Center, with severe, advanced heart disease. He had checked in after suffering chest pains. "Surgery was recommended," said a doctor familiar with Pope's medical history.[2] But Pope refused an angiogram and checked himself out of the hospital.

"This was a sick man who was known to avoid doctors and physicals," said the doctor. "Look, when Mr. Pope, a powerful man and a benefactor of the hospital, checks himself out, well, he checks himself out. But he was apprised of his condition."[3]

Pope did give up smoking, but too late. Several months later he died of his first heart attack, a massive one, on October 2, 1988, at sixty-one. But he couldn't give up the deepest addiction of all, the *National Enquirer*. A month

This formal portrait of Pope was taken at the 1987 charity ball he sponsored for JFK Memorial Hospital, where he would be declared dead on arrival in 1988. (Photo by Alan Zlotky / *Palm Beach Post*)

after his sixtieth birthday Pope told a reporter, "If you took this away from me, I'd probably die."[4]

On the Sunday morning Pope died, the *New York Times* carried Alfred Kazin's review of Dorothy Gallagher's book, *All the Right Enemies: The Life and Murder of Carlo Tresca*. The book made it clear that the prime suspect in the murder by contract of Tresca in 1943 was his fascist archenemy, Generoso Pope Sr. "After an admirably close and careful review of all the evidence, Ms. Gallagher says that the instrument was most probably Frank Garofalo, who as far back as 1934 had tried, as Generoso's agent, to silence Tresca," Kazin wrote. "She believes that the continuing tension between Pope and Tresca led to Pope's loss of face and thus to Garofalo's discredit as an enforcer of Pope's will."[5] The prominent review beginning on page 3 of the book section was quite unusual for a modestly published academic book by a scholarly writer, and it was also unusual for a heavyweight like Kazin to review such a book. So it seems likely there was a certain buzz regarding Gallagher's book, which sought to resuscitate the charismatic Tresca, who was passionately left wing without being a communist.

Did Pope read the *New York Times* book review? He certainly liked to be kept informed, and the Sunday edition of the *New York Times* was available in Palm Beach County Saturday evening. If Pope had any social connections from the old days in New York (Roy Cohn had died of AIDS two years before), it's plausible someone would have called him about the review, though he remained alienated from his brothers and mother. Could Pope have read the review on the day he died? Could the exhuming of these secrets, so long buried, have stressed him to the point that, combined with his heart disease, it brought on his fatal heart attack? That would certainly be a cosmic irony, since Gallagher also makes it clear that she believes Pope Sr.'s political connections shielded him from the consequences of a murder by contract. The public will never know unless Lois Pope knows and chooses to tell. But the timing of the review and the fatal heart attack is at the very least a poignant irony.

There were other ironies in Pope's death—one being that the purveyor of junk medical science ignored sound medical advice. Another was the fact that Pope expired in a special rescue vehicle he had donated to JFK Medical Center, sometime during the twenty or thirty minutes it took to get from his Manalapan house to the hospital. The new $7 million DeBakey Cardiac Care

Unit, which he had donated in part and helped dedicate a year earlier, never got a crack at him. "Essentially he was dead on arrival [of cardiac arrest]," said hospital spokesman Larry Schwingel, who confirmed that Pope had been hospitalized for three days in July after complaining of chest pains. "Pope was looking extremely well until today," Schwingel elaborated. "Some people at the hospital saw him on Friday and said he looked in very good health."[6] *Enquirer* reporter Roger Capettini said in a press statement that Pope had been very much himself the previous week and "looked vibrant and healthy." Iain Calder, as executive editor, said in a statement, "No one can replace him, but his wife and family are determined to continue publishing the *Enquirer* with the same dedication and high standards Gene demanded."

Head gardener Mike Harris discovered the personal tape recorder Pope had been carrying his last Friday on earth. Pope used the small recorder as a notebook. "Someone must have turned it back to office services. I picked it up and turned it on, and there was Pope's voice from his last day at work," Harris said. He was amused that one of Pope's final concerns was about the timed lawn sprinklers at his house: "He was bitching that the sprinklers came on at 5:10 instead of 5:15."[7]

Melvin Laird, Nixon's secretary of state from 1969 to 1973, delivered a eulogy at Pope's funeral.[8] His presence was somewhat a mystery to those who did not remember that Laird had obliged Pope by giving a group of supermarket executives a tour of the White House, including a session with Nixon, when Pope was trying to wangle his way to their checkout counters. The *New York Post* mocked Pope gently, headlining his obituary, "*National Enquirer Owner Goes to Meet with Elvis.*"[9]

Within months the *Enquirer* was up for sale. The *Palm Beach Post* ran a cartoon of Elvis coming down in a spaceship to buy the paper. (Some *Post* reporters, like Rafe Klinger, had migrated to the better-paying *Enquirer,* and a few fired *Enquirer* reporters had found a resting place at the *Post* after their stint in tabloid journalism.) Among the bidders for the company, which included the *Weekly World News,* were two groups of employees, one led by Paul Pope and the other led by Calder. Also reportedly among the paper's suitors were British publisher Robert Maxwell, France's Hachette, West German publisher Heinrich Bauer, and the German-based multinational Bertelsmann AG. Like Hachette, Bertelsmann was one of the five biggest media conglomerates, owner at the time of Doubleday, Bantam, Dell, and the Literary Guild Book Club, along with RCA, Arista Records, and forty magazines.[10]

The winning bid—$412.5 million—was submitted by a dark horse, Boston Ventures, which included McFadden Holdings, a publisher of romance and trade magazines, which incurred $300 million of debt to make the purchase. Within the year the new owners bought the *Star* for $400 million and renamed the holding company American Media Inc.[11]

The new owners immediately economized, downsizing the editorial staff and canceling Pope's six-year-old Enquiring Minds advertising campaign. They also canceled the Christmas tree. "[The tree] was like stapling $3 to the last 150,000 copies," Mike Boylan, president of McFadden complained to a reporter.[12] "There's no way in the world we can throw a million-dollar Christmas party on our own," he added, as he also defended the immediate layoff of forty-seven employees, mostly in editorial. "Mr. Pope was Santa Claus, we just can't afford to be."[13]

Boylan wasn't exaggerating. To make the winning bid, McFadden Holdings had assumed such an enormous amount of debt, it appeared to haunt the new operation at every turn. Although Calder, in his memoir, makes it clear that top executives, very much including himself, were getting rich, in general the operation was downsized and streamlined. Prices were up, total pages were down. Gladiatorial journalism was out; editors and reporters would not waste time competing with one another. No longer would every one of the thousands of letters from readers be dignified with a personal reply. Calder said the yearly editorial budget never again come close to the $18 million it had been in 1988 under Pope: "Where Gene had preferred high sales to high profits, the new owners reversed those values immediately."[14] Yet the new owners managed to put out an *Enquirer* with enough continuity that probably few readers noticed the change in management, though to South Floridians the missing Christmas tree was a sure mark of Pope's absence.

Though the will and the sale made young Paul Pope a millionaire, in failing to provide for Paul's expected inheritance, or even a role at the *Enquirer,* Generoso Jr. somewhat duplicated his own father's behavior. In some sense he orphaned Paul as his own orphaned father had orphaned him, an uncanny repetition through the generations. Failing to get the *Enquirer* devastated Paul, who at the time made a heroic attempt a few weeks after he turned twenty-one to mount a winning bid for the paper, which was expected to sell for between $150 million and $300 million. He had backers from Shearson Lehman supporting a bid up to $400 million, quite close to Boston Venture's winning bid. Paul came away from the sale thinking that his mother had conspired against him. Like his father with his mother before him, he broke off relations. "All the women in Pope men's lives have been domineering, controlling," said Paul. "My father didn't speak to his mother for 40 years. It's a family trait."[15]

It had often been assumed that Paul, Gene Pope's youngest boy, would inherit the *Enquirer*, though there were contradictions and complexities in the situation. The extent to which Pope Jr. treated his son Paul as his father treated him is remarkable, too. Paul always believed he was going to inherit the paper. *Enquirer* staffers remembered him as a nerdy brat who was fond of telling experienced and worldly reporters, when he was interning at the paper, "Someday you'll all be working for me."[16] Pope's former executive editor Tom Kuncl remembers an incident at a staff Christmas celebration that supports Paul's perceptions, as well as staffers' conclusions that the boy was a brat:

> Once Pope's then teenage son, Paul, whom we assumed to be the dauphin and heir to the throne, walked up to his dad and a group of executives listening to the band. "Where did you find these stiffs, at a garage sale?" he pointedly asked pater, with a look in his eye so undeniably genetic that I reached for my pulse and found none to count. Pope first looked shocked, annoyed. Then a monster movie grin spread across his face. "You're all going to be working for this kid someday. How do you like him so far?" Pope chuckled.[17]

Gene Pope repeatedly told reporters how he had been introduced into the world of newspaper publishing at a tender age: "My father took me to work on his newspaper when I was six—I've got printer's ink in my blood." It seems he did the same for his son Paul and inoculated him with ink: "I had worked at the *Enquirer* since I was 10," Paul recalled. "It was in my blood, just like it was in his blood."[18] "I was being groomed to take the paper over," Paul told another reporter.[19] Paul worked in various departments: at the printing plant in Pompano Beach, with the marketing department in London, the advertising department in New York, and finally in editorial in Lantana. "He was training me in every aspect of the job to be a publisher," Paul told another reporter.[20] "He had me working in every department, from circulation to distribution to the business side, and lastly and most importantly, in editorial. Hell, I even loaded papers onto the truck at the printing plant in Pompano Beach. There's not one shadow of doubt in my mind that he wanted me to take over."

Yet there is evidence of the father's ambivalence. Pope told an afternoon editors meeting in 1974 (when Paul was only six), "When I go, my trustees have been told to sell the *Enquirer* because no one in my family can run it." He said, "My executives are instructed to sell it and set up trust funds for my family. Of course, the employees would have first option to buy it, since nobody in the family could run it."[21] In 1976 he went on record as saying, "The worst thing you can do [for children] is to leave them money,"[22] suggesting he was perhaps contemplating his own father's act of cutting his children out of his fortune. When Pope died in 1988, his most current will, dated 1983, instructed his trustees to sell the paper to the highest bidder, dashing Paul's expectations. However, according to the other provisions, proceeds from the sale went to his children and widow, who ended up multimillionaires. Paul's share of the $412.5 million sale was $40 million, according to Calder.[23] And much of Generoso Jr.'s wealth, like his father's, went to charity, in the form of a philanthropic foundation named for him and overseen by his third wife, Lois. "Like father like son" is no empty bromide in this case.

TWENTY

THE *ENQUIRER* AFTER POPE

In the last years Pope was at the helm of the *Enquirer* its circulation was running steadily in the middle four millions, and the paper remained a reliable cash cow, always easily existing on its cover price, as was the *Weekly World News,* still a lucrative shoestring operation. The *Enquirer* had slipped from its position of the late seventies and early eighties, when its circulation ran steadily in the five millions and occasionally spiked into the six millions. Pope had to back down from advertising the paper as the nation's largest, but his Enquiring Minds Want to Know television ads were holding the paper steady at the lower mark, even after cover-price increases. At that point the paper seemed to have found its niche in the enlarged tabloid culture it had an enormous role in creating.

That was to change as media culture entered the new decade without Pope. The nineties were dubbed "the Tabloid Decade" in *Vanity Fair* as David Kamp looked back from the perspective of 1999 in an article that announced "the tabloidification of news, culture, and even human behavior."[1] Kamp went on to explain, rather joyfully, that "the tabloidification of American life—of the news, of the culture, yea, of human behavior—is such a sweeping phenomenon that it can't be dismissed as merely a jokey footnote to the history of the 1990s. Rather, it's the very hallmark of our times . . . virtually

As Pope's longest-term and most loyal editorial employee, Iain Calder lived in his boss's shadow his whole career, even after he took over the *Enquirer*'s helm in 1988. (Staff photo by Chris Matula / *Palm Beach Post*)

nothing and no one has been left unaffected by tabloid's sweep."[2] Kamp observed pointedly, "What set the 1990s apart from any previous yellow-tinged epoch are two factors: advanced technology and increased vulgarity."[3]

That growing media culture continued to carve a bigger and bigger chunk out of the *Enquirer*'s share of the tabloid market. That was ironic because the mainstream press had looked down on the *Enquirer* at the same time it was stealing and adapting the tabloid's practices—and noting and envying its profitability. Even the staid cover of the *Reader's Digest* began to look more tabloid: bulleted, simplified, and racier. Celebrity and scandal-heavy *Vanity Fair* itself was a manifestation of tabloid moving up through the glossy magazines as upscale tabloid, a pairing of words that once would have been oxymoronic. *Vanity Fair* was reincarnated in 1984 from a stylish magazine of the twenties, long defunct, and under the editorship of Tina Brown blossomed into something at once fresh and gaudy. Brown was a Brit who had tremendous influence on American magazine journalism, as she moved on from *Vanity Fair* in 1992 to change the *New Yorker* into what it is today—not tabloid but certainly trendier and racier than the staid literary magazine it had been. Both *Vanity Fair* and the new *New Yorker* still flourish by working what remains essentially Brown's formula. Then Brown overreached or stumbled, teaming up with Rupert Murdoch, who financed a ground-up original startup, *Talk* magazine, which must have looked like an opportunity of a lifetime. *Talk* was also upscale tabloid, but it fizzled and folded in early 2002 after barely two years on the stands, without showing a profit.

"Imagery, shock [certainly tabloid qualities], and merchandizing" were the touchstones of Brown's editorial method, according to Stefan Kanfer, who in 1998 wrote a two-part series for the *Columbia Journalism Review,* "Tina Brown and the Coming Decline of Celebrity Journalism." Kanfer concluded that Brown "misreads the times." He opined, "Celebrity journalism has reached its apogee. There is a limit to how much information readers can absorb about . . . film stars and rock stars and senatorial stars and media stars and criminal stars and Clintons and Starrs—especially since they can get them for free on TV and in a score of supermarket checkout-counter newspapers."[4] Kanfer was wrong, and his logic was flawed, since celebrity journalism wasn't exactly deceased if TV and supermarket tabloids were practicing it. Also, there were only six supermarket tabloids at the nation's checkouts, not a "score." And supermarket tabloids were cheap but not free.

The proximity of *Talk*'s failure to the terrorist attacks on the World Trade Center were conflated by the media pundits, who concluded that tabloid (insofar as it coincided with celebrity journalism) was in decline, or over, as Americans recovered their wits to cope with the serious challenges of a new age. One of the most notable and articulate of the pundits was Brown's fellow Brit Andrew Sullivan, who was also recolonizing American journalism, then as editor of the *New Republic*. Writing about Brown in the *Wall Street Journal*, Sullivan picked September 11 as "the watershed for Tinaism—not because of what it did to the economy, but because of what it did for the culture. That day reminded us that there are more important things than winning the news cycle, that the old virtues still matter, that substance counts, and that the opposite of 'hot' is sometimes *true*. This culture is here to stay for the foreseeable future and it is one in which Tina Brown, as epitomized by *Talk,* has simply nothing to say."[5] Sullivan says he felt the shift of cultural change even before the terrorist attacks: "What did her in was the changing culture. By the turn of the millennium, you could feel a shift. The burst of the dot-com bubble, the slowing economy, the election of George W. Bush, the retreat of Hollywood from Washington, the emergence of Internet media—all these began to generate a new, more substantive mood. Tina didn't seem to see it."

Aside from *Talk*'s demise, Kanfer, Sullivan, and their like we can see were as wrong as the fashion pundits who from time to time prophesy that jeans culture is on its last legs. Perhaps there was a short cultural moment contributing to the sinking of *Talk,* but knowing why a publication is failing or succeeding is always difficult, owing to the lag time in measurable readership reaction. Putting a startup magazine into the black takes longer than two years. Besides, Kanfer contended that Brown ran the *New Yorker* in the red her whole term there and that magazine and her editorship there were still regarded as a grand success. Nevertheless, Brown had a lot of detractors.

Was the *Enquirer* losing circulation because Pope was gone and Calder was not up to the task, or because of the overall editorial downsizing in the name of profit? Or was it shrinking because other publications were encroaching on its previously exclusive tabloid preserve? The new owners apparently chose to believe the latter, at least until they sidelined Calder in 1995. And perhaps they were even looking forward to selling the declining paper to a sucker, as they more or less did in 1999.

In 1997 *Time* magazine chose Steve Coz, who two years before had risen to become the *Enquirer*'s new editor, as one of its "25 most influential Americans." "Every single network, every single magazine in America has gone more celebrity," Coz told *Time*. "That's the *Enquirer*'s influence, whether you like it or don't like it."[6]

By the Monica Lewinsky scandal the tabloidization of the mainstream press had gone so far that *Time* (whose parent company had founded *People* magazine in the early seventies to garner a share of the tabloid market) collaborated with the *Enquirer* to buy the remarkable amateur snap that ran on the covers of both publications: a wide-angle shot capturing Bill Clinton at close range smiling and pressing the flesh, with gaga-eyed intern Monica close enough to kiss, wearing her signature beret, at his reelection party on the White House lawn, savoring the secret that would soon be revealed.[7]

Testimony regarding the preempting of tabloid culture by the mainstream comes also from an unlikely source, underground and independent moviemaker John Waters, author of the essay "Why I Love the *National Enquirer.*" A longtime subscriber to the *Enquirer,* Waters told *Vanity Fair* he thought the supermarket tabloids had been outflanked by other media on the Lewinsky scandal: "My sense is that they hate the Monica story because they've been robbed of it. They feel gypped. It should be theirs and it's everyone's."[8] Circulation figures for the first half of 1998 bear out the theory that the tabloids lose circulation as the rest of the media take over their subject matter. During those six months of Monicagate, the *Enquirer*'s circulation declined 18.8 percent. It seems the auteur of *Pink Flamingos,* himself a master of the abject, had his finger on the tabloid pulse.

In 1998 "R.P." wrote in a special fortieth-anniversary supplement of the *Columbia Journalism Review* that what was remarkable about the Monicagate scandal "was the extent to which the [tabloid] beast's tail began wagging the mainstream-media dog. The new prurience of the 'established' media also had much to do with the changing economic, institutional, and cultural structures of the media business itself," he continued. "It was a time of massive competition for fickle public attention in a world of hundreds of cable channels and billions of web sites, of quarterly demands for great profits from network news divisions and newspapers owned by publicly held corporations, and in a society of coarsening standards of judgment."[9]

Similar sentiments were expressed by *American Journalism Review* editor Carl Sessions Stepp: "Almost as fast as you can say O. J. or JonBenet, the supermarket tabloids are tanking, finding themselves out-tabloided and outsleazed, at least as they see it, by the mainstream press they once sneered at.

When oral sex can dominate the national news for a year and cable channels can go all-celebrity all-the-time, what's left to lure us at the checkout counter?"[10]

After Pope the *Enquirer*'s circulation declined steadily from its 4.3 million mark in 1988. The paper's new owners put Iain Calder at the helm, since he had been the closest to Pope and could surely best serve as his surrogate after so many years as his No. 2. The strategy was to keep the *Enquirer* the same as it had been with Pope. Although Calder no doubt knew the professional side of Pope intimately, it was in his role of second-guesser, since that's what everyone was under such a tyrannical, hands-on boss. In the subtitle of his memoir, "*My 20 Years Running the* National Enquirer," Calder had extended his full stewardship of the paper a decade or more back into the Pope years, a bit of tabloid hype. Anyone who knew Pope knew that no one else came close to "running" the paper while he was alive. Calder became editor in chief in 1991 and in 1995, by his own account, began working part-time for the holding company on new magazine projects, and thus was effectively sidelined from the main day-to-day operations of the *Enquirer*. In the four years Calder indisputably "ran" the *National Enquirer* its weekly circulation figures fell from 3.75 million to 2.75 million by his own account.[11]

Pope was always tweaking his formula. While he had gradually stabilized that formula as he aged and mellowed, it's still an open question what he would have done when he saw his circulation plummeting from the three millions into the two millions, as it did in those four years under Calder. Without Pope an essential ingredient of the *Enquirer*'s journalistic discourse was missing. For a while under the new ownership the formula seemed frozen and endlessly reprised. It drifted ever more into celebrity coverage and lost the variety of Pope's wider formula. It continued to emphasize the one thing every-one remembered about the *Enquirer,* and its tabloid portfolio was no longer as diversified. It was no longer anything close to the poor man's *Reader's Digest.* Mike Rosenbloom's clones could think of nothing better to do than continue to imitate the *Enquirer,* so the *Globe* and *National Examiner,* staffed largely by recycled *Enquirer* reporters and editors, continued to chase the *Enquirer* in its nosedive, and their circulations crashed and burned, too.

Under Pope, celebrities were never more than half the formula.[12] Perhaps Calder went reluctantly toward the heavier celebrity formula, because he also observes in his book that he no longer had the lavish editorial budget that Pope provided, the $18 million that Calder thought was bigger than *Time* magazine's budget. In Pope's time the *Enquirer* never had more than $17 million in yearly profit; but within four years under the new management profits (which included income from the newly acquired *Star*) exploded to $120 million, according to Calder.[13] The new profit hunger might have been defensible or even necessary, because American Media Inc. was encumbered with the immense debt incurred to win its bid for its tabloid empire. But the strategy wasn't good for the health of the *Enquirer.* Under Pope, the *Enquirer* was privately owned and its financial numbers had been closely held, but it appears that after he got the *Enquirer* into the black in the late sixties, he had operated without any debt whatsoever, and his holding company was completely clear of debt when he died.

One of the mysteries of Pope's biography is why he didn't exploit tabloid TV, an opportunity that dangled before him like ripe fruit. It might not have interested him, a study of his character suggests, because his operation would have grown to the point that he could not personally dominate it. He would have had to delegate. But Hearst was somewhat like Pope, and he did manage to expand his empire considerably and still maintain tight control. Of course, Hearst had many other interests that he enjoyed and was much more of a social persona. Pope's life became so circumscribed that it suggests a borderline psychological pathology, possibly Asperger's.

But it isn't right to assume that Pope never would have expanded his market and wouldn't have changed the *Enquirer*. Everything in his early biography suggests the opposite. His creation of the *Weekly World News* in 1979 involved scouring the market for talent and delegating control of the operation. Eventually it might have become obvious to him that he should move into tabloid TV and other media.

Could Pope possibly have sat and watched the *Enquirer* sink into oblivion like a cannonaded pirate's prize? He always managed to keep the *Enquirer*'s circulation healthy, even if he had to step down from the high circulations of the late seventies and early eighties. His advertising campaign kept the paper's circulation and profitability high. What could the new owners have been thinking when they canceled it? Their loser strategy quickly became a self-fulfilling prophecy, although they, and Calder, became wealthy in the process. Surely Pope would have kept tweaking his formula.

Right now, as the *Enquirer* appears to be heading toward its finish, what's robbing its circulation is the slicker format of the new magazine weeklies. Their luxurious photos of celebrities, who have tremendous influence on fashion, tap into the enormous circulation for fashion magazines. The *Enquirer* was always too newsprint tacky to wield much clout there, and Pope seemed personally color blind and tone deaf to fashion. But a glance at the oversize and arty fashion magazine *W* discloses a formula of mixing beautiful photography, high fashion, celebrities, and gossip. A recent issue featured a soft-core-porn layout of David and Victoria Beckham modeling haute couture, frolicking and showing their tattoos, an exotic mix of high and low culture. Would Pope have been observant enough to see what was coming and stay ahead of the game? Very likely. David Pecker, heading the second ownership of American Media, was trying to turn the *Star* into a slick, but the unoriginal strategy came far too late and placed his offering as a trailing supplicant in an overcrowded market.

In the mid-nineties, after Steve Coz became editor in chief, the *Enquirer* appeared to be moving toward legitimate journalism. It's possible that this is a strategy Pope would have followed, had he lived. That would be close to where he started out with the *New York Enquirer*. He might have exploited this moment when the borders between tabloid and mainstream seemed in flux. This shifting border was particularly evident during the paper's coverage of the O. J. Simpson murder trial, which stretched from January to October 1994. Increasingly the paper was scooping the mainstream on the facts, as its devious and energetic tabloid reporters had previously shown they could—if they wanted to. Moreover, many of journalism's pundits noted that the mainstream was also moving closer to the supermarket tabloids.

In 2002 *Time*'s law reporter Andrea Sachs wrote in the *Columbia Journalism Review:*

> Increasingly in recent years, the *Enquirer* has won grudging respect from its mainstream rivals for the thoroughness and accuracy, if not always the taste and fairness, of its coverage

of the *Enquirer*'s kind of hard news story. And increasingly, the *Enquirer*'s kind has become the mainstream's kind—Gary Hart, William Kennedy Smith and the woman who accused him of rape, Gennifer Flowers, Michael Jackson, Tonya Harding, and most spectacularly, O. J. Simpson. Supermarket tabloids and their broadcast cousins, David Broder wrote scathingly in the *Washington Post* last year, "have demonstrated the capacity to 'launch' stories—often of the sleaziest kind—that the mainstream press feels it necessary to follow."[14]

Many, like Sachs, felt the merging of tabloid and mainstream began in 1987 with the Gary Hart story: "A melding of mainstream culture and *Enquirer* culture has been in the cards ever since the *Enquirer* helped end Gary Hart's political career by publishing a photo of a beaming (and married) Hart with Donna Rice perched on his knee."[15] In support, Sachs quotes Everette Dennis, executive director of the Freedom Forum Media Studies Center at Columbia University: "The *National Enquirer* earned its spurs with the Gary Hart story. It established them in a new way. The fact that it happened made it more acceptable for mainstream publications to look at the *National Enquirer* as a lead for news."[16]

This kind of discussion in such publications as the *Columbia Journalism Review* was new and significant in itself, aside from the writers' conclusions. The *Enquirer*'s journalism was no longer beneath serious recognition, as it had been for most of its existence. When the *Enquirer* had been covered at all, it was as a circus act or a freak show. The mainstream sneered and snickered up its sleeve but remained on the whole gently critical of the paper's dubious practices.

According to Sachs in the *Columbia Journalism Review,* O. J. Simpson's so famously chased "white Bronco blazed a trail where high culture and low culture meet." Certainly Steve Coz, who guided the *Enquirer* through the Simpson trial and boasted of being asked for his autograph in the courtroom, would agree. In the *Enquirer's* coffee-table book, subtitled *Thirty Years of Unforgettable Images,* Coz points with pride to the fact that his reporters, scrutinizing thousands of archival photos, finally, after months of work, found an image of O. J. wearing Bruno Magli shoes (which Simpson had denied ever owning) like those that left incriminating bloody footprints at the murder scene. The Magli shoes photo came too late for the criminal trial, but Coz believes it was essential to the $33 million judgment against Simpson in the civil suit.[17] The *Enquirer's* circulation rose during the trial and fell after it was over: during its most Simpson-soaked stretch, twenty-four of thirty-four *Enquirer* covers featured the case.[18]

When David Margolick, covering the Simpson trial for the *New York Times,* quoted the *Enquirer's* story, former reporter Marvin Kalb, then director of Harvard's Shorenstein Center on Press, Politics, and Public Policy, objected. "To cite the *National Enquirer* as his only source is, I think, dead wrong," said Kalb on CNN's *Crossfire.* The *Enquirer,* countered Margolick in a *Washington Post* interview, was a "reliable source."[19]

It was certainly a great change for the *Enquirer* to be considered a reliable source, a long journey from Walter Cronkite's spurious UFO sighting. The change sparked this headline from the Sunday *London Independent:*

"The *National Enquirer* Has Gone from Scandal Rag to Giant-Killing Paper of Record." In his review in 2001 of the *Enquirer*'s photo book that followed that headline, David Keeps recalls his visit to the Tabloid Triangle in Boca Raton and his "shocking" discovery that "the *National Enquirer,* contrary to its tawdry image, is a respected news organization," having "solved" the murder of Bill Cosby's son Ennis (the *Enquirer* offered a hefty reward to bring witnesses forth), as well as scooping the media on Simpson and exposing Jesse Jackson's allegedly illegitimate child,[20] a story the mainstream press chased with passion. *Washington Post* media critic Howard Kurtz, who observed that the *Enquirer* was breaking stories "worthy of being chased by the mainstream press," called the *Enquirer* "the hottest publication in America" in February 1991.[21]

This "legitimized" *National Enquirer* of the nineties led Steve Dunleavy, Murdoch's veteran tabloid ace in the hole, then a columnist for the *New York Post,* to crow: "They used to call us sleazebags. These nitwits who sneered at us, they want to open their veins now that the *New York Times'* front page actually has to recognize the *National Enquirer.*"[22]

In early 1999 American Media Inc., described by the *Washington Post* as "a publisher that has suffered from slipping sales," was acquired for $837 million by Evercore Partners. Evercore hired David Pecker, who resigned as chief executive of Hachette Filipacchi Magazines, which published *George, Elle, Premiere,* and *Mirabella,* to serve as AMI chairman and chief executive. At the time the *Enquirer*'s circulation was put at 2.24 million, down from 2.72 million in June 1997.[23] Legit or not, the paper had shrunk nearly by half in the previous decade.

Before 1999 was out AMI acquired Globe Communications, publishers of the *Globe, National Examiner,* and *Sun,* for $105 million, establishing a tabloid monopoly that included all six of the major supermarket tabloids.[24] When Evercore bought AMI, the supermarket tabloid circulations had been sinking for a decade, and they continued their decline in the ever-widening tabloid culture of the twenty-first century. In August 2003 Britain's *Observer* reported that the *Enquirer*'s weekly circulation had fallen in 2002 to a meager 1,788,000 copies a week, down 7.6 percent from the previous year.[25] David Pecker, who was an accountant, not a journalist, sought to woo advertisers by pursuing respectability in his acquired tabloids, but without success.

"The *National Enquirer* has been striving to remake its image during the last few years," said the *Montreal Gazette* at the time of the second sale, "weaning itself off stories about alien abductions, but it has continued to struggle with declining circulation and a taboo among advertisers unwilling to have their names associated with it."[26] Respectability was a troublesome issue in the history of the *Enquirer:* the paper lost advertising without it, but lost readers whenever it was cleaned up, even under Pope. It was the old Scylla and Charybdis, the rock and a hard place, that had troubled Pope from the beginning.

Pecker stuck to his cleanup strategy and decided to make the *Star* his lead tabloid, blindsiding Steve Coz, who had risen first to take the helm of the *Enquirer,* then to become editorial director of the entire AMI tabloid monopoly. In 2003 Coz resigned, as Pecker hired a high-profile New York editor, Bonnie Fuller, who had made her mark bolstering sales of *Rolling Stone* publisher Jann Wenner's *Us Weekly* magazine by taking it deeper into tabloid territory.[27] But Pecker wanted Fuller to navigate the *Star* the other way, toward respectability, advertising, and *de*-tabloidization. Pecker downsized his other tabloids, raiding them for talent to send to the *Star,* which he moved to New York City.

Pecker tasked Fuller with turning the *Star*—which had always trailed the *Enquirer* in Pope's time—into one of the New York–based glossy magazines, fat with advertising. But by then the tabloid trend in American culture had gone so far that Pecker was swimming upstream, competing far too late in an increasingly flooded market. What Fuller did to *Us,* and to five other magazines she headed in the previous decade, was to make them more tabloid. As *Vanity Fair*'s Judith Newman so breezily put it in her profile of Fuller, she had "become the symbol for the End of Journalism as We Know It—not so much a beneficiary of our culture's debased taste as a creator of it."[28] Later circulation figures suggested Pecker's northward strategy out of tabloid was fatally flawed. According to *Vanity Fair,* AMI conceded that during the first six months of Fuller's reign the *Star*'s circulation declined 10,000 copies a week, while the circulation of *Us,* still working Fuller's tabloid formula, continued to rise by 20 percent. The gap Pecker wanted to close was widening.

By fiscal 2005 *Enquirer* had lost 200,000 more in circulation, down to just over 1 million, a six-zero figure that lit up as a negative benchmark: this was the level where the paper had stalled as a gore paper way back in the sixties, before Pope took it into the grocery stores, and up and away. The *Weekly World News* had fallen to 122,000, approximately the level of its initial printing in 1979, a mere starting point from which it had quickly rocketed up. So while America feasted on the glossier celebrity tabloid presentations of *Us, People,* and new entries to the market, the original supermarket tabloid, the *Enquirer* as well as its clones, seemed stranded in suspended animation, endlessly reprising old formulas.

Meanwhile, the *Weekly World News,* marching to a different beat, writing a celebrity-free variation of tabloid, was reading like a satire of itself, and even then not itself at its best. When the paper began, it had subsisted mainly on real news stories from clips hyped to a tabloid level. Somewhere in the middle of its existence, under the editorship of Eddie Klontz, the black-and-white paper's formula had moved ever more deeply into tall-tale fiction, so called top-of-the-headers, and the late formula was fictional hype hyped, which is hard to do without becoming fatally silly or dumb. Writers like Rafe Klinger, with a deft touch and an ironic sense of humor that worked both for college kids and blue collars, were long gone. It seemed that the *Enquirer's* dark sister had worn out its formula and lost the beat entirely, and not at all because others were encroaching on its market share. Just plain bad management was the most likely culprit.

As the remade *Star* under Fuller continued to disappoint, CEO Pecker turned his attention back to the *Enquirer* in another rash move. In the spring of 2005 he told the *Enquirer* staff they had to pack and move to New York City (the *Sun,* the *Globe,* the *Examiner,* and the *Weekly World News* would remain in Florida). He deposed editor David Perel, who had served the empire for nineteen years, in favor of Paul Field, thirty-three, a brash veteran of such mass-market British dailies as the *Sun,* who was to bring what the Manchester *Guardian* called "24 British hacks" to replenish the *Enquirer* staffers who would presumably choose not to make the northward trek and would take a buyout. Pecker estimated that he would lose 50 percent of his current staff in the transfer to New York, but moving day dawned as a violent mix of blood and tears as Pecker suddenly laid off all but four editorial employees, a move that the *Observer* described—all the way across the Atlantic—as "savage."[29]

"The *Enquirer*'s lost its reader interaction and it's lost its identity," the newly installed Field told the *Observer*, which reported that Pecker had "one eye on the British market, where celebrity titles and women's weeklies have grown hugely in recent years despite a saturated market."[30] Britain, after all, remained the mother culture of Big Tabloid.

This return to the old formula with a Brit cadre and Fleet Street style seemed illogical and rash, especially after sending Bonnie Fuller on a mission in the other direction. When quarterly earnings were announced a few months later on June 30, it was evident why Pecker seemed to have lost his compass: the numbers were stunningly bad, and he was obviously desperate. The *Enquirer*'s weekly sales had dropped into the low 800,000s, and the parent company's quarterly loss was $2.9 million, compared to a profit of $11.5 million a year earlier.[31] This was a neon code-red emergency in the supermarket monopoly, and Pecker lost his cool, as the *New York Post* noted screaming matches between editor Field and CEO Pecker.

Fourteen months after he was named editor of the *Enquirer* and mastermind of the new strategy, Paul Field was called upstairs to David Pecker and unexpectedly fired. The *Enquirer* was moving back to Boca Raton, and David Perel was to be reinstalled as editor. Most of the twenty-odd Brit staffers would have to move back home, as their O-1 visas were invalid without media sponsorship, though they might have to stow away or hitchhike. Pecker rewarded the British buccaneers' courage with a measly two weeks' severance. Few blamed Field for failing to turn the paper around in such a short time.

American Media entered into default with its bondholders in April 2006. Under the headline "He Just Keeps Peckering Away at AMI," the *New York Post* wrote of another round of layoffs and cited rumors that the *En-*

quirer and the *Star* were soon to be put on the block. A year later bondholders were still extending filing deadlines for AMI as Pecker announced that the *Star* had fallen to a record low in the second half of 2006, to 560,000 copies.

The future of the *Enquirer* looks dire, but there are only a certain number of possible endings. It could go all the way down, as giant national publications have before, like the *Saturday Evening Post, Collier's,* and *Life* (although *Life* has zombied back from time to time in various special editions). It could be bought by a publisher with ambitions of bringing it back up. Or it could be bought by a management skillful in profiting from publications that live more or less in suspended animation forever.

Looking back, it's certainly worth wondering if Mike Boylan and Peter Callahan, president and chairman respectively of McFadden Holdings, had a role in taking the *Enquirer* down with strategies that became a form of self-fulfilling prophecy. Immediately after McFadden and Boston Ventures won the bidding war for the *Enquirer*, Boylan told the *New York Times,* "We've been known as bottom fishermen: we took other people's troubles and turned them around."[32] The *Enquirer* obviously never turned around. Rather, the new owners rode it down while it was still profitable, then sold it to a second ownership that was bold or arrogant enough to think it could make the *Enquirer* work again.

In August 2007 the *Weekly World News* folded; its circulation had fallen to 80,000, far below its original startup figure of 122,000, and far, far, far below its top figure of 1.1 million. Its obituaries ran worldwide: not only in the *New York Times,* the *Los Angeles Times,* and the *Washington Post* but also in *Advertising Age,* the *Irish Times,* Canada's *Globe and Mail,* and Sydney, Australia's *Morning Herald.* Many writers noted that the spirit of the *News* survived in TV's *Daily Show* and the satirical newspaper the *Onion.* AMI offered little explanation in its bleak one-paragraph statement that changes in the marketplace forced the closing. Former sitcom scriptwriter Mark Miller, one of the later writers at the paper, gave up his trade secrets to *Agence France Presse* and *Time* magazine, including the fact that he used ten pseudonymous bylines: "We gave the stories bylines and included quotes from experts. We made up the quotes and the experts and added research—that we made up." The old *News* at its highest circulation still had connections to reality—admittedly stretched and distorted reality, but it might be an important difference. The *Weekly World News,* it seemed, under a new management that hired comedy writers instead of journalists, had floated away from its readers. *Time's* obituary essayist also reminded us that the old *News* had penetrated the culture to the point that the paper was appearing in movies like *So I Married an Axe Murderer* and *Men in Black,* in which Tommy Lee Jones praises the *Weekly World News* for the "best damned investigative reporting on the planet." It told you a lot about a character when you saw him reading the *Weekly World News,* as Emilio Estevez does in the 1984 cult classic *Repo Man.*

The worldwide attention given to the *Weekly World News,* which had seemed to be languishing unnoticed on the diminishing supermarket racks, was surprising, even to tabloid journalists, who were used to functioning unheralded in the realm of the abject. Pope always thought of the *News* as a sideshow, and it was only 20 percent of his circulation even in its best days. The *National Enquirer* should make a much bigger splash if it goes down.

TWENTY-ONE

POPE IN PERSPECTIVE

In his lifetime and in the years since his death in 1988 Pope has never achieved recognition. Some of this lack of recognition is related to the "authorlessness" of tabloid: in a real sense Pope was the constructive author of every story the *Enquirer* published, but his work was unsigned and anonymous. This fit the low-profile godfatherish life he had constructed for himself. Pope had failed to behave like a tycoon: he missed the opportunity to pioneer tabloid TV. He seemed too happy in his tropical bower in small-town Florida, tweaking his formula, controlling every story, scribbling his red *Z* on pieces of paper he could hold in his hand.

By the year of Pope's death Rupert Murdoch was poised to become the torchbearer of tabloid. Murdoch did behave like a tycoon. While most of his progress in television came after Pope's death, he founded *Current Affair* in 1986, two years before Pope died, as well as launching his Fox network with *The Late Show* starring Joan Rivers. Fox started out with six independent stations—in New York, Los Angeles, Chicago, Washington, Dallas, and Houston—and by 2001 owned thirty-two stations and had become our fourth network, the first new one since ABC's startup in 1951. His shows—*The Simpsons, Ally McBeal, The X-Files, Married with Children, Roseanne,* former

Enquirer reporter Steve Chao's *Cops,* and *America's Most Wanted*—were solid hits, as well as being recognizably tabloid.

But if Murdoch was behaving like the global Hearst of our time, wouldn't Pope qualify as our Pulitzer? Hearst had advanced the yellow journalism pioneered by Pulitzer into an empire that included at his death nine magazines and eighteen newspapers in twelve cities.[1] In the end, though, Hearst's empire was hollowed out by debt, at least partly to finance his grand lifestyle, while Pope had no debt at all, and his empire was discovered to have been vastly underestimated when it was put on the auction block. Yellow journalism was a recognizable antecedent of Pope's style of tabloid, and, significantly, Hearst had helped found the *New York Enquirer* in 1926, nearly three decades before Pope bought it. Pope commanded a circulation easily greater than that of Pulitzer's two papers, the *St. Louis Post-Dispatch* and the *New York World,* and was comparable with Hearst's more thinly spread empire. He was probably as wealthy as either Hearst or Pulitzer at their peak. Pope's influence on American journalism is comparable, too. So once his story has come to light, shouldn't Pope be elevated to stand in the pantheon with Hearst and Pulitzer?

An argument against admitting Pope to the pantheon might be that many regard him as vulgar popularizer. But that is precisely how Hearst and Pulitzer were seen in their own time. It is ironic that the most prestigious prizes in American journalism are named for Pulitzer. Both of the old press moguls lowered the common denominator of American journalism or, to choose a less value-weighted metaphor, widened it. They reached deeper or further into the American millions for their mass circulations, and so did Pope, continuing their work. Pulitzer's first paper, the *St. Louis Post-Dispatch,* was considered vulgar and radical, and the city's leading citizens snubbed the upstart Jewish-Magyar immigrant publisher. Pulitzer prefigured Hearst, who then vanquished Pulitzer in the early circulation wars in New York between his *Journal* and Pulitzer's *World,* in the first decades of the twentieth century. Together Pulitzer and Hearst, who outlived his rival by forty years, defined the trend of yellow journalism, which took its name from Richard Outcault's early cartoon of the Yellow Kid. The Kid was debuted in 1896 in Pulitzer's *World,* and Hearst promptly stole him, by making Outcault a salary offer he couldn't refuse, a characteristic tactic that Pope, too, was fond of using.[2] Yellow journalism became so dominant in many cities in those years that there was hardly any point in distinguishing it by calling it yellow. So it is easy to link the yellow journalism of the beginning of the twentieth century to the tabloid culture at the beginning of the twenty-first.

Pulitzer pitched his papers to the masses, and Hearst courted the common herd even more passionately, among other things as a successful strategy to outflank Pulitzer in their circulation war. H. L. Mencken said of Hearst, "He did not try to lift up the mob like Pulitzer; he boldly leaped down to its level."[3] Pulitzer, a self-educated man of cultivation with fine tastes in art, music, and literature, appeared to want to help the masses follow in his footsteps. Hearst, who seems to have squandered his years at Harvard largely from a lack of attention and interest, appeared much less concerned with making the newspaper the poor man's university, as Mark Twain so famously said it was. His method was closer to pandering, which he was routinely accused of.

According to biographer W. A. Swanberg, Pulitzer's first paper "breathed a quality so newly animated by Pulitzer that one might say he invented it—*sensationalism*" and "catered to the businessman, the workman, the housewife."[4] Pulitzer bought the *Dispatch* in 1878 for $2,500 at a bankruptcy auction. He immediately merged it with the *Post,* owned by a colleague and friend, and set about making the paper the city's leading daily. St. Louis was then the nation's fourth-largest city, after New York, Philadelphia, and Brooklyn.

Seven years later Pulitzer was able to pay financier Jay Gould $346,000 for the *New York World,* with a sagging circulation of eleven thousand. Pulitzer immediately called his editors and reporters together and made it clear that his momentum was from the elite to the common. "Gentlemen," he said, "you realize a change has taken place in the *World.* Heretofore you have been living in the parlor and taking baths every day. Now I wish you to understand that in the future, you are all walking down the Bowery."[5] Pulitzer insisted on short sentences, violent verbs, and tight writing. "Condense! Condense!" was his cry in the city room. That paleo-tabloid credo reverberated long after in the newsrooms of supermarket and city tabloids.

Hearst, too, learned from Pulitzer and also began originating and formulating journalistic practices that would continue to serve the strain of journalism that flowed into the supermarket tabloid. In 1887 Hearst took over the San Francisco paper his father had bought and used solely as an instrument for his political ambitions, which culminated in his election to the U.S. Senate from California. The front page consisted of nine columns of uninviting, dense text. Young Hearst seemed to have had a firm instinct for design. He doubled the size of the headlines and reduced the number of columns. Although it was not then feasible to publish photographs in a daily newspaper, Hearst understood the value of illustrations and introduced line drawings to his front page.

These embellishments, he explained to his father, "attract the eye and stimulate the imagination of the lower classes and materially aid the comprehension of an unaccustomed reader and thus are of particular importance to that class of people which the *Examiner* claims to address."[6] Hearst was moving toward the mass-market tabloid formula, picture heavy, with big headlines and a layout inviting to the eye. His editorial formula, evolved from Pulitzer, included sex, crime, and insults to the mighty.

The most glaring of several important differences between Pope and his mogul forefathers lies in the realm of politics. Hearst and Pulitzer were drenched in politics, but Pope, after he moved into gore, then on to the supermarkets, seemed to have no politics at all. Some cultural critics, especially British ones whose theory has neo-Marxist underpinnings, eagerly read politics into tabloid culture, but to do so seems to require a fairly fundamentalist vision of the Marxist relationship between economics and culture. And their critique seems to work better with Pulitzer and Hearst than with Pope, especially concerning the politics of parties, policies, votes, and revolutions.

That was precisely the kind of politics that obsessed Pulitzer and Hearst, who both served briefly in Congress. Hearst even had ambitions to become president, and Hungarian-born Pulitzer, who was banned by the Constitution from serving as chief executive, wanted at least to become a kingmaker. Grassroots politics existed at the turn of the twentieth century to a degree that we can scarcely imagine now, when many feel that the crucial moves and choices are made behind the scenes and in corporate boardrooms, before the votes are even cast. Hearst's father, an illiterate Forty-niner who had struck it rich, had used the *San Francisco Examiner* solely as a political instrument for his election to the U.S. Senate: young Hearst when he took over said he still thought of readers as voters. Politically, Pulitzer was considered a radical in his own time, though he was left wing in a peculiarly American way, in a style that was perhaps characteristic of the foreign-born who came with nothing and grew rich. Although Pulitzer was on the left, he was fiercely opposed to socialism or communism (like Generoso Pope Sr.). Both Pulitzer and Hearst were crusaders, and crusading journalism became synonymous with yellow journalism.

Newspapers were part of a robust political dialogue, as newly immigrated ethnic groups—Jews, Catholics, Italians, Irish, East Europeans—and classes struggled passionately for their share of power. Newspapers were part of a metanarrative of truth and progress through news and reportage, a discourse that supermarket tabloids have seriously eroded. Pope's tabloids invited readers to forget serious concerns and move deeper into the kind of fantasy world film and TV created. In its simplest form this involved reporting the private romances and lives of celebrities. But even more serious reportage—of medical news, for instance—was also simplified and hyped to the point that it became part of a fantasy world where cancer was cured once a week.

Pope and Pulitzer constantly recycled their staffs, and firings were frequent, though both mellowed in this regard as they grew older. Pulitzer was mercurial and passionate, and once had a city-room fistfight with one of his reporters over an assignment, while Pope, by contrast, was personally aloof and distant. Pulitzer, like Pope, believed his reporters and editors performed better under battlefield conditions; he stressed them, moved them from job to job, and was widely regarded as a "nasty, vituperative, foul-mouthed martinet."[7] Pope deliberately fostered competition between his own editors and reporters, since he felt rival tabloids failed to supply enough in the way of battlefield conditions. Hearst by contrast was considered a kindly master who offered his reporters and editors high salaries and security. Although he leaned heavily, even tyrannically, on his key editors, he was always a gentleman, even under deadline pressures.

When Hearst began raiding Pulitzer's editorial ranks—a tactic he believed would both strengthen him and weaken Pulitzer—the outrageously high salaries he offered weren't the only incentive to defect. Hearst also offered calm and stability in place of Pulitzer's chaos. Hearst inspired loyalty, offered security, and kept his editors and reporters. Pope failed in this even more surely than Pulitzer—he seemed to inspire hardly any loyalty at all—although like Hearst he knew the value of offering high salaries. In the late seventies Pope's journalists became the best paid in the nation, and he relished tempting top editors away from top jobs with lucrative offers.

Hearst and Pulitzer also kept a close watch on their publications, though neither more thoroughly than Pope. He picked the stories, read them several times in production, asked questions, then killed a number of them for various reasons, or just because. To say he was hands-on is an understatement. Hearst kept close watch but not at the expense of his personal life. He used the telephone to manage the *Journal*'s daily lineup of stories. When he entertained at San Simeon, an exact time for dinner was never set. Guests knew dinner began when Hearst finished talking on the phone with his editors about the next morning's story lineup. Pulitzer certainly managed his papers, but as he grew older and his health failed, he relinquished day-to-day control and spent more and more time on his yacht.

Pope, Pulitzer, and Hearst—all three were socially marginalized in their different ways. Pulitzer had hardly any formal education and initially was hardly able to speak English. His part-Jewish ancestry through his father made him vulnerable to anti-Semitism. Pulitzer's obsessive, eccentric personality isolated him still more, and Swanberg describes him as "an active nervous wreck" and wonders whether in more modern times Pulitzer would have been diagnosed as manic-depressive.[8]

Hearst was sent to Harvard by his father, but the son had little interest in his studies and never graduated. Like his father, Will Hearst avoided polite society. Although Hearst's personal life was often in the limelight, he was never accepted into high society, for which his fortune and power might have otherwise qualified him. All his life he chose women from the demiworld and was a stage-door johnny who loved musical comedy. Hearst gushed over chorus girls, the younger the better. He eventually married one, Millicent Willson, but not before he scandalized New York by traveling everywhere with her and her sister Anita. Marion Davies was a starlet of eighteen when he first latched onto her, and he immediately employed his fortune to foster her film career. She stayed with Hearst, more than thirty years her senior, for thirty-six years, becoming a stone alcoholic along the way.

Pope's father's rise from impoverished immigrant to power and fortune mimicked Pulitzer's career in its rough outline. Like Hearst, Pope made the jump to elite education, at Horace Mann and MIT, in one generation. Later, in Florida, Pope lived apart from wealthy Palm Beach society. Generally the only parties he attended were the rare ones he hosted himself, including a yearly charity ball for JFK Hospital (later JFK Medical Center) in nearby Lake Worth, where he was chairman of the board of trustees. Like Hearst, Pope was shunned by America's social circles, isolated both by his birth and by the nature of his work, perceived as vulgar. But neither Pope, Pulitzer, nor Hearst seemed to want social prominence anyway.

One reason Pope has never loomed so large in the public imagination as

Hearst or Pulitzer is that he was not showy or colorful, as Hearst certainly was, and Pulitzer, too, in a more refined way. Pope was virtually invisible to the public, in the manner of a Mafia godfather, though he did grant press interviews willingly and usually said the same things in all of them. Pope wore a nondescript uniform around the office, drove a nondescript car (aside from the vanity plate), didn't spend ostentatiously or collect world-class art like Pulitzer (but rather electric trains), didn't womanize like Hearst—or have a yacht, as did both Hearst and Pulitzer. He probably didn't even eat that well. By his own account he lived in a cheeseburger culture, and his culinary adventures seemed limited to once-a-week trips to his favorite small-town Italian restaurant, where he ate the Friday before he had his heart attack.

Pope lived in a twelve-thousand-square-foot oceanfront house—which perhaps barely made it into the mansion category the press always accorded it—but it was nothing like Hearst's grand San Simeon or the five castles Hearst owned. Pulitzer owned homes in Bar Harbor, Maine; Jekyll Island, Georgia; Lakeside, New Jersey; and Cape Martin on the French Riviera, as well as a house in Brooklyn that burned down with many of his art treasures and beloved jewels. Pope's mansion was a fraction of the size of the houses Hearst bought for his estranged wife, Millicent, and for his notorious mistress, Marion Davies.

Both Hearst and Pulitzer constructed major public buildings to house their publications. Hearst constructed a handsome building at Market and Third for his *San Francisco Examiner* in 1888; he considered the building an important statement and a notice of his presence. In 1890, to house his *World,* Pulitzer built a 309-foot, twenty-story skyscraper, at the time the tallest building in New York. Hearst owned a block in lower Manhattan to house his

Journal and its plant. Pope, by contrast, housed his *Enquirer* in the sprawling, homely, one-story bungalow-like plant he built in a small town in South Florida. He proceeded to hide the *Enquirer* from the town's main road, U.S. 1, Dixie Highway, with a high hedge; the only notice of the paper's presence was its name and the current temperature on a modest sign that a small-town bank might have displayed.

Even Pope's second-place competitors in Florida's Tabloid Triangle built, by contrast, an ostentatious five-story building in a corporate park in Boca Raton, with a fountain, a tasteless statue of Hercules, or someone, holding up the planet, a circular driveway around the statue, and underground parking. It was soon dubbed the Taj Mahal by the employees of Globe Communications. After AMI acquired Mike Rosenbloom's tabloids in 1999, David Pecker moved the *Enquirer* and *Weekly World News* into the big Boca Raton building, but abandoned it in 2001 after the anthrax attack that killed photo editor Bob Stevens. The contaminated "Taj Mahal" has remained unoccupied, and it appears that decades of exclusive photos that Pope collected are degenerating there.

Libel law is, of course, the major legal discourse that regulates the press, the issue that is the constant concern of nearly every editor and reporter. Shortly before he died, Pulitzer defended the *World* against a libel suit brought by President Theodore Roosevelt. Pulitzer was accused not only of insulting and libeling the mighty but also of libeling the American people and the American government, in the *World*'s coverage and editorial commentary concerning the shady dealing in financing the Panama Canal. It was also clear that Roosevelt, using the overwhelming powers of a sitting president, wanted to make an example of Pulitzer and send the sick, blind, and ailing publisher, who would die within a year of winning the lawsuit, to prison. Roosevelt even attacked Pulitzer in a message to Congress. Pulitzer fought the suit for two years, all the way to the Supreme Court, spending amounts that only a millionaire publisher could afford, and won a unanimous decision in 1911.[9] The case was a landmark in the defense of a free press.

Pope, too, fought a landmark lawsuit for tabloids, but his was over the sixty-five-word gossip item that insinuated that Carol Burnett had been drunk in a restaurant in 1976. Determined to punish the *Enquirer* for making up an item about her, Burnett fought an exorbitantly costly lawsuit in which a jury awarded her $1.6 million in damages. But the amount was reduced to $200,000 after a number of appeals, and then settled out of court for an undisclosed amount, as low as $50,000 according to some sources.[10] Though Pope's victory over Burnett was Pyrrhic, he nevertheless successfully defended an area where tabloid journalism, his own and his imitators', continued to flourish, in celebrity gossip and at its extreme, celebrity bashing.

Pulitzer and Hearst were denigrated in their own time, then elevated in our historical evaluation by virtue of their achievement and influence. Pope has suffered even more than they have in being dismissed as a mere popularizer, and his personal invisibility has lengthened his period of obscurity. But once the differences in lifestyle are accounted for, we might decide that Pope casts a shadow as long as theirs. We might recognize him as the late twentieth century's equivalent of Pulitzer (even as Rupert Murdoch begins to loom larger as Pope's successor, as Hearst did over Pulitzer).

Perhaps one obstacle to putting Pope up as one of journalism's saints is that we have yet to decide whether this influence he wielded was positive. Certainly there are reservations. The mood of the nation, and clearly the jury, during the Carol Burnett libel suit seemed to go decisively against the *Enquirer*. The schizoid complexity, which needs to be resolved, was that five million Americans were also buying the paper. Another imponderable is how much the mainstream media, in high dudgeon over the *Enquirer*'s shoddy journalism, cast a pall on the proceedings. Pulitzer and Hearst, whatever their flaws, are now seen as markers on the way to a feisty, energetic journalism that supports, whatever its momentary failings, the discourse toward truth, or at least toward progress, through information and news. Far from fostering the continuation of that discourse, Pope seems to have distracted us from it with trivialities, fantasies, and cheap, even mean, pleasures, forms of cultural decadence in Frederic Jameson's taxonomy of schlock.

Pope's widow, Lois, has been known to say that the lasting achievement of her husband is that he brought Americans closer to our true feelings. There seems some value and self-knowledge in understanding that we are not as good as we pretend or want to be; in fact that seems a peculiarly postmodern judgment, compatible with postmodernists' reservations about elite culture. Yes, we might be low-minded enough to prefer celebrity gossip over the *Wall Street Journal*. The irony in that comparison is that Pope's successor in tabloid culture, Rupert Murdoch, has bought the *Journal,* which many fear will be the end of civilization as we know it. Could the binary that the *Journal* and the *Enquirer* represented in the seventies when their circulations were tied at five million weekly be collapsing? That's something posterity will have to shake down for us.

At least no one can accuse Pope of doing harm, unless diversion is harmful. At least Pope never had it on his head that he fostered a war, as the *New York Times, CNN, Fox News,* and much of our mainstream media did in the run-up to the war in Iraq, as Hearst did in his time in the run-up to the Span-ish-American War. Through much of the time Pope was publishing the *En-quirer,* we were engaged in the Vietnam War, but you would never have known it by reading his tabloid.

The issue of Pope's future image brings up a fundamental ambivalence in his personality. He read the great biographies of Hearst and Pulitzer and ex-horted his editors to read them. Articles editor Phil Brennan felt that Pope was inviting a comparison. Executive editor Tom Kuncl remarked on Pope's grandiosity, that somewhere "in his own mind" he was a media baron. Yet by the mid-seventies, just a few years after getting into the business, Pope stood as the single-handed creator of a weekly paper with a circulation of more than five million. How could he not be a media baron? Did the abjectness of his tabloid journalism disqualify him, the junk and schlock that he peddled? Maybe.

Frank Zahour and other reporters registered Pope's self-consciousness, in that he seemed to enjoy creating his own legend in his own small pond. That part of Pope clearly wanted a place in some pantheon. But Pope always ex-pressed contempt of journalism prizes, including the Pulitzer, and seems to have taken pleasure in firing mainstream prizewinners when the opportunity arose. That could have been sour grapes from the practitioner of abject jour-nalism. Or there could have been more to it; when he canvassed the Ivy League for reporters, he stipulated that he didn't want any journalism majors. What a paradox Pope presents: he wants to be a legend and a recognized mo-gul, yet he buries himself in a small Florida town. Pope had a wide streak of Groucho Marx and, it seems, wouldn't have wanted to stand in any pantheon that would have admitted him.

NOTES

The author conducted the following interviews in preparing this book:

Bill Bates, personal interview, April 1992.
Phil Brennan, telephone interview, 10 May 2001.
Phil Bunton, telephone interview, 10 June 2004.
Steve Coz, telephone interview, 3 March 2004.
Chris Currie, telephone interview, 7 May 2001.
Beatrice Dexter, telephone interview, 18 July 2001.
Vince Eckersley, telephone interview, 9 June 2001.
Mike Harris, telephone interview, 6 May 2001.
Brian Hogan, personal interview, March 1982.
Mike Hoy, personal interview, December 1980.
George Hunter, personal interview, December 1980.
Susan Jamison, telephone interview, 12 June 2001.
Rafe Klinger, telephone interview, 2 March 2004.
Tom Kuncl, telephone interview, 14 May 2001.
Paul Levy, personal interview, August 1989.
Val Virga, telephone interview, 5 April 2004.
Frank Zahour, telephone interview, 22 May 2002.

Introduction

1. Central Intelligence Agency File 4, MORI DocID 226001, obtained courtesy of Frank Zahour.

1. The Man in Perspective

1. Kuncl interview.

2. Quoted in Tim Page, "Personal History: Parallel Play," *New Yorker,* 20 August 2007, 37.

2. Family Connections

1. "Girl Sues Married Man," *New York Times,* 17 July 1920, 4.

2. Dorothy Gallagher, *All the Right Enemies: The Life and Murder of Carlo Tresca* (New Brunswick, NJ: Rutgers University Press, 1988), 189.

3. Ibid., 188–89.

4. Ibid., 191.

5. "Generoso Pope Backs U.S.," *New York Times,* 14 September 1941, 4.

6. Nicholas Von Hoffman, *Citizen Cohn: The Life and Times of Roy Cohn* (New York: Doubleday, 1988), 82.

7. Gallagher, *All the Right Enemies,* 196.

8. Ibid., 260.

9. Alfred Kazin, "Who Hired the Assassin?" review of *All the Right Enemies,* by Dorothy Gallagher, *New York Times Book Review,* 2 October 1988, 3.

10. Von Hoffman, *Citizen Cohn,* 69.

11. Sidney Zion, *The Autobiography of Roy Cohn* (Secaucus, NJ: Lyle Stuart, 1988), 30.

12. Von Hoffman, *Citizen Cohn,* 72.

13. George Wolf, with Joseph DiMona, *Frank Costello: Prime Minister of the Underworld* (New York: William Morrow, 1974), 12.

14. "Notorious Mafia Leader Bonnano Dead," Associated Press, Yahoo! News, http://dailynews.yahoo.com, 12 May 2002.

15. Wolf, *Frank Costello,* 9.

16. Zion, *Autobiography of Roy Cohn,* 64.

17. Ibid., 60.

18. Ibid., 61.

19. Ibid., 61.

20. Ibid., 61.

21. Ibid., 61.

22. Ibid., 61.
23. Ibid., 62.
24. Ibid., 64.
25. Ibid., 12.
26. Von Hoffman, *Citizen Cohn,* 132.

3. Kid Wheeler-Dealer

1. "Pope: The High Priest of Lowbrow," *New York Daily News,* 10 October 1999.
2. Tom Wolfe, "Dangerous Obsessions," review of *The Autobiography of Roy Cohn,* by Sidney Zion, *New York Times Book Review,* 3 April 1988, 1.
3. John A. Byrne, "Slugging It Out in the Supermarkets," *Forbes,* March 1981, 78–79.
4. "High Priest of Lowbrow."
5. Ibid.
6. "Murphy Dismisses Generoso Pope Jr. as Honorary Police Deputy," *New York Times,* 26 October 1950, 1.
7. "Estate of G. Pope Mainly to Charity," *New York Times,* 10 May 1950, 47.
8. "Mayor at Service for Generoso Pope," *New York Times,* 2 May 1950, 27.
9. Howard Rudnitsky, "How Gene Pope Made Millions in the Newspaper Business," *Forbes,* 16 October 1978, 77–78.
10. James Lardner, "Publisher Nixes Gore, Plugs Self-Help: The Man behind the *Enquirer;* Generoso Pope," *Washington Post,* 2 April 1978, F1.
11. Rudnitsky, "How Gene Pope Made Millions," 79.
12. Zahour interview.
13. Kuncl interview.
14. Ibid.

4. Friends in Low Places

1. Gallagher, *All the Right Enemies,* 253–54.
2. Gay Talese, *Honor Thy Father* (New York: Ballantine Books, 1981), 184–85.
3. Gallagher, *All the Right Enemies,* 254.
4. Talese, *Honor Thy Father,* 256.
5. "High Priest of Lowbrow."
6. Lardner, "Publisher Nixes Gore."

7. Von Hoffman, *Citizen Cohn,* 134.

8. "High Priest of Lowbrow."

9. Ibid.

10. Ibid.

11. Jonathan Mahler, "The *National Enquirer*'s Thwarted Heir Lashes Out," *Talk,* January 2000.

12. Zion, *Autobiography of Roy Cohn,* 11.

13. Ibid., 13.

14. "Generoso Pope Buys *New York Enquirer,*" *New York Times,* 4 April 1953, 15.

15. Lardner, "Publisher Nixes Gore," F1.

16. Kuncl interview.

17. Byrne, "Slugging It Out," 78.

18. "High Priest of Lowbrow."

19. Mahler, "Thwarted Heir Lashes Out."

20. Jim Hogshire, *Grossed-Out Surgeon Vomits in Patient! An Insider's Look at Supermarket Tabloids* (Venice, CA: Feral House, 1997), 99.

21. Carl Sessions Stepp, "A Treasure Trove of Tabloid Tales," *American Journalism Review,* March 2001, 69.

22. Mahler, "Thwarted Heir Lashes Out."

23. Sid Kirchheimer, "Gigantic Smash!" *San Diego Union-Tribune,* 22 February 1987, D3.

24. "Costello Is Shot Entering Home; Gunman Escapes," *New York Times,* 3 May 1957, 1.

25. Wolf, *Frank Costello,* 254–57.

26. Ibid., 266.

27. CIA File 4.

5. From Gore to Groceries

1. Mahler, "Thwarted Heir Lashes Out."

2. Malcolm Balfour, "Enquiring Minds Will Want to Know," *NYPost.com,* 8 August 2000.

3. "High Priest of Lowbrow."

4. George Stein, "Generoso Pope: Millionaire Owner of *National Enquirer,*" *Los Angeles Times,* 3 October 1988, 16.

5. Lardner, "Publisher Nixes Gore."

6. "High Priest of Lowbrow."

7. Mahler, "Thwarted Heir Lashes Out."

8. Rudnitsky, "How Gene Pope Made Millions," 77–78.

9. Tom Kuncl, "The Last Christmas Tree," *Miami Herald,* 19 November 1989, 1.

10. "High Priest of Lowbrow."

11. Lardner, "Publisher Nixes Gore."

12. Currie interview.

13. Kuncl interview.

6. A Second Start

1. James McLaren, "Generoso Pope Jr., Owner of *National Enquirer,* at Age 61," *Bergen (NJ) Record,* 3 October 1988, A11.

2. Iain Calder, *The Untold Story: My 20 Years Running the National Enquirer* (New York: Miramax Books, 2004), 23.

3. Ibid., 109.

4. Kirchheimer, "Gigantic Smash!" D3.

5. McLaren, "Pope, at Age 61," A11.

6. Eckersley interview.

7. Brennan interview.

8. "*Enquirer* Charged on Alien Laws," *New York Times,* 21 November 1981, 8.

9. Arthur Golden, "Ah, Those Days on a Tabloid," *San Diego Union-Tribune,* 24 December 1988, D1.

10. Brennan interview.

11. Eckersley interview.

12. Ibid.

13. Ibid.

14. Alex Jones, "Hart Photo: Asking Price Set at $25,000," *New York Times,* 31 May 1987, 24.

15. Eckersley interview.

7. Rocketing Up

1. Balfour, "Enquiring Minds."

2. Elizabeth Peer and William Schmidt, "The *Enquirer:* Up from Smut," *Newsweek,* 21 April 1975, 62.

3. Calder, *Untold Story,* 174.

4. Zion, *Autobiography of Roy Cohn,* 421.

5. Brennan interview.

6. Bates interview.

7. Brennan interview.

8. Rudy Maxa, "Lucky: Doggone Hype," *Washington Post Sunday Magazine,* 16 July 1978, 4.

9. Kuncl, "Last Christmas Tree," 1.

10. Dexter interview.

11. Peer and Schmidt, "*Enquirer:* Up from Smut," 62.

12. Golden, "Ah, Those Days," D1.

13. Elizabeth S. Bird, *For Enquiring Minds: A Study of Supermarket Tabloids* (Knoxville: University of Tennessee Press, 1992), 95.

14. Ibid., 95.

15. CIA File 6.

16. Calder, *Untold Story,* 125.

17. Harris interview.

18. Brennan interview.

19. Calder, *Untold Story,* 91.

20. Brennan interview.

21. Calder, *Untold Story,* 97.

22. Eckersley interview.

23. Calder, *Untold Story,* 50.

24. Bunton interview.

25. "Now the Story Can Be Told! How Tabloids Survived the Recession," *Business Week,* 7 November 1983, 145.

26. Calder, *Untold Story,* 100.

27. Kirchheimer, "Gigantic Smash!" D3.

28. Hogan interview.

8. Perfecting the Formula

1. Kuncl interview.

2. Ibid.

3. Ibid.

4. Coz interview.

5. Kuncl interview.

6. Ibid.

7. Talese, *Honor Thy Father.*

8. Jay Gourley, "I Killed Gig Young," *Washington Monthly,* September 1981, 32–38.

9. Calder, *Untold Story,* 186.

10. Jack Vitek and Jerry Oppenheimer, *Idol: Rock Hudson: The True Story of an American Film Hero* (New York: Villard Books, 1986), 56–63.

11. David Kamp, "The Tabloid Decade," *Vanity Fair,* February 1999, 61–78.

12. Wolfe, "Dangerous Obsessions."

13. See chap. 15.

14. Byrne, "Slugging It Out," 78–79.

9. Lantana 33464

1. Kirchheimer, "Gigantic Smash!" D3.

2. Zahour interview.

3. Golden, "Days on a Tabloid," D1.

4. Ibid.

5. Ibid.

6. Ibid.

7. Andrea Sachs, "Mud and the Mainstream," *Columbia Journalism Review,* May/June, 1995. Available at http://backissues.cjrarchives.org/year/95/3/mud.asp.

8. Calder, *Untold Story,* 85.

9. Kuncl interview.

10. Ibid.

11. Ibid.

12. "Special Car Tags Quickly Renewed," *New York Times,* 18 December 1935, 30.

13. Kuncl interview.

10. The Million-Dollar Tree: Ho! Ho! Ho!

1. Kuncl, "Last Christmas Tree."

2. Zahour interview.

3. Ibid.

4. Kuncl, "Last Christmas Tree."

5. Ibid.

6. Ibid.

7. Currie interview.

8. Ibid.

9. Ibid.

10. Ibid.

11. Ibid.

11. Washington Garbage

1. Jay Gourley, "Beyond the Pail: The Theory and Practice of Garbage Journalism," *Washington Monthly,* October 1975, 46.

2. Gourley, "Beyond the Pail," 48.

3. Ibid., 48.

4. Ibid., 46.

5. Ibid., 48.

6. Ibid., 49.

7. Ibid., 49.

8. Ibid., 49.

9. Ibid., 50.

10. Ibid., 49.

11. Ibid., 48.

12. Manufacturing "Truth"

1. Neal Travis, Neal Travis' New York, *New York Post Online,* 26 November 1997. Quoted in UFO Updates, http://www.virtuallystrange.net/ufo/updates/1997/nov/m29-009.shtml; accessed 10 May 2002.

2. Kuncl interview.

3. Ibid.

4. Virga interview.

5. Gourley, "I Killed Gig Young," 38.

6. Quoted in Barry Smart, *Michel Foucault* (London: Tavistock, 1985), 380.

13. The Peak of Tabloid: Elvis

1. Kuncl interview.
2. Eckersley interview.
3. Calder, *Untold Story,* 156.
4. Hogshire, *Grossed-Out Surgeon,* 107.
5. Rudnitsky, "How Gene Pope Made Millions," 77.
6. Kuncl interview.
7. Charles C. Thompson II and James P. Cole, *The Death of Elvis: What Really Happened* (New York: Delacorte Press, 1991), 258.
8. Kuncl interview.
9. Thompson and Cole, *Death of Elvis,* 258.
10. Kuncl interview.
11. Charles Melcher and Valerie Virga, *The* National Enquirer: *Thirty Years of Unforgettable Images* (New York: Talk Miramax Books, 2001), 6.
12. Kuncl interview.
13. Thompson and Cole, *Death of Elvis,* 54.
14. Kuncl interview.
15. Ibid.

14. Reporter as Gladiator

1. Brennan interview.
2. Hogshire, *Grossed-Out Surgeon,* 103.
3. N. R. Kleinfield, "What Acquiring Minds Want to Know," *New York Times,* 7 May 1989, C1.
4. John Harris, "My Search for Utopia," *Gentlemen Ranters,* http://www .gentlemenranters .com/3.html#utopia; accessed 8 June 2008.
5. Calder, *Untold Story,* 104.
6. Ibid., 106–7.
7. Zahour interview.
8. Ibid.
9. Ibid.

10. Ibid.

11. Ibid.

12. Ibid.

13. Ibid.

14. Coz interview.

15. Ibid.

16. Melcher and Virga, *Unforgettable Images*, 5.

17. Coz interview.

18. Gourley, "I Killed Gig Young," 36.

19. Ibid., 36.

20. Ibid., 37.

21. Ibid., 37.

15. Star Wars: Hollywood versus the *Enquirer*

1. Robert Lindsey, "Carol Burnett Given $1.6 Million in Suit against *National Enquirer*," *New York Times,* 27 March 1981, A1.

2. Aljean Harmetz, "Hollywood Stars Are Fighting Back against *Enquirer*," *New York Times,* 12 November 1980, C1.

3. Harmetz, "Stars Are Fighting Back," C1.

4. Ibid.

5. Ibid.

6. Ibid.

7. Ibid.

8. "Trial Opens in Carol Burnett's Libel Suit," *New York Times,* 12 March 1981, A14.

9. Ibid.

10. Lindsey, "Burnett Given $1.6 Million," A1.

11. Jonathan Friendly, "Double-Edge Challenge to Press Freedom?" *New York Times,* 27 March 1981, A17.

12. "Price of Libel," *New York Times,* 31 March 1981, A18.

13. Jonathan Friendly, "In Libel Suits, Juries Exact Damaging Dues for Damaged Reputations," *New York Times,* 5 April 1981, E8.

14. James C. Goodale, "The Burnett Award," *New York Times,* 9 April 1981, A23.

15. "Burnett Libel Award Cut," *New York Times,* 20 July 1983, C17.

16. "Miss Burnett Will Aid 2 Journalism Programs," *New York Times,* 6 June 1981, 10.

17. "Court Backs Reduction in Burnett Libel Award," *New York Times,* 8 October 1983, 34.

18. "*National Enquirer* Agrees to Settle with Shirley Jones in Libel Suit," *New York Times,* 27 April 1984, A17.

16. Wacky World News (Tabloid II)

1. Klinger interview.
2. Bunton interview.
3. Klinger interview.
4. Ibid.
5. Ibid.
6. Jamison interview.
7. Klinger interview.
8. Bunton interview.

17. Anger as Satire

1. Klinger interview.
2. Ibid.
3. Ibid.
4. Ibid.
5. Coz interview.
6. Virga interview.

18. Second Peak (Two Gardeners' Stories)

1. Harris interview.
2. Ibid.
3. Coz interview.
4. Ibid.
5. Calder, *Untold Story,* 179.
6. Peter Prichard, *The Making of McPaper: The Inside Story of* USA Today (New York: Andrews, McMeel & Parker, 1987).

7. Jones, "Hart Photo."

8. *"Donna Rice Photos," Editor & Publisher*, 6 June 1987, 15.

9. Calder, *Untold Story*, 211.

10. Ibid., 212.

11. George Childs Kohn, ed., *The New Encyclopedia of American Scandal* (New York: Checkmark Books, 2001), 173–74.

19. Sudden Death, Ironically

1. *Palm Beach Report*, 14 May 2000. Online posting. Accessed 25 February 2002.

2. Ibid.

3. Ibid.

4. Kirchheimer, "Gigantic Smash!" D3.

5. Kazin, "Who Hired the Assassin?" 39.

6. Stein, "Pope: Millionaire Owner."

7. Harris interview.

8. Hogshire, *Grossed-Out Surgeon*, 52.

9. Calendar, *Los Angeles Times*, 16 October 1988: 31.

10. Hogshire, *Grossed-Out Surgeon*, 107.

11. Ibid., 107.

12. Ibid., 47.

13. "Inquiring Minds Might Ask: Where Are Jobs, Yule Lights?" *San Diego Union-Tribune*, 15 June 1989, AA1.

14. Calder, *Untold Story*, 233.

15. Balfour, "Enquiring Minds."

16. Dexter interview.

17. Kuncl, "Last Christmas Tree."

18. *Palm Beach Report*.

19. Kirchheimer, "Gigantic Smash!" D3.

20. Balfour, "Enquiring Minds."

21. Ibid.

22. *Palm Beach Report*.

23. Calder, *Untold Story*, 427.

20. The *Enquirer* after Pope

1. Kamp, "The Tabloid Decade," 61.

2. Ibid., 66.

3. Ibid., 70.

4. Stefan Kanfer, "Tina Brown and the Coming Decline of Celebrity Journalism," *Columbia Journalism Review,* September/October 1998. Available at http://backissues .cjrarchives.org/year/98/5/tina.asp.

5. Andrew Sullivan, "Some Like It Hot: Tina Brown Was the Bill Clinton of Journalism," *Wall Street Journal,* 24 January 2002. Available online at http://opinionjournal.com/editorial/feature.html?id=95001767.

6. "25 Most Influential Americans," *Time,* 21 April 1997, 50.

7. Melcher and Virga, *Unforgettable Images,* 5.

8. John Waters, *Crackpot: The Obsessions of John Waters* (New York: Macmillan, 1986), 66.

9. R. P., "Monica! Bill Clinton Had an Affair, and the Tabloid Tail Began Wagging the Mainstream Dog," *Supplement: Special 40th Anniversary Issue, Columbia Journalism Review,* December 2001, 124.

10. Stepp, "Treasure Trove of Tabloid Tales," 69.

11. Calder, *Untold Story,* 236.

12. Ibid., 186.

13. Ibid., 231.

14. Sachs, "Mud and the Mainstream."

15. Ibid.

16. Ibid.

17. Melcher and Virga, *Unforgettable Images,* 10.

18. Sachs, "Mud and the Mainstream."

19. Ibid.

20. David Keeps, "American Tabloid," *(London) Independent on Sunday,* 25 November 2001, 33.

21. Jay Cheshes, "Sex, Trash & Videotapes," *Talk,* October 2001, 130.

22. Ibid.

23. "Publisher of *National Enquirer, Star* to Be Sold," *Washington Post,* 17 February 1999, E2.

24. Darcie Lunsford, "Taming the Tabloids," *American Journalism Review,* September 2001, 56.

25. "Sinking U.S. Tabloids to Make it OK," *Observer,* 17 August 2003, 8.

26. "Tabloid Marriage Spawns Six-Headed Monster," *Montreal Gazette,* 3 November 1999, D2.

27. "Editor Is Leaving *Us Weekly* to Try Her Hand at Tabloids," *New York Times,* 27 June 2003, C1.

28. Judith Newman, "Bonnie Fuller's Fear Factor," *Vanity Fair,* March 2004, 300–311.

29. Keith Kelly, "Tabloid's Big Apple Cuts," *Observer,* 6 April 2005, 36.

30. James Robinson, "Brit Pack to Revive *Enquirer* Glories," *Observer,* 20 February 2005, 7.

31. Kelly, "Tabloid's Big Apple Cuts."

32. Kleinfield, "Acquiring Minds," C1.

21. Pope in Perspective

1. W. A. Swanberg, *Citizen Hearst: A Biography of William Randolph Hearst* (New York: Scribner's, 1961), 531.

2. David Nassau, *The Chief: The Life of William Randolph Hearst* (New York: Houghton Mifflin, 2000), 108.

3. Quoted in Nassau, *The Chief,* 593.

4. W. A. Swanberg, *Pulitzer* (New York: Scribner's, 1967), 50.

5. Ibid., 70.

6. Nassau, *The Chief,* 75.

7. Ibid., 105.

8. Swanberg, *Pulitzer,* 165–69.

9. Ibid., 359ff.

10. Hogshire, *Grossed-Out Surgeon,* 81.

SELECTED BIBLIOGRAPHY

Adorno, T. W. "Culture Industry Reconsidered." In Ashley, *Reading Popular Narrative,* 43–48.

Ashley, Bob, ed. *Reading Popular Narrative: A Source Book.* London: Leicester University Press, 1997.

Barthes, Roland. "Authors and Writers." In *A Barthes Reader,* edited by Susan Sontag. New York: Hill and Wang, 1983, 185–93.

Baudrillard, Jean. "Symbolic Exchange and Death." In *From Modernism to Postmodernism: An Anthology,* edited by Lawrence Cahoone. Oxford: Blackwell Publishers, 1996.

———. "Simulacra and Simulations." In *Selected Writings,* edited by Mark Poster. Stanford, CA: Stanford University Press, 2001.

Bergson, Henri. *Laughter: An Essay on the Meaning of the Comic.* Translated by Cloudesley Brereton and Fred Rothwell. New York: Macmillan, 1911.

Bird, S. Elizabeth. *For Enquiring Minds: A Study of Supermarket Tabloids.* Knoxville: University of Tennessee Press, 1992.

Byrne, John A. "Slugging It Out in the Supermarkets." *Forbes,* March 1981.

Cahoone, Lawrence, ed. *From Modernism to Postmodernism: An Anthology.* Oxford: Blackwell Publishers, 1996.

Calder, Iain. *The Untold Story: My 20 Years Running the National Enquirer.* New York: Miramax Books, 2004.

Cassidy, John. "The Hell-Raiser." *New Yorker,* 11 September 2001.

Cheshes, Jay. "Sex, Trash & Videotapes." *Talk,* October 2001.

Chomsky, Noam, and Edward S. Herman. *Manufacturing Consent: The Political Economy of the Mass Media.* New York: Pantheon, 1988.

Derrida, Jacques. *Adieu to Emmanuel Levinas.* Translated by Pascale-Anne Brault and Michael Naas. Stanford, CA: Stanford University Press, 1999.

"Donna Rice Photos." *Editor & Publisher,* 6 June 1987, 15.

Fiske, John. *Reading the Popular.* Boston: Unwin Hyman, 1989.

————. *Understanding Popular Culture.* Boston: Unwin Hyman, 1989.

————. *Power Plays, Power Works.* New York: Verso, 1993.

Foucault, Michel. "Nietzsche, Genealogy, History." In Cahoone, *From Modernism to Postmodernism,* 360–78.

————. "Truth and Power." In Cahoone. *From Modernism to Postmodernism,* 379–81.

————. "Panopticism, from *Discipline and Punish.*" In *The Foucault Reader,* edited by Paul Rabinow. New York: Pantheon Books, 1984.

————. "What Is an Author?" In *Rethinking Popular Culture: Contemporary Perspectives in Cultural Studies,* edited by Chandra Mukerji and Michael Schudson. Berkeley: University of California Press, 1991.

Gallagher, Dorothy. *All the Right Enemies: The Life and Murder of Carlo Tresca.* New Brunswick, NJ: Rutgers University Press, 1988.

Geertz, Clifford. "Thick Description: Toward an Interpretive Theory of Culture." In *The Interpretation of Cultures: Selected Essays.* New York: Basic Books, 1973, 3–32.

Gonser, Sarah. "American Media Expansion Plan: Tabloid Giant to Tap U.S. Latino Market." Intertech Publishing Co., 1 March 2001.

Gourley, Jay. "Beyond the Pail: The Theory and Practice of Garbage Journalism." *Washington Monthly,* October 1975.

————. "I Killed Gig Young." *Washington Monthly,* September 1981.

Gross, Daniel. "Tabloid Shocker! Enquiring minds want to know why the *National Enquirer* and its parent company are doing so badly." *Slate.com,* 14 March 2006. http://www.slate.com/id/2137277/?nav=fo.

Hall, Stuart. "Encoding, Decoding." In *The Cultural Studies Reader,* edited by Simon During. New York: Routledge, 1993.

Harris, John. "My Search for Utopia." *Gentlemen Ranters.* http://www.gentlemenranters.com/3.html#utopia, 24 August 2007.

Hessler, Peter. "Letter to China: Straight to Video." *New Yorker,* 15 October 2001.

Hogshire, Jim. *Grossed-Out Surgeon Vomits in Patient: An Insider's Look at Supermarket Tabloids.* Venice, CA: Feral House, 1997.

Jameson, Fredric. "The Cultural Logic of Late Capitalism." In Cahoone, *From Modernism to Postmodernism,* 556–72.

Kamp, David. "The Tabloid Decade." *Vanity Fair,* February 1999.

Kanfer, Stefan. "Tina Brown and the Coming Decline of Celebrity Journalism." *Columbia*

Journalism Review. September/October 1998. http://backissues.cjrarchives.org/year/98/5/tina.asp.

Kristeva, Julia. *Powers of Horror: An Essay on Abjection.* Translated by Leon S. Roudiez. New York: Columbia University Press, 1982.

Liebling, A. J. *The Press.* New York: Ballantine, 1961.

L. J. "Murdoch Expands His Global Empire." *Columbia Journalism Review,* November/December 2001.

Lunsford, Darcie. "Taming the Tabloids." *American Journalism Review,* September 2001.

Lyotard, Jean. "The Postmodern Condition: A Report on Knowledge." In Cahoone, *From Modernism to Postmodernism.*

Mahler, Jonathan. "The *National Enquirer*'s Thwarted Heir Lashes Out." *Talk,* January 2000.

Melcher, Charles, and Valerie Virga. *The National Enquirer: Thirty Years of Unforgettable Images.* New York: Talk Miramax Books, 2001.

"Min's Analysis of Magazine Circulation, Second Half 2003," part 1. *Min Media Industry Newsletter,* 23 February 2004.

Mooney, Paul. "Phoenix Rising." *Newsweek,* Atlantic edition, 12 November 2001.

Nassau, David. *The Chief: The Life of William Randolph Hearst.* New York: Houghton Mifflin, 2000.

Newman, Judith. "Bonnie Fuller's Fear Factor." *Vanity Fair,* March 2004.

"Now the Story Can Be Told! How Tabloids Survived the Recession." *Business Week,* 7 November 1983.

Page, Tim. "Personal History: Parallel Play." *New Yorker,* 20 August 2007.

Peer, Elizabeth, and William Schmidt. "The *Enquirer:* Up from Smut." *Newsweek,* 21 April 1975.

Prichard, Peter. *The Making of McPaper: The Inside Story of* USA Today. New York: Andrews, McMeel & Parker, 1987.

R. P. "Monica! Bill Clinton Had an Affair, and the Tabloid Tail Began Wagging the Mainstream Dog." *Supplement: Special 40th Anniversary Issue, Columbia Journalism Review,* December 2001.

Rudnitsky, Howard. "How Gene Pope Made Millions in the Newspaper Business." *Forbes,* 16 October 1978.

Sachs, Andrea. "Mud and the Mainstream." *Columbia Journalism Review,* May/June 1995. http://backissues.cjrarchives.org/year/95/3/mud.asp.

SELECTED BIBLIOGRAPHY

"Sex, Lies and Celebrities." *Newsweek,* Pacific edition, 20 August 2001.

Sloan, Bill. *"I Watched a Wild Hog Eat My Baby!" A Colorful History of Tabloids and Their Cultural Impact.* New York: Prometheus Books, 2001.

Smart, Barry. *Michel Foucault.* London: Tavistock, 1985.

Stallybrass, Peter, and Allon White. *The Politics and Poetics of Transgression.* London: Methuen, 1986.

Stepp, Carl Sessions. "A Treasure Trove of Tabloid Tales." *American Journalism Review,* March 2001.

Swanberg, W. A. *Citizen Hearst: A Biography of William Randolph Hearst.* New York: Scribner's, 1961.

———. *Pulitzer.* New York: Scribner's, 1967.

Talese, Gay. *Honor Thy Father.* New York: Ballantine Books, 1981.

Thompson, Charles C., II, and James P. Cole. *The Death of Elvis: What Really Happened.* New York: Delacorte Press, 1991.

"25 Most Influential Americans." *Time,* 21 April 1997.

Vitek, Jack, and Jerry Oppenheimer. *Idol: Rock Hudson: The True Story of an American Film Hero.* New York: Villard Books, 1986.

Von Hoffman, Nicholas. *Citizen Cohn: The Life and Times of Roy Cohn.* New York: Doubleday, 1988.

Waters, John. *Crackpot: The Obsessions of John Waters.* New York: Macmillan, 1986.

Wolf, George, with Joseph DiMona. *Frank Costello: Prime Minister of the Underworld.* New York: William Morrow, 1974.

Zion, Sidney. *The Autobiography of Roy Cohn.* Secaucus, NJ: Lyle Stuart, 1988.

INDEX

INDEX